THE LITTLE FOX OF LA CAPILLA DE GUADALUPE

Adventures, Mischief, and Tragedies:
A Beautiful Mexican Childhood

By
Liborio Gutiérrez Martín del Campo
and
José Gutiérrez González

Copyright
© 2024 by Liborio Gutiérrez Martín del Campo and José Gutierrez González
All rights reserved. No part of this publication may be reproduced, distributed, or transmitted in any form or by any means, including photocopying, recording, or other electronic or mechanical methods, without the prior written permission of the publisher, except in the case of brief quotations embodied in critical reviews and certain other noncommercial uses permitted by copyright law.

Hardback
ISBN# 978-1-963925-00-5

Paperback
ISBN# 978-0-9884025-7-7

E-Book
ISBN# 978-1-963925-08-1

Published by New Trends Press
P.O. Box 3001, Beaumont, Ca 92223
WWW.NewTrendsPress.Com
First Edition

Library of Congress Cataloging-in-Publication Data
Names: Gutiérrez Martín del Campo, Liborio, Author. | Gutiérrez González, José, Author.
Title: The Little Fox of La Capilla de Guadalupe / Adventures, Mischief, and Tragedies: A Beautiful Mexican Childhood / by Liborio Gutiérrez Martín del Campo and José Gutiérrez González.
Description: First Edition. | Beaumont: New Trends Press, 2024.

Identifiers: ISBN: 978-0-9884025-7-7

Subjects: LCSH: Los Altos de Jalisco, Mexico – History. | Los Altos de Jalisco, Mexico – Biography. | BISAC: HISTORY / Latin America / Mexico. | BIOGRAPHY & AUTOBIOGRAPHY / Personal Memoirs.
Cover design by José Gutiérrez González
Interior layout by José Gutiérrez González
Printed in the US

Contents

Prologue 3
Chapter 1 6
Chapter 2 20
Chapter 3 24
Chapter 4 34
Chapter 5 51
Chapter 6 54
Chapter 7 68
Chapter 8 80
Chapter 9 102
Chapter 10 110
Chapter 11 124
Chapter 12 137
Chapter 13 148
Chapter 14 164
Chapter 15 179
Chapter 16 185
Chapter 17 190
Chapter 18 209
Chapter 19 233
Chapter 20 246
Chapter 21 257
Chapter 22 269

Chapter 23 277
Chapter 24 289
Chapter 25 298
Chapter 26 303
Chapter 27 314

WARNING!

Not everything written here is one hundred percent verified, but it is a collection of memories from individuals, books read, and other forms of information gathered throughout the life of

Liborio Gutierrez.

My Beautiful Village, La Capilla de Guadalupe

"¡Ay Jalisco no te rajes!"

By

Jorge Negrete

Prologue

In life, we encounter challenges that, in a way, become part of our mission. This has precisely been the case with my father and his desire to transcribe his memories, experiences, and knowledge so that they may pass on to posterity, even when he is no longer with us.

And it is in this context that I, as his son, am here with the responsibility and privilege to continue his dream.

My father, Liborio Gutiérrez, wrote this autobiography where he tells us about his adventures, mischief, and tragedies during his childhood in his beautiful village. You will enjoy many anecdotes involving the families he wrote about in the prequel titled "For the Love of God," where he made a detailed journey through Mexico's history from colonization to the mid-last century, focusing mainly on the Los Altos de Jalisco and a beautiful exposition of the ranches, lineages, customs, and traditions of the people who lived in these places.

There are two points I wish to highlight about the composition and structure of this work.

First, my father did not manage to publish and finish it in his lifetime; he had advanced work and it is clear that he was already in the phase of compiling his notes, polishing them, and giving the book structure.

Second, when I took on these tasks, I came across a lot of fascinating information and also found it very complicated to synthesize or eliminate some notes, as my father surely would have done.

That's why it's important for me that you understand if there are similar paragraphs because I have transcribed them even from manuscripts in his agendas, wanting to respect his voice and, if a note had a nuance or point of view, I preserved it so that it would truly be he, with his experiences and memories, who would speak to us through this book.

I leave below an introduction written by my father that I have decided to add to this prologue.

José Gutiérrez

Words from my father, Liborio Gutiérrez

This book unfolds a story told in three crucial segments. It is a story that I have carefully constructed using inquiry and reason to uncover truths that were once hidden and unknown. The most notable of these three segments is the third, a portrayal of my personal life beginning from the innocence of my early years and culminating at the threshold of my sixteenth year. Within these pages lie many revelations that offer deep insights into my journey in life. These written words now immortalize those cherished moments because, as time inexorably moves forward and my health declines, I will no longer be able to express them myself.

My sincere dedication

In writing the history of my life, along with the historical colonization of my ancestors in and around the mountainous area of Los Altos de Jalisco, Mexico, I am deeply grateful to my son, José, the guiding light on this journey. His encouragement and belief in the value of my experiences have been crucial in bringing these pages to life.

José, more than a son, you have been my anchor and inspiration. Your support and insight have transformed the challenge of writing this autobiography into a path of self-discovery and sharing. This book is a legacy that we have created together, a reflection of our shared journey and enduring bond.

To José, I owe the fulfillment of a long-cherished dream to immortalize my stories. José, your patience and unwavering understanding, even in my imperfect moments, mean so much to me. My hope is that this book will bring us all closer to understanding and peace.

Above all, I extend my deepest thanks to all my children. In times when I have faltered, showing less warmth and kindness than they deserved, their patience and understanding have remained steadfast. The depths of my love for all of you are known only to the divine. As I reflect on the mosaic of my life, colored by triumphs and mistakes, my heart yearns for your forgiveness. My earnest hope is that this understanding will pave my way to eternal peace with God.

With all my love and deep gratitude,

Liborio Gutiérrez

CHAPTER 1

My Parents' Marriage and My Birth: A Chapter of Life

The union of my parents in January 1933 was an event blessed both by the government and divinity. Their marriage marked the beginning of a new family, born from love and hope in uncertain times.

My older brother, the first child of my parents, was born in my grandmother's large house, where they initially lived. Despite the economic difficulties my father faced, his love for my mother was unwavering. He, a well-favored mestizo with dark skin, and she, of a beauty that captivated his heart, demonstrated that love transcends all barriers, including economic ones.

In August 1934, it was my turn to be born, on a rainy and stormy Friday, the 3rd. I have always believed that my affinity for rain comes from that rainy day I came into the world. At that time, the fields in my region of Los Altos were green and flourishing–a perfect backdrop for a birth.

My family then lived in my grandmother's house, surrounded by pastures where cattle and animals grazed and fattened. It was a time when nature showed its splendor, and the popular saying "put that animal in the Agostadero meadow" resonated with truth. By the end of August, the landscape transformed into a tapestry of flowers and greenery, a testament to life continuing its course despite adversities.

Giant Garden of Floriculture: A Birth Among Colors and Scents

I was born in a place that resembled a giant garden, brimming with beauty and life. This garden was adorned with flowers of every conceivable color, creating an impressive visual spectacle. Among them, the Santa María stood out with its unique yellow flower, and the mirasol, similar to a sunflower but smaller, decorated the landscape with its pink and purple flowers.

The "cinco llagas," a small mamey-colored flower, was notable both for its beauty and its medicinal properties, even used in treatments against brain tumors. The variety of the "maravilla," with its multiple colors, added a vibrant touch to the environment. Not to forget the galiza, an intense blue bell-shaped flower with white stripes in the center, and the "mano de león," a plant with white flowers that resembled the Santa María but was larger.

In this garden, botanists would find a paradise, an inexhaustible source of plants for their collections and medicinal studies. It was in this setting, on August 3rd, that I began my life, amid colorful and fragrant fields, where even the air seemed to change, becoming imbued with a sweet and fresh scent characteristic of that region.

Childhood Memories: The Early Years of Life

Now I set out to narrate the earliest events of my life, the ones that marked my childhood. As a newborn, my brother Miguel was already a year and a half old. At that time, he faced a health problem: annoying worms in his stomach. While undergoing treatment, he was kept in his crib to prevent him from playing on the ground, as it was said that contact with the earth could worsen his condition.

Interestingly, Miguel developed an unusual hobby: he would scratch the adobe wall next to his crib and eat the adobe, something my mother later discovered with surprise. For my part, being just a baby of one or two months, I developed an abscess on my neck, the size of a tennis ball. People felt sorry for me, predicting the worst, but in the end, only a scar remained as a reminder of that incident.

These stories were told to me by my mother, as I was too young to remember them. However, there is a vivid memory that remains in my memory from when I was between six and eight months old, an experience so peculiar that many doubt its veracity, perhaps because of my young age at that time.

Memories and Changes: From My Childhood to My Father's Departure "Those Unforgettable Moments"

When I was just a child who could not yet walk, my mother had a helper, a young lady who was my caregiver and used to take me to her house, located on the outskirts of town. I remember one particular day, she carried me in her arms, and on the way, she met a young man who, I assume, was her boyfriend. Wishing to be alone with him, she left me sitting on the threshold of a window. There, feeling jealousy and abandonment, I began to cry. Although the window was not high, for me it felt like an insurmountable mountain. This is one of my earliest memories, lived when I was less than a year old.

Not long after, my father made a crucial decision for our future. Although he worked as a tailor, the earnings were minimal and did not offer an encouraging future perspective. In the great house of my grandmother, my father's mother, we never lacked food or a place to sleep. But seeking better opportunities, my father decided to emigrate to the United States. He went with his sister, my aunt Chole, who lived in South San Francisco, California with her husband, whom we called Uncle José. He was Navarro, belonging to the same family lineage as us. They lived happily with their son Reynaldo and three daughters with whom God had blessed them.

My father spent several years there, facing new experiences and challenges, in a land that was foreign yet promising to him.

My Childhood and the Days at Rancho El Cinco: Road to Rancho El Cinco

When I was about two years old, my father had already been working in the United States, often referred to as "the North" in Mexico, for a year. During this time, my mother had changed residence. Thanks to the dollars my father sent, she was able to move to her own house, seeking independence, although she always maintained an affectionate relationship with my grandmother, her mother-in-law.

At that age, I was already walking confidently. I especially remember the trips to Rancho El Cinco. My mother, along with several relatives and friends, used to visit the ranch, especially during corn harvest time. At the ranch, owned by a relative named Idelisa, they gathered to prepare traditional dishes like elotes (cooked corn), tamales, and tostachos, a kind of thick tortilla.

Idelisa, cousin of my grandmother María and second cousin of my other grandmother, Chitos' mother, was known for her hospitality and the delicious fresh cheese she prepared. This cheese, combined with the elotes and freshly made tamales, created an exceptionally delicious and unique flavor.

My Childhood: Adventures at Rancho El Cinco

From my earliest childhood, Rancho El Cinco held a special fascination for me. What attracted me most about that place were the lush ash trees and the large corral, where between thirty and forty round stone piles were stored to feed the numerous cows. Watching the milking and receiving a jug of frothy milk from the hands of Aunt Idelisa's sons, who also participated in these chores, was a true delight for me. They were kind and hardworking people.

Once, my mother left me at home with my brother Miguel, under the care of a young woman who worked with her. Taking advantage of a moment of carelessness, I escaped to Rancho El Cinco. Crossing the pasture known as El Llanito, near La Capilla and heading north, I came across a stone fence. Although it seemed very high, I managed to find a lower point to jump over. However, instead of heading towards Rancho El Cinco, I inadvertently took the path to Cerro Gordo. During that journey, the herbs and the landscape seemed immense to me, as if I were venturing into an unknown world.

Lost in Nature: A Childhood Adventure

In my early childhood, I embarked on an adventure that remained etched in my memory. The sunflowers, tall and majestic, stood around me, exceeding one meter in height. I was fascinated by the variety of herbs and plants in the field, though they also harbored spider webs with spiders painted yellow and black. Despite knowing that these spiders were not venomous, their presence caused me great panic.

As I delved deeper and deeper among the herbs, the spiders clung to my clothes. I tried frantically to remove them, feeling fear and confusion. Soon, my adventure turned into disorientation. Fear completely overtook me, and the thought of finding my mother vanished from my mind. I was lost, not knowing the way back home.

I walked for what seemed like an eternity, and it was beginning to get dark. Unknowingly, I was heading toward the skirt of Cerro Gordo, near Rancho San Antonio, a place often mentioned. Fortunately, I did not encounter any rattlesnakes, dangerously abundant in that area.

Just when I was almost overcome by fear and uncertainty, I heard voices in the distance. They were those of a woman and her granddaughter, returning from the hill after cutting firewood. They needed the wood for their kitchen, where the lady made tortillas.

My Guardian Angel: Doña Paulina and the Unexpected Encounter: The Rescue of a Lost Child

In those days, my mother, affectionately known as Paulina, was famous for her delicious white atole made from corn dough. But the story I want to tell you today is different, an episode from my childhood that deeply marked me.

Lost and disoriented, I encountered Doña Paulina and her daughter. Seeing me alone, they dropped their load of firewood and began to seek help for me. Doña Paulina approached me and, with a mix of concern and tenderness, asked about my mother. Unable to speak and still confused, I didn't know what to answer.

Doña Paulina, becoming my guardian angel, decided to take me to the town square. There, we sat on a bench, hoping to find someone who recognized me. Aware of my vulnerability, Doña Paulina chose not to take me to her home, as she was unaware of my origins.

Fortune was on my side when a man named Santos approached. Recognizing me immediately, he exclaimed, "But this is Cuca's child!" Doña Paulina explained to him how she found me at the foot of the Hill, lost and frightened. Santos hurried to inform my mother, assuring Doña Paulina that they would soon contact her to thank her for her kindness and the time spent looking after me.

The First of Many Adventures: Rescue and Revelations

This story, my first great adventure, has been deeply etched in my memory, and I will never forget it. I was just two years old when I first displayed my adventurous spirit; a trait that, I believe, runs in my blood from my ancestors.

It all started when Santos arrived with my mother, who was visibly frightened, fearing something serious had happened to me as I was nowhere to be found. Santos explained where I was and what Doña Paulina had said. My mother, relieved, hurried to bring some money as a thank you to Doña Paulina for looking after me.

Since that incident, I have lived countless adventures. Being a bold and mischievous child, I always liked to challenge danger. Fortunately, I have always had divine protection. In the pages of this book, I will try to share as many adventures as possible, recounting the experiences that have shaped my life.

In Guadalajara, with my aunt María M. del Campo, I lived another unforgettable episode. As my uncle would say, "I will never forget it," for I believe it was a divine intervention. This event occurred before my father returned from the North (United States), and I had the opportunity to spend some time in Guadalajara with a beloved aunt, María, my mother's sister. Aunt María was an admirable person: kind, intelligent, and newly married. She lived in Guadalajara with her husband, whom we affectionately called Uncle Gustavo Uribe, a native of Autlán de la Grana and from a distinguished family.

I remember with special affection a visit that Aunt María made to La Capilla. On that occasion, she came alone and, upon returning, took me with her. I, with my adventurous spirit and fondness for new places, was excited about the trip. This episode happened the same year I got lost and was found by Doña Paulina.

The house of my aunt in Guadalajara was spacious and welcoming. The rooms, although separate, were connected without doors. We slept in two beds in the same room: one for them and one for me. I believe I was about three years old at that time.

An Unsettling Night at Aunt María's: My Childhood in Guadalajara with Aunt María

One night, when the lights were turned off to sleep, I noticed the absence of electric bulbs, which seemed strange to me, since electricity was common at that time. Instead, they used a high-quality kerosene lamp, which provided excellent illumination. That night, when the light was extinguished for sleep, I began a nocturnal experience I will never forget, at that house in Guadalajara, owned by my aunt María. That night, several hours had passed since my uncles and I had fallen asleep. Suddenly, I woke up, feeling the presence of someone beside me. In the dim light, I thought it might be my uncle or aunt, but upon closer inspection, I realized they were still in their bed. A faint glow lit the room, enough to confirm that no one else was with me.

Frightened, I began to scream desperately, waking up my uncles. My aunt, concerned, got up to see what was happening. Uncle Gustavo lit a candle, and together they searched around, even under the bed, thinking I might have a fever or was having a nightmare. After verifying I was fine, they managed to calm me, and we went back to sleep.

However, later that night, I woke up again. This time, I didn't see anyone in my bed, but when I looked toward the other room, the one without a door, I thought I saw two people dressed in long white robes. It seemed as if they were blocking other people, preventing them from approaching me. This unusual vision left me perplexed, and that night at my aunt María's house was one of the most unforgettable of my childhood. After my first scream of fear, my uncles woke up and began searching the room, thinking perhaps someone had entered. However, they found no one. They went back to sleep, but shortly after, once again, I was forced to wake them with my screams. This time, I claimed to have seen figures moving from one room to another. My uncles, already tired, conducted another thorough search, but again, there was no one but us.

Eventually, I managed to calm down and let my uncles rest. This experience has never faded from my memory. I have always believed it was not just a mere nightmare but something more, something real. In my heart, I feel they were angels who came that night to protect and defend me, as I was not ill nor did I suffer from nightmares at that time.

In that house also lived a cousin of my uncle Gustavo, named Ángel, whom everyone called Angelito. I vividly remember his tricycle, which fascinated me. Aunt María and Uncle Gustavo had a spacious house where other families lived. My uncle Gustavo had a black bicycle with a rack, and he took me for a ride on it once, a memory I also deeply treasure.

Memories of Guadalajara and My Father's Return: Childhood with Aunt María

During my childhood, I lived experiences in Guadalajara that still resonate in my memory. Once, my uncle took me to a place with a square cement tank used for storing water. At that time, the tank was empty. I remember seeing many people around, as if it were a business place where everyone worked. My uncle apparently had to speak with someone and, for some reason I did not understand then, left me inside the empty tank, asking me to wait there. This anecdote, experienced when I was about three years old, remained etched in my mind.

My Father's Return from the United States to La Capilla

After my return from Guadalajara, nearly at the age of three, my father was still in the United States. During his absence, my mother decided to move to a new house, where she felt happier and more comfortable in her own space. It was over a year in this large house on Guerrero

Street, which still stands today, before my father returned from the North. This house, once owned by Timo Alcalá, now deceased, was a special place in our family and an important part of my childhood memories.

The awaited return of my father from the United States happened when I was about to turn four years old. Initially, I was reluctant to approach him, as my childish memory barely retained any image of him. However, over time, everything changed. My father brought us toy airplanes made of tin that worked with a wind-up mechanism; they performed aerial acrobatics and emitted sparks of light. One was for me and the other for my brother Miguel. Those toys seemed fascinating, and through them, my father began to earn my affection. Soon, I started to love him deeply; he was always very kind to us and everyone around him.

I also remember the clay animals he molded, an artistic skill he had developed at the lagoon. He was a true artist in creating figures of horses, pigs, bulls, chickens, and roosters. His skill was remarkable; everything he tried to do, he achieved with exceptional ability. Although I tried to imitate his works as I grew up, I never managed to match his mastery.

Friends of my father, like Santiago Padilla, told me that in his youth he had created small armies of horses with federal soldiers, inspired by the scenes he had seen during the Cristera War. He even modeled carts with oxen, reflecting his passion and talent.

Memories of a Busy Childhood: Moving Houses and the Birth of a Brother

Reflecting on my childhood, I clearly remember when my father, after returning from the United States about a year earlier, decided that we should move to another house. This new residence belonged to his first cousin, Felipe González, who kindly facilitated our move. The memories of that time at my Uncle Felipe's house are varied and vivid.

One of the most significant events that marked me during our stay at that house was the birth of my third brother, an event that occurred on May 25, 1939. I remember that day with surprising clarity: it was a typical afternoon, playing on the sidewalk in front of Uncle Felipe's house, when a lady entered our home. My grandmother Chita, my mother's mother who lived with us at that time, came out shortly after and told me to keep playing outside because they were very busy.

Time passed, and just as I was about to go back inside, an extremely strong dust storm began to lash out. The wind was lifting small stones with such force that it was uncomfortable and difficult to move forward.

The Birth of My Second Brother Amid a Dust Storm

The day of my second brother's birth is etched in my memory due to an unusual event. As a dust storm raged with intensity, I found myself forced to sit against the house door, protecting my face with my arms and legs. The wind was so strong that I had to seek shelter in that corner, waiting patiently for it to pass.

When the wind finally calmed down, I was about to return home when I saw a lady coming out, who turned out to be the midwife who had assisted my mother during childbirth. It was a birth marked by chance and the force of nature, something that has always made me reflect.

Interestingly, my own birth was also surrounded by unique circumstances, and I have always thought that these coincidences – my birth amid a storm and my brother Rubén's during a strong dust storm – might have a special meaning, perhaps a message or a divine sign.

Unfortunately, that childbirth was traumatic due to mistakes made by the midwife, which had lasting consequences for my mother. These events have stayed with me, deeply marking my view of life and the interconnectedness with nature's elements.

The Red Trucks of Los Altos and My Father's Initiative: My Childhood and the Limited Cooperative Society

During those years, an important transportation line known as "Red Trucks of Los Altos S.C.L.," a Limited Cooperative Society, was formed. The general offices were located in Tepatitlán, but it had partners from the entire Los Altos region of Jalisco. Each partner began their participation by contributing 200 pesos, a considerable sum at that time.

My father had the chance to join this initiative thanks to the help of my aunt Chole, who lived in California. To gather the necessary two hundred pesos, my father had to make a tough decision: to sell a valuable watch he had brought from the north for my mother. He sold it to a doctor, affectionately called "el Pildorista" for his preference for homeopathy, in exchange for almost the amount needed to complete the investment.

After gathering the money, my father started working as a collector for the cooperative, as he did not know how to drive and never learned. He began on the Guadalajara to Arandas route, often passing through La Capilla. Sometimes, he was assigned to other routes, as the cooperative had several destinations, including major cities like León, Guanajuato, Irapuato, and San Luis Potosí.

In the afternoons, we used to watch him while he repaired the trucks in our house's garage. It was hard work, but he did it with dedication. Moreover, he loved to tell us stories about his travels and experiences on the road, fueling our imagination and adding a touch of adventure to our lives.

In those days, the cooperative's Red Trucks expanded their route, reaching places like Lagos de Moreno, Aguascalientes, Zacatecas, Durango, and even Torreón. I was always filled with joy when they passed through my town, especially because they followed the route to Arandas and passed by the street where we lived. Often, while we played in the street, the driver would throw us copper coins of twenty cents and white nickel coins of ten and five cents, as well as those of fourteen and twenty-four cents.

Our house had a large room where we slept and another where we stored coal for cooking, as we still did not use petroleum stoves at that time. The backyard was large and elongated, with a big square cement tank at the end. I remember a photo of the three siblings: Rubén, holding a white cat, was just one year old.

Saving Mamá Hita and Advancing in the Los Altos Truck Cooperative: A Fright and a New Beginning

On one of those days, my grandmother, affectionately known as mamá Hita, had an accident at our home. While trying to light a cigarette, her long, loose hair caught fire. The flames rose quickly, and she, paralyzed by fear, did not know what to do. My mother, seized by panic, could only scream for help. Fortunately, my father, realizing the gravity of the situation, acted quickly. He took a blanket and placed it over my grandmother's head to smother the fire, saving her from serious burns.

CHAPTER 2

The New House on Guerrero Street

Thanks to the success my father was having with the Red Trucks Cooperative, our financial situation improved significantly. Soon, he gathered enough money to buy a new house, located on the same block as our previous residence on Guerrero Street but closer to the square. It was a fairly large house, though not as much as my grandmother María's. My father carefully remodeled it, adding a distinctive touch: an arched window with a unique railing at the front, and above it, he placed a Virgin of tiles, surrounded by decorative bricks.

The house my father bought and remodeled became a symbol of our family's growth. On the facade, an image of the Virgin of Guadalupe, acquired in San Pedro Tlaquepaque, stood out. This representation, still present today, gave a special character to our home. Made between 1940 and 1942, the house still stands, retaining its original charm.

The interior of the house was equally impressive. My father decorated the kitchen with pots and jugs hung on the dining room walls, creating a cozy and traditional atmosphere. There was a regular-sized patio where he built a portal giving access to the living room, near the window adorned with an exquisite railing. From there, one passed to the hall and the two bedrooms.

At the back, there was a large corral and, beyond, an even larger one with several stables. A second floor was used to store straw (dry corn leaves), used to feed the animals. Another corral reached another street, where pigs were raised.

We lived in this house, located at Vicente Guerrero Street No. 20, until 1949, when my father moved to San Luis Potosí. It was in this house where, at seven years old, I began to better understand the daily life and material realities of the people in my town.

The Other House and My Childhood Years

At that age, I remained a child brimming with energy and curiosity, captivated by uncovering every nook of my town and its surroundings. The countryside was particularly alluring, and sometimes I ventured into it alone, despite the risks. I always carried my slingshot, which for me was a tool of defense against any danger, especially the dogs that tried to bite me. I'd like to share with you what my town and its daily life were like from the perspective of an adventurous child.

My explorations and adventures truly began around the age of 8. Even as a child, I was starting to form a clearer idea of my surroundings. The heart of my town was the square and the church. The square, with its great beauty and size, was a fascinating place for me. It measured approximately 75 x 75 meters, though in my child's memory, it seemed even grander. Like many squares in Mexico, it was the center of community life and a space that, over time, I learned to appreciate even more.

The square in my childhood: The square in my town and my childhood

The square of my town, though it has been remodeled and decorated today, will always hold a special place in my childhood memories. Now it features a beautiful kiosk and cement benches, but in the 40s, when I was a child, it had a different charm.

Back then, the square was full of lush trees: flamboyants, Indian poplars, and some ashes. Birds' singing filled the air all day long. I particularly remember the grackles, black birds that arrived in flocks to rest in the afternoons. At night, their chirping was so intense it seemed like a natural symphony. The next day, the ground under the trees would be covered with their droppings, meaning a lot of work for the sweepers.

The benches were made of wood, supported by cast iron stands. The ground was covered with red brick, and there were benches around the entire square and also around the four gardens. These gardens were full of plants and flowers of different kinds, creating a colorful and attractive landscape. In the center of the gardens, there stood a typical and very picturesque kiosk, located near the edge of the square.

The heart of my town: The square and the church in my childhood years

The square of my town, the center of our community life, and the imposing church are vivid memories of my childhood. In those days, the square was adorned with benches and cast-iron light posts, topped with iron dragons at the tips, each holding an oval bulb, as if they were little luminous balls. The cobblestone streets were typical of the era, adding a rustic and traditional touch to the urban landscape.

On the west side of the square, it was beautified with majestic porticos, architectural elements that gave it a distinctive character. Although today the square has been modernized and looks prettier, unfortunately, it has fewer trees. It seems that the town has favored cutting down trees to avoid the work of cleaning leaves and bird droppings.

On the east side of the square stands the great church, the most important and emblematic building of the town. Now turned into a large parish, its construction was started in the 1850s and 1860s by Felipe Navarro, my great-great-grandfather. This church replaced the small chapel that had been built by his grandfather, Don Antonio de Aceves, also known as "el Amo Aceves."

My town and my childhood - The church and the quarries

In front of the church, on the street to the right, for many years, large pieces of quarry stone were piled up. It was common to hear the constant noise of the hammer and chisel, tools used by artisans in crafting pieces to decorate the church. The quarry loads mainly came from San Miguel el Alto, known for its excellent quality stone, ideal for carving.

One of the most significant projects where this quarry was used was the construction of the new church tower. For years, the temple had only one tower, which had two floors and ended with a domed cupola, topped with an iron cross. The skill and expertise with which this structure was erected are admirable; only God knows how they managed to raise that imposing cross to the top.

The blacksmiths of that time did exquisite work at the tip of the cross, where they installed a lightning rod. This device was connected to a rod that extended to the ground, ensuring that any lightning striking it would be conducted to an underground reservoir. Thus, the church was not only beautified with the quarry and the blacksmiths' art, but also incorporated elements of protection and safety.

CHAPTER 3

The Church Bells of My Childhood

In my childhood, the most emblematic image of my village was the church's bell tower. A lightning rod, curiously adorned with hair from barbershops, was placed atop to protect it. Indeed, I witnessed lightning striking the cross and traveling down the rod, a spectacle visible from my grandmother's house opposite the church.

Within that tower was a gigantic and beautiful copper bell, whose unique sound could be heard for miles around. I often wondered how they managed to hoist it due to its significant weight. This main bell was accompanied by three smaller ones. Unfortunately, the large bell developed cracks and had to be replaced by a smaller one, which, though new, never matched the original's special sound. It was rumored that the first bell contained a bit of silver, providing its distinctive tone.

Of the other three bells, one particularly small bell was used both in conjunction with the others and solo for special occasions. For instance, when someone passed away, this bell would emit a special sound, tolling slowly and solemnly, marking moments of agony and mourning.

My Childhood and the Sounds of the Small Bell

During my childhood, a small bell in the church played a special role in community life. Each ring it emitted had a specific meaning. For instance, during times of agony, its unique sound announced that someone was nearing the end of their life. This sound alerted us that the priest, accompanied by acolytes, was en route to administer the Last Rites. Dressed in their liturgical vestments and carrying the Eucharist, their passage commanded deep respect from the parishioners, who would kneel in reverence as they passed.

The bell also had a significant role during baptisms. At these events, it would ring quickly and joyfully, signaling the ceremony's end. This was a cue for the godparents to throw coins into the air in celebration. I remember, as a child, running excitedly toward the church upon hearing the bell, knowing it was time to collect the scattered coins, a tradition that filled us with joy and anticipation.

Baptism Traditions and Santos, the Bell Ringer

A vivid childhood memory is the "Bolo" tradition at baptisms. When the godparents tossed coins, the village children would erupt in excitement, shouting: "Bolo, bolo, and more bolo!"—a local expression describing the joy of collecting the coins after a child's baptism. This custom was a moment of great anticipation and happiness for all of us.

Another emblematic figure from my childhood was Santos, the church bell ringer. While I don't recall his last name, his humility and calmness were well-known to all. I never saw him angry or heard of him being upset. Santos, esteemed by everyone for his kindness, must have been over 85 years old back then. He began his bell-ringing duties at the tender age of 10, assisting the previous bell ringer who had replaced another who tragically died after slipping from the bell tower.

When the former bell ringer died, Santos, with 10 years of experience, took over the role. To the date these memories are penned, he remained the devoted bell ringer, preserving an essential tradition in our village life.

Santos, the Tireless Bell Ringer of My Village

It's astonishing but true: Santos, the bell ringer of our village, has dedicated over 70 years to his task, ringing the bells day in and day out. From the first mass at 5 a.m. to the evening rosary at 8 p.m., his commitment never wanes. On Sundays and holidays, with their numerous masses and special celebrations, he is always there, ensuring the bells toll for each event.

Though he often had volunteer helpers like myself during times when I loved climbing the belfry to assist him, Santos seemed to possess endless energy and spirit. He would ascend the spiral staircase to the tower's top multiple times a day, never showing fatigue and always with a smile.

Whenever I visit my village, I make it a point to see Santos in the belfry. I greatly enjoy our chats, where he shares stories of our ancestors. The joy in these meetings is mutual. We hold great esteem for each other. Sometimes, I wonder why no one has acknowledged this world record, as I doubt there's anyone with such a long and dedicated tenure as Santos in the art of bell ringing.

The Legacy of Santos, the Bell Ringer, and The Chapel of Guadalupe

Santos, the bell ringer of our village, truly deserves extraordinary recognition. Finding another bell ringer with a comparable career seems unlikely, as he has devoted over 70 years to his daily duties. What's most admirable is that even at his advanced age, he ascends the spiral staircase with the agility of his youth. Perhaps it's a miracle from God, and if so, maybe at 100, Santos will continue his labor. In my view, Santos is worthy of a monument for his dedication and humility.

The Chapel of Guadalupe and the Church

Originally, the church had only one tower. The baptistery inside, right next to the main entrance, was shielded by a gate. A baptismal font made of quarry stone stood at the floor's center. The vast exterior atrium, with its brick flooring, and the eastern residence of Father Morales with a porch, fell into disuse after the priest's demise.

My Childhood and Memories of the Temple and Father Morales's House: The Temple in My Early Years

Father Morales's house, situated near the temple, stands out in my childhood memories. It remained almost in ruins for years as his successors chose not to live there, leaving it without necessary repairs. Even today, it awaits someone willing to restore it. When Father Morales was alive, the house was quite beautiful.

During my childhood, I was part of a musical band with my brother Miguel and grandfather Tacho. A tradition was serenading Father on his birthday. After playing several musical pieces, he would invite us to his dining room, where we all fit at a long table, the white walls creating a cozy atmosphere. I fondly recall the hot chocolate and delicious picón breads made by Gregorio Trujillo that were served to us.

We also enjoyed a small glass of rompope, relishing its taste. Father Morales was dearly loved in the village. When we arrived with the band, we weren't alone; his atrium filled with people coming to enjoy the serenade, singing and celebrating in a joyful, communal spirit.

The Father's House, the Spiral Staircase, and the Choir

In my childhood, Father Morales's house was a focal point of gathering and celebration. After the serenades, he thanked everyone, offering each a small glass of rompope. We, the band members, were privileged to be invited inside, though I never knew exactly why. Meanwhile, the party continued outside, some with guitars, others with accordions, extending the joyous occasion.

Father Morales was greatly appreciated for his relentless work in the church. He was an active, charitable, understanding, and intelligent priest. His multi-story house, with numerous rooms, was directly connected to the temple, allowing easy access to the sacristy for his religious duties. A corridor ran the length of the house, elevated by about four or five steps.

Around the atrium's perimeter, there was a wall with round, elegant quarry stone pillars. Near the tower, a door led to the spiral staircase up to the belfry. Before this, another door accessed the choir, where the organ or piano resided. This area, known as "the choir," was dedicated to music and singing during religious services.

The Temple Interior and the Painting of the Virgin of Guadalupe

Inside my village's temple, seating arrangements for parishioners during mass and celebrations were specific: women on one side of the central rows, and men on the other. These rows formed a cross, at whose center stood a beautifully crafted quarry stone altar, adorned with golden candlesticks and a large chalice.

Atop the altar, framed elegantly, was the painting of the Virgin of Guadalupe, brought by Don Antonio de Aceves from his ancestral Castilian city. This painting, along with other sacred items, including a Divine Face I own, enriched the altar. Yet, it was the Virgin's image that captivated all, further beautifying the altar.

Beneath the altar lay the tabernacle, also ornately decorated, a sacred place housing the Eucharist, symbolizing Christ's enduring presence in the church.

My Childhood: The Lord of the Afflicted and Other Saints in the Temple

In the temple of my childhood, various religious figures deeply impressed me. Beneath the altar, to the right, was an alcove housing several saint statues. On the left, a similar arrangement existed but featured a particularly special piece: a Christ sculpture carved from Cerro Gordo's wood. This figure, known as the "Lord of the Afflicted," bore striking beauty, closely resembling Tepatitlán's "Lord of Mercy" and the "Lord of Forgiveness" from Los Sauces ranch at Cerro Gordo's base.

It was rumored that these three Christs were baptized on the same day, though I might be mistaken. Some believed these sculptures were the work of a highly skilled, yet anonymous sculptor, their origins shrouded in mystery, dating back to around 1840 or 1850. The undeniable similarity among these figures suggested they were crafted by the same hand, embodying a unified vision and profound sentimental reverence for Christ on the Cross.

Don Luis Gutiérrez's Shop and Family: A Legacy of Love and Business

Leaving behind the temple, whose architecture is distinct and different from other temples in nearby towns, I head towards the large wooden door that opens onto the plaza on the western side. Here lies a beautiful arcade that now spans the entire block. In the middle of this arcade is the region's most famous and oldest clothing store, which I have known since my childhood. Its owner, Don Luis Gutiérrez, is an exceptional businessman and a highly respected figure in our town.

Don Luis is a true source of pride for La Capilla. I am not sure if he was born in our town or brought as a child by his father from San Miguel. I have known him since he was very young, as well as several of his sisters and a brother who died young, already married, leaving behind a beautiful wife and two daughters. Don Luis married a lady from La Capilla, and it is possible that he might even be related to me, as almost everyone in our town is somehow connected.

Don Luis's store is not just a business but a meeting point and a symbol of history and everyday life in La Capilla. Among us, there are those who live nearby and others further away, some more well-off and others less so, but all of us are descendants of those ancestors who might have been luckier financially.

Don Luis and his wife, Doña Rebeca, who I believe has the surname Navarro, are the perfect example of a typically Castilian family, devoted to the temple of their home. Their love story is admirable: they fell in love, married, and remain in love to this day. As Don Teófilo used to say, their love will last until the end of their days, and God willing, that will be many years from now.

The Gutiérrez marriage has not only built significant wealth, but also a united and prosperous family. Their daughter Rebequita, known for her business acumen, is a real whirlwind, just like her parents. She became a young widow with two children and, although she has been advised to remarry due to her youth and beauty, she is open to the idea but asserts she will only do so if she finds someone truly worthwhile.

All of Don Luis Gutiérrez's children inherited his entrepreneurial spirit and commitment to the community, continuing the family legacy with pride and dedication.

Notable Families and Businesses Around the Square

When talking about the families of my town, one cannot overlook the diversity and character of these. While some descendants of affluent families may indulge in extravagance, as can happen anywhere, the children of the notable couple formed by Don Luis Gutiérrez and his wife have responded with responsibility, even surpassing their father's capital in some cases. This is just one example of the many exemplary families in my town.

Focusing now on the surroundings of the square during my childhood, there was a well-known grocery store owned by Don José María Navarro. Like Don Luis, Don José María moved out of La Capilla to live in Autlán de la Grana. His store was then an important meeting point in the town. Later, it became the property of Juan Alcalá, the son of the famous commander Herminio Alcalá.

Another prominent figure in the area was Don Juan Casillas, whose house was also near the square. Today, that place has been transformed into a bank. Don Juan, belonging to the Casillas del Terrero family, was married to a cousin of my mother, both great-granddaughters of Don Miguel Franco el Grande. Their marriage is also remembered as an example of dedication and commitment to the community.**What There Was in My Town and Its Surroundings**

In my childhood, I vividly remember the characters and places that brought life to my town. Just crossing the corner to the east, there was Don Juan Casillas's office, a prominent associate of Los Camiones de los Altos, where he sold tickets. Next to this office was Don José Navarro's house, another notable figure in town. Both he and his wife, Doña María Navarro, a first cousin of my grandmother María, were examples of the good families in the area. Their marriage, however, was marred by the sad circumstance of three of their daughters being born mute, and two of them also becoming blind, just like my Aunt Matilde, my mother's cousin.

Don José Navarro's house was actually an inheritance from my great-great-grandfather Don Felipe Navarro, who owned the entire block. Doña María received this property as part of her inheritance. I remember Don José had an impressive herd of dairy cows, more than 50. He owned several pastures north of La Capilla, and at his home, he had a large corral where the cows slept. In the mornings, the sound of the cows and the activity in the corral were a regular part of my childhood's soundscape.

Don José Navarro and His Cows

Early, after milking and feeding the cows, they would be led down the street to the pasture to graze and exercise. When they were herded, the street would be filled with cows, and it seemed as though they were heading en masse to the pasture. There were so many that, to avoid encountering them, we would run through other streets not to be overwhelmed. Thus, in the afternoon, they were brought back for milking and then rested in the corral.

Don José Navarro was a gentleman who always wore pants in an old-fashioned style, almost like those of a charro but simpler. He wore a large, round hat, not too big, made of palm or straw. He was a very cheerful and talkative person. His laughter resonated, and he always had jokes and witty comments that made us laugh. He seemed to have an endless supply of anecdotes and jokes that we didn't know where he got from. He was a very intelligent person and had the gift of making people laugh with his wit.

Don José was very happy with Doña María, his wife, who was also a very kind person. In their presence, we knew no bitterness, as they were a good-hearted family, like most of the Navarros. Don José disliked seeing anyone in need, as he believed that helping others brought joy. He was always ready to assist in whatever way he could.

El Tajo and Laguna Carelasa

Continuing with the narrative, I delve into the description of the houses located to the east of Don José Navarro's house. The next in line was the house of Don Zacarías Navarro, who was also a first cousin of my grandmother María and heir to Don Felipe Navarro, his grandfather. Immediately after, I reached the imposing house of my grandmother, the place of my birth.

Moving towards the town center, I remember the streets, 70% of which were paved. From the square extending westward, the same street aligned all the houses I previously mentioned. This street, which used to be about five blocks long, has grown over time and now has more extensions.

To the south of the square, the street narrowed to only two blocks because it met the lagoon, which tended to increase in size during the rainy seasons. Despite this, it was a beautiful sight, as it filled with lilies and was frequently visited by ducks and herons. There was a stone fence in the center of the lagoon that was almost submerged by the water. Along this fence, numerous eucalyptus trees were aligned along the lagoon's edge.

In the eastern part of the lagoon, a large pond was constructed, known as "El Tajo," a name that still endures. This pond served as a water reservoir for the entire year and, additionally, as a beautiful landmark in the landscape.

Chapter 4

El Tajo

In this chapter, my account focuses on the land use in the town and its surroundings, specifically in relation to the pond. Around this pond, there was a high edge of deep black soil, which seemed to have been excavated previously when the pond was cleaned.

Below the soil layer, another layer of tepetate was found, quite deep. It is believed that this tepetate layer formed from the lava that flowed from Cerro Gordo millions of years ago. I share this information because tests and evidence support the existence of this tepetate layer, whose thickness seems endless. Allow me to explain why.

When a government-funded federal highway was built through this area, instead of using crushed stone, they opted for tepetate. This turned out to be a mistake, as during construction, a very large pit, about seventy five by seventy five meters and fifteen to twenty meters deep, was discovered. Surprisingly, in the process, they found that beneath the tepetate, along with the black soil, black stones were also extracted. These stones, not very large, varied in size from a baseball to a soccer ball, but notably, they showed their volcanic origin.

This finding puzzled us, as in the same stratum where the tepetate is found, these lava stones were also discovered. Thus concludes my account of "El Tajo," a place that remains an enigma in our lands.

The Enigmatic Tajo

In this segment, I wish to explore a mystery that has long intrigued me. It concerns a round well that Don Juan Casillas excavated on the land. After digging about twenty meters, Don Juan decided to continue digging, making the well even deeper and reaching about fifteen additional meters. However, the surprise was that he did not find the end of the tepetate layer, which added to the intrigue. This enigma, perhaps only known to God or possibly scientists, has no clear solution.

I prefer to leave this mystery here, as I have detailed in previous chapters the amazing surroundings of "El Tajo," the lagoon and its surroundings, as well as the Tajo River. It is worth mentioning that the name "Tajo" probably comes from our Castilian ancestors, who lived in Castilla before coming to this region of Los Altos de Jalisco. It was precisely this generation of Castilians and their descendants who founded my beloved town, La Capilla, in 1823.

Those who arrived from Castilla brought with them the memory of their homeland, a dreamy place they shared in communion with the Tajo River. This river, the longest in Spain, crosses beautiful and enigmatic landscapes, leaving an indelible mark on the memory of those who were fortunate enough to live near its waters.**El Tajo and the Lagoon**

This whole narrative brings to mind that, in the Castilla region, heading towards Toledo, there is a majestic river named El Tajo. Additionally, in the same direction, there is a quaint town called Tajo. This River Tajo, after winding its way, flows into the majestic Atlantic Ocean, crossing through Portugal along its route. I cannot help but think of these places, but I must return to the heart of my village and all that surrounds the Tajo.

What I am about to describe took place long before they began extracting tepetate to build the road. Allow me to take you back to that place, the Tajo and the lagoon, in the final days of August, when everything was at its peak of beauty. At that time, the lagoon was a stunning dream come true. It was brimming with water, stretching for about a kilometer and a half in length and roughly the same in width.

The lagoon was encircled by a fence running from east to west, adjacent to the line of tall and lush eucalyptus trees.

The Tajo, located between the east and the north, was at that time a large water reservoir, measuring about 40 by 40 meters. Its depth reached down to the layer of tepetate, estimated at about a meter and a half or perhaps two meters. I am not certain if those who excavated the Tajo encountered any water-related challenges, but if they did, I am confident they overcame them.

Around the Tajo, there was a high rim of black soil that had been dug out to create it. This rim added even more allure to the landscape that I fondly remember.

The Lagoon and Its Beauties, and the Boats

Long ago, when the lagoon was at its fullest, recalling this place fills me with nostalgia. There were measures to ensure that the lagoon's water did not go where it should not. I remember there was a trough or a long but not very high drinking place, so that the animals could drink water. There were also several stone washbasins where women would come to wash clothes. Additionally, there were numerous eucalyptus trees and many marigold bushes, with flowers that looked like tiny bells of various colors.

In the eastern area, outside the lagoon, there were plentiful marigold bushes. Women used to make colorful and beautiful necklaces with these flowers. When they gathered and strolled around the area, many looked lovely with their necklaces. Some of them had a special talent for singing, which added even more beauty to the place with their enchanting melodies.

As I write these lines, I fondly recall those times when I lived among these people and their customs. I cannot forget to mention the boats that were built to navigate the lagoon. If I remember correctly, two of them were constructed, and their building was overseen by a good friend and cheerful companion named Zacarías, though I am not sure of his last name.

Zacarías was a friendly and jovial man. Besides his skill in building boats, he was a talented musician. He rented these vessels to those who wished to explore the beauty of the lagoon.

The Enchanting Pond of La Grifa

I doubt anyone got rich from it, but what is certain is that our friend embarked on a wonderful initiative for our community. By the way, I own a photo capturing one of those moments in a boat, featuring several beautiful women, including my mother, wearing the famous marvel necklaces. At that time, these women were in the prime of their youth.

The pond was adorned with a profusion of lilies that, when blooming, lent it a truly enchanting appearance. They came in two colors, white and pink. Even though my friends and I were just children at the time, we loved attempting to swim in these waters. We had a real passion for bathing at a time when water was readily available everywhere.

I, for instance, spent my days basking in the sun, and as a result, often had a peeling nose due to the blisters that would form from spending so much time under the sun while swimming. But my favorite place to bathe was in a small pond known as "the pond of La Grifa." The pond's owner was known as "La Grifa," likely because he appeared to be in good spirits or enthusiastic all the time (the term "grifado" denotes being in a cheerful mood). It was in this pond I learned to swim. In fact, I delved so deeply into swimming that even my mother would punish me on occasion. I would sneak away two or three times a day to indulge in that pleasure. Though I didn't fully understand it at the time, my mother had every reason to be concerned and reprimand me.

The Stream of Los Linos and Its Secrets

Near La Capilla, to the east, lies a special place that has left indelible marks on my memory: the pond of Los Linos. Although this pond still exists, it is now enclosed by the urban development that has taken place in the area. Nonetheless, the memories of my youth, when I used to revel in its charms, remain vivid in my mind.

I was also particularly drawn to bathing in the stream that meandered through the region, known as the "stream of Los Linos." To this day, I don't have a clear answer about the origin of that peculiar name. Unlike the crystal-clear waters one might expect, the water in this stream had a rather brownish hue.

My childhood friends and I found indescribable joy in diving into the stream's puddles. However, my enthusiasm for these adventures often got me into trouble with my mother. She was adamant that we eat daily at 2 p.m., and my fondness for the water led me to have a reddened and peeling nose from the sun's blisters. Moreover, the bruised buttocks were a reminder of the scoldings my mother would administer with quince branches.

Nevertheless, these quince branches were not used for punishment; they served to air out the wool of our mattresses. Each year, my mother would take apart the mattresses, wash the wool, expose it to the sun to dry, and then place it back in the mattresses, stuffing and sewing them carefully.

But these branches had another purpose: to keep us in line. If we misbehaved, my mother knew how to use them to make us understand that we needed to correct our behavior. Despite this, in my youth, I did not understand why my mother always seemed ready to administer corrections at the slightest sign of disobedience.

The Adventure at La Grifa Pond

I vividly remember that as a mischievous child, my mother used to send me to swim in La Grifa Pond. Every time I faced the idea of diving into the water, I would make quite a spectacle. I would start screaming desperately and crying like a champion. Despite this, my mother would give me a slap or two, seeing that I was misbehaving and fearing something bad might happen to me. Although the slaps hurt, they were not that severe. My screams frightened my mother, and I, being a very ingenious child, often exaggerated the situation. From a very young age, I exhibited a playful and mischievous spirit. These memories date back to when I was about eight to thirteen years old, around 1947 or 1948.

In those days, when I was about eight, I had an anecdote at La Grifa Pond. I still did not know how to swim, and all the children my age were trying to learn. One of the older children challenged me, saying, "I dare you to jump into the water to learn how to swim." While some bigger kids held the smaller ones in the water, this part of the pond was not too deep for them; the water came up to their chests. This happened in a section of the pond where we used to take the cattle to drink.

One of the older children grabbed me by the jaw and pretended to teach me to swim. However, for fun and because of his sense of humor, he suddenly let go of me. It was a huge scare, but there was no real reason to worry, as the other children were close by. Although I was frightened at first, I eventually learned to swim in that same pond.

A Dramatic Experience at La Grifa Pond

At La Grifa Pond, I had an experience that left a mark on me. We were there to have fun, and I, as a restless child, was playing in the water. But the fun took an unexpected turn. Suddenly, I realized I was in trouble. I was in a place where I couldn't stay afloat and struggled desperately in the water. I could only move my hands, trying to grasp something at the bottom.

A friend tried to pull me out and reached his hands in, but couldn't find me. My frantic movements under the water didn't help him locate me. I was on the verge of drowning when, somehow, he finally found me. He grabbed me by the hair, and in a desperate act, I emerged from the water, coughing and spitting out the water I had swallowed. This was the third time I escaped a dangerous situation in my life. The first was when I had an inflammation in my neck that people thought would lead to my death, and the second was when, at two years old, I ventured to look for my mother at the ranch and got lost on the paths of Cerro Gordo until I was rescued by Doña Paulina, my guardian angel.

Throughout my life, I have faced more difficult situations, and I could tell at least fifty more stories, although not all will be in this book, as here I focus on my life up to fifteen or sixteen years old. Now, let us continue with my story about the Lagoon to the south.

The Youth Soccer Team

Just past the stone fence to the south, a beautiful landscape unfolded where herons, ducks, gallinules, and dowitchers were plentiful. In that same pasture, there was a small path or breach that served as a route for vehicles, including trucks and pickups.

Upon reaching the stone fence, we found a "cattle guard" made of wooden beams, designed to prevent livestock from crossing. To the west of that "little plain" was a soccer field officially used by a soccer team. Back then, our sports symbol was the team called "Nacional." The team's uniform was very attractive, featuring the colors of the Mexican flag: green jersey, white shorts, and red socks.

I remember some of the players from that time: the talented goalkeeper, Juan Carranza, nicknamed "Pollo"; the composed Gerardo Castellanos in defense, known as "Churica"; his brother Victoriano Castellanos, sometimes goalkeeper and other times defender; Eleazar Casillas, son of Don Juan Casillas, excelling in midfield, along with two players from Rancho Domínguez, who were also very good. Sometimes, some of them would play in defense.

The Nacional soccer team was a source of pride for us and represented a true symbol of unity and passion for the sport.

The Soccer Team

In the soccer team affectionately known as "Nacional," there were several standout players who left an indelible mark on our community. Among them were:

- "Chuyanga" Navarro and his brother José.
- Arnulfo, another brother, who played as a fullback.
- "Chava," the son of José María Navarro, excelling as a left fullback, a very agile player and a leader on the field.

- A player nicknamed "the one who kicked the ball," one of the team's stars in the forward position. He was skillful and talented, capable of performing wonders with the ball.

Besides these players, there were others whose names I can't recall at the moment. What I distinctly remember is the dedication and passion of those from Rancho Domínguez, who would come to train on foot, even in rainy weather. The playing field turned into a magical place on those days, with lush, natural green grass that seemed like a delicately cared-for carpet.

Back then, some of us wore "huaraches" (traditional sandals) to train, as they were more comfortable for walking on the grass and kept our feet clean. However, when we trained together, we all wore socks, bandages, and had our own youth team. Regarding shoes, I should clarify that I did not have proper soccer shoes, but the Domínguez brothers would wear them only on sunny days, taking them off for training, which we would now consider brave.

The Shoeless Team

The soccer team players showcased their skill and agility, even while playing barefoot. They seemed stronger and more nimble without shoes. The Domínguez siblings, in particular, stood out on the field, despite being tall and slender. The ball seemed to spark when they kicked it, and there was a risk of bursting it with their thickened nails from fieldwork.

It's worth noting that, back then, the Domínguez were farmers and applied the same focus and energy to their cornfields as they did on the soccer field. They worked the land barefoot, even when weeds were obstacles, which speaks volumes about their determination and strength.

The children's football team was also an essential part of our community. In that team, I was quite popular and nicknamed "the Fox" due to my agility and ability to dribble past opponents. I played as a center forward, though sometimes I also played as a left back.

The children's team was a source of unity and friendship, taking us to face teams from other localities, like Tepatitlán and San José de Gracia. These matches were always challenging, given their talented teams, and they represented significant tests for us.

The Children's Football Team

The children's football team consisted of a group of talented young people who shared a passion for the sport. Among the members were:

- "Goyo Trujillo," who sometimes played in various positions as the team needed.
- "Chava," his brother, who occasionally served as goalkeeper.
- "Pilló," a good friend of mine, also had his moments in goal.
- "La Sandunga," who usually was the goalkeeper.
- "Salvador," nicknamed "la Rana," was key in the forward line due to his skill.
- "Cisto," another team player contributing his talent.
- "Tachín," my cousin, the son of Eulogio.
- "Heriberto González Mereage," my uncle Felipe's son.
- "Javier Paredes," son of Don Pancho Paredes.
- "Chayo," also known by his nickname.

- Additionally, we had some of my relatives, sons of Don Leandro Martín de Mirandilla, like "el Garbanzo," whose real name is Ramón, and his brother "Chicharra," both excellent players.

Our team had an unbreakable spirit, playing with passion and heart in every match. We were supported and cheered by the entire village, creating memorable moments on the field. Notable among the spectators were individuals like Pedro, known as "Eligio's," and Pepe, always present to encourage us.

As we shared these football experiences in El Llanito, we will continue to explore other aspects of that life stage in the next chapter.

El Llanito, Football Matches, and Cheers

In El Llanito, besides the natural grass, various plants bloomed, adding beauty to the surroundings, like the lion's hand and galusa, known for its beautiful blue bell-like flowers, and the marvel, recognized for its larger bell-shaped flowers. We also found mixosol, Santa María, and yellow flowers adorning the area.

Weekends, especially Sundays, were celebration times in El Llanito. Young women gathered to enjoy afternoons together, often engaging in activities on the grass where fun and camaraderie were central. Song choreographies were common, filling the atmosphere with joy.

Sundays became even more special with football matches. On these days, El Llanito buzzed with excitement. While men were the primary attendees, women joined too. When a visiting team arrived, the cheers became passionate and loud.

Our local cheer squad, led by a sister of "la Churica" and "el Tinaco," known as Mercedes, showed unmatched enthusiasm. Although kind elsewhere, her support for the team was fervent. Sometimes rivalries with visiting cheers emerged, and we, the youth, were ardent defenders of our team.

Looking back, I believe the passion and energy we displayed in matches and cheers were an expression of our love for football and our community.

Soccer and Mischief in Zacarías' Orchard

Soccer was a passion in our community, and we savored each match as if it were a grand event. When visiting teams arrived in their stake trucks, we organized to welcome them at the exit of La Capilla. We would hide in silence, waiting for the perfect moment to surprise them. Suddenly, we would burst from our hiding places, shouting and throwing stones, which truly made us unbearable. We were undeniably the champions of mischief, but when it was time for our team to visit the others, we too were exposed to a good dose of stone-throwing, as the league's rules dictated that mischief was part of the game.

In those times without television, we had much more time to devise our "malice", and our misdeeds seemed endless. But setting aside our pranks, we explored everything around the lagoon. Heading west, we found a gate that led to Zacarías' orchard. There, Zacarías had his house and a considerable orchard. It was mostly a tranquil place, and we often went to steal guavas when they were ripe. At first, we tried to be stealthy and acted as if no one was in the house. We would jump nearby and climb the guava trees to pick the juicy fruits. However, sometimes, a guard dog would spot us, and our getaways became even more thrilling.

The dog would chase us, but it was cunning and would veer off when Zacarías' grandmother took down the shotgun. We ran like true champions, aware that the orchard owners were after us. Once out of the orchard, we found ourselves in a pasture where we entertained ourselves by looking for talayotes and chirles. The talayote plant spread across the ground and produced a peculiar fruit, similar to a hen's egg but flatter. Inside, it had fibers and flattened seeds, silver-looking, like velvet. Although tasteless, it was prized for its unique texture. My mother, when we brought her several talayotes, would bathe them in whipped cheese, making them delicious. I believe this region was the only place where these fruits were found, as I have never heard of them elsewhere. Moreover, chirles, small vegetables of crystalline white, tasteless and about the size of a finger, were another of our favorite culinary delights. The leaves of these plants resembled miniature palms, akin to an umbrella, and grew to about 40 centimeters tall.

Ranches Near the Lagoon in the North

In the vicinity of the lagoon to the north, there were various ranches, each with its own history and uniqueness. The closest of all was Rancho El Cinco, which I have already mentioned. In this place, two families coexisted in harmony: the family of my aunt Idelisa González, and the Domínguez, peaceful people with big hearts.

Continuing north along the Camino Real that came from Zacatecas and ended at Rancho Los Sauces, where it crossed the Camino Real from

Guadalajara to Mexico City, was a special place: La Capillita. In this humble corner, the Lord of Forgiveness was venerated with deep respect and devotion.

Moving east, we arrived at the beloved Rancho de San Antonio, a place full of memories and anecdotes, largely thanks to the work of my father, Simón Navarro, who built an impressive house on that land. This estate would become a backdrop where countless stories were woven.

After my father's death, San Antonio passed into the hands of my great-grandmother Matilde, who was Simón's wife. Then, the responsibility of the ranch fell to my grandmother and later to my mother, who continued the legacy of caring for and managing this beautiful property.

At one point, my grandmother Chita and her two sisters, who were the wives of my father Demetrio and my aunt Matilde respectively, made a momentous decision. They chose to sell all the properties, which included the illustrious Rancho San Antonio and an exceptional livestock operation. At that time, there was no other property like it in my entire town.

Among these properties was a majestic chapel belonging to Rancho San Antonio de los Franco, a renowned and appreciated family in the region. The Francos also resided in San Antonio and had other properties in the same locality. The relationship between our two families dated back several generations, starting with my great-great-grandfather Simón, and had solidified over time.

Our friendship was so strong that we lived as one family. When needed, we supported and defended each other, united by the esteem we held for one another. In times of need, we were ready to fight together, even against the cattle rustlers who often stole livestock in the area. The Francos, like us, were relentless in their determination to protect their properties and livestock and did not hesitate to teach a lesson to those who tried to steal in the region.

Ultimately, the Francos of San Antonio themselves decided to acquire all our properties, giving a new direction to the story of these valuable lands and fostering a final chapter in this exciting saga.

With great satisfaction, I observe how the Francos of San Antonio take over, as I believe they truly deserve it. Who better than them, who shared such deep esteem for each other? The connection of my grandmother Chita (doña María de Jesús Estrada) with my grandfather Antonio Martín del Campo Franco, who was the grandson of the illustrious don Miguel Franco el Grande, resulted in a connection with the Francos themselves. Thus, although we are now somewhat distant relatives, we remain part of the same family.

As a result, the renowned Francos have established their presence throughout San Antonio, including the chapel that my father Simón built in the 1860s. This structure houses a fascinating history, with a dozen rooms and an adjacent castle that he erected near the Camino Real. This castle features unique architecture, with a round shape that allows for panoramic views from the floor to the ceiling. It is adorned with numerous skylights that enable shooting with rifles from within, essential given the constant threats along that path.

In summary, this house is a true work of art where every detail, from the arrangement of the stones to the creation of the skylight windows, shows the meticulousness and dedication that Simón put into its construction.

He must have been an expert in his craft, as he designed the square in such a way that it was perfectly accommodated with polished and carved stone, wide and perfectly level. It seems that no slope was felt when walking through it. In addition to serving as a square for various activities, it was also used for shoeing cattle, given that the family of don Juanillo Franco owned a large amount of livestock in the region. In fact, to this day, they remain one of the largest livestock owners in the area, maintaining a tradition that dates back to our ancestors.

Due to this cattle wealth, the first authentic Charros began to emerge in the region. As I mentioned earlier, the most famous of those times was don Miguel Aceves Galindo. His renown was such that they even erected a monument to him at the eastern entrance in Guadalajara, in the roundabout facing La Paz, near San Pedro and Lázaro Cárdenas. This beautiful monument depicts don Miguel Aceves Galindo dressed as a charro, brandishing a rope that flourished impressively. In his time, there was no other charro who could handle the rope in that manner. Today, there are likely many talented charros, but it is important to acknowledge that don Miguel Aceves Galindo was a true pioneer in this art.

CHAPTER 5

Champion Charros

Today, the Francos of San Antonio, who are my relatives, are a source of great pride in my town and throughout the Los Altos de Jalisco region. If Don Miguel Aceves Galindo were alive, he would undoubtedly be immensely proud of them. Despite the existence of hundreds of charro teams in Mexico, this particular team has managed to win the National Champions title twice. The trophies and recognitions they have received are so numerous that I could not even count them all without spending a lot of time.

I had the privilege of visiting the house of Miguel Franco, the eldest of the Franco brothers and leader of the charro team. Additionally, the team's president, Miguel, is someone my age and married a cousin of mine named Beatriz, daughter of my uncle Felipe González, who is known both for her skill in music and for being a great wife.

In the living room of the house, which is quite spacious, trophies filled all the walls. They even had to place them in three or four rows to accommodate them all. And that's not all, as they also had another room full of awards. It is truly a source of great pride that we must preserve in memory for future generations.

The charro team is mostly composed of members of the Franco family, with Miguel as the president of the team and Chava, who is the tallest of all.

Among the standout members of the charro team is Rafael, a typical Franco about 2.10 meters tall, with blond hair and very fair skin. He is a great person in every sense. Another outstanding brother on the team is Arturo González, a childhood friend and an exceptional person, married to a wonderful woman who is also a great mother and wife.

In addition to those mentioned, there are other valuable members on the team, like the Franco Palao, talented young men residing in Tepatitlán and proud to be part of the La Capilla team. These young men are our close relatives, as they are grandsons of a brother of Mama Dolores Franco, who is the daughter of Don Miguel Franco el Grande.

Although I cannot remember all the team members at this moment, what I do remember is that the first time they won the Championship, they reached the semifinals, competing against teams from all over Mexico. Among the teams in the semifinals were Mexico City and one of the teams from Guadalajara, specifically the Charros de Jalisco, with some members having lineage from La Capilla.

One of my best childhood friends, whom we used to call "Juven," was the son of Don Juventino Aceves, a man of great nobility and a generous heart. He and his family moved to Guadalajara, a city that, compared to my small town, seemed immense. Mexico City had twenty million inhabitants, Guadalajara had three million, and in contrast, my beloved Capilla had just fifteen thousand inhabitants.

However, what a surprise and pride when the Charros de La Capilla became National Champions! They demonstrated that they come from determined and brave people, with a strong tradition in charrería that has endured over time. Their heirs reached the pinnacle of the National Championship, and this is a source of great pride for all of us.

The most astonishing thing is that they achieved this title in their first participation, with a unique record in the history of Mexican charrería. An impressive feat, as no charro team had achieved such a feat. We are all very proud of them and their great champion charro team.

Thus, I have shared a bit of the pride we feel in La Capilla de Guadalupe for our great charro champions and their feats in charrería. Now, I will continue with the mischief that I experienced when I was about seven or eight years old.

My Friends and My Mischief

As I mentioned, I was about seven or eight years old. My father was seldom at home due to his job with the Red Trucks traveling from one city to another. We saw him when he had to work near Arandas, and sometimes, he stayed with us overnight. My mother spent most of her time alone taking care of us; we were three siblings, but I was the one who gave her the most trouble.

I had several friends I would hang out with, but I also enjoyed exploring and getting to know the surroundings of my town on my own. At the same time, I attended school and, once or twice a week, went to church to study Catechism. I remember a young lady named Ivanita, sister of Zacarías, the musician who played the trumpet and had created the chalupas that were rented for rides on the lagoon.

I also have memories of Miss Clica Navarro, who lived right across from my grandmother María's house, where I was born. She was also a relative, a descendant of Papa Felipe Navarro. Another lady I remember fondly is Cuca, a very kind and religious person, just like her sister Lupe.

These were some of the people who were part of my life back then, and in the following chapters, I will share more about my friends and the mischief I experienced during that stage of my life.

Chapter 6

My Mischief: My Friends and Activities in My Town

Teacher Lola Cacillas, the daughter of founder Don Juan Casillas, was one of our most esteemed teachers. All of us who studied with her in high school considered her an excellent person and professional. Lola Cacillas had something special, a way of teaching that captivated all of us. Her stories and the way she told them were unique.

She married Salvador Navarra, a man equally respectable and devout. Together they formed a beautiful family, which was deserving of all our admiration. Doña Lola, in addition to being an excellent teacher, was deeply respected and loved in the community. She dedicated herself passionately both to her work at the school and to her role in the local church.

She was always at the service of the community, willing to help wherever necessary. Her kindness and dedication were known to everyone in the town, and it can be said that her legacy is indelible. We all remember her with great affection and admiration for her noble work and the beautiful life lessons she taught us.

I especially remember the times she would meet with us at the Carmen church. We gathered after mass to talk and learn from her wise words. Those moments are unforgettable and deeply marked our lives.

School Life and Promises

In those times, numerous ladies and young women of great virtue fervently participated in religious ceremonies, following beliefs originating when Mary, the mother of Christ, appeared at the same place where she passed away, on Mount Carmel, on July 16, 1257. For this reason, the Virgin of Carmen is venerated, whose image is associated with that sacred place, which at the time was a monastery.

The story goes that she appeared to one of the monks of the monastery, named Saint Simon Stock, of English origin. The Virgin gave him a scapular and made a promise that those who died wearing it would not suffer the pains of hell. Those who accept the scapular must believe in this promise. It is common for parents to bring their children, around the age of 10, to an initiation ceremony in the Brotherhood, where they begin to wear the scapular as part of their faith commitment. From that day, it is expected that they keep the scapular for life. Some forget or diminish its importance, while others always carry it with them. Generally, they are small scapulars and are renewed when they wear out. In my town, this religious custom is still maintained with deep faith.

My Teachers: Miss "La Chona"

Continuing with my school memories, I want to talk about my beloved teachers during my childhood. Among the ladies who marked my early education, I particularly remember one whose father was affectionately known as "La Chona." This teacher gave classes in her own home, and it was with her where I started my first school year. Lessons were given in a spacious corridor, next to a pond of crystalline water, a place I still vividly remember.

It was during this time that I began to show my naughtier side and earn the nickname that would accompany me for years. In La Capilla, almost no one was spared from having a nickname. We played a game called "The Enchanted Ones" during recess, which consisted of standing still when we were "enchanted" by another child, while the others ran to avoid being touched.

I remember one day, playing this game, no one could catch me because of my agility; I was very light on my feet. In front of the courtyard was a pasture enclosed by a stone wall. Even though I was small, I could jump with the agility of a squirrel, which we called "Zorritas." That day, when I easily leaped over the stone fence, one of my classmates, known as "La Sandía," exclaimed: "Look at him, he looks like a Zorrita!" Thus, my nickname "El Zorrito" was born, which eventually evolved into "El Zorro." However, my stay at that school was not very long; my mother decided not to allow me continue there after a disagreement with "La Chona."

La Chona's First Gas Station

One day, someone went to my house to tell my mother that I had taken a gasoline cap from one of La Chona's trucks. I was always a mischievous child, but never a thief. Such behavior was not like me from a young age, and my mother knew it. That's why she trusted me and did not scold me. The real culprit was a very good young man who, over time, became a priest. But, unfortunately, some of the boys blamed me.

La Chona owned two trucks as a business. She dedicated herself to transporting goods and moving gasoline from Guadalajara. It was the only gas station in the area. I remember she had countless two hundred-liter barrels lined up. That was her gas station. Additionally, she brought petroleum to supply the shops and stalls, which was used in devices that lit up at night.

"El del Zorrillo"

Just to the north, on the other corner, there was another pond known as "el del Zorrillo," named after its owner. This pond also had very clear water, and the owner made a business selling it. One day, my mother sent me to fetch water from this pond. I carried square containers, each capable of holding several liters. It was a common task for everyone in town since that was the main water source.

My Friends and My Mischief

It was our routine to carry water to homes for the animals and for daily use. The only way to have water was to fill the common containers we used to transport on a structure we affectionately called "la Burra." We carried it on our shoulders, holding the containers that weighed about fifty kilos. Despite being heavy for me, I transported them with intermittent rests.

I remember one particular day when I went to fetch water from Zorrillo's well. I was carrying my usual containers and had to pass by Miss Senaida's school. There, I encountered a group of boys who had not yet entered the class; they were just arriving. Among them was a boy from a neighboring ranch. He was a bit older than me, and we met while I was carrying the water. The older boys often looked for fun by provoking fights among others. And that day, without fully understanding the situation, I found myself involved in a scuffle with the ranch boy, right next to Zorrillo's pond.

Childhood and Mischief Outside Teacher Senaida's School

In those days of my childhood, despite never admitting I was scared, I got involved in a fight. The confrontation started when neither I nor my opponent, a boy equally brave, wanted to show fear. The fight lasted quite a while, exchanging blows until we were exhausted. Neither of us wanted to continue fighting. In my case, I already had a black eye and longed for someone older to intervene. I was about to give up when, a second before, my opponent declared, "That's enough, you won." It was a bittersweet victory, as in reality, no one won.

Reflecting on the incident, I realized that I had given in to the pressure of the older boys, showing bravery only to not admit my fear. In a hurry and somewhat battered, I returned home to deliver the water. My mother, seeing me in that state and suspecting something had happened, scolded me with her famous quince sticks. The purple marks from the fight added to the black eye the boy had caused me. Now, leaving that episode behind, I continue with the stories of the Posadas.

My Town's Activities from Ages 6 to 10

I would like to recount the experiences and activities of my town during my childhood, especially between the ages of six and ten. December is a particularly active month in our Chapel, as in many other places, due to the Christmas celebration, which is celebrated on December 25th. In our Chapel, preparations for Christmas began with the Posadas, starting a week before Christmas Eve, about an hour before the rosary, which always began at 8:00 p.m.

The Posadas were a kind of pilgrimage that began around 7:00 p.m. From six in the evening, many people began to gather in the square, turning it into a spectacle to see so many people together. People from neighboring ranches came to the square, which was filled with candy stalls, sugar canes, fruit stands, and especially peanuts, affectionately called "nail noise" due to the sound they made when peeled. With the cold, people consumed many calories, and peanuts were particularly coveted. It was a joy to see the square at night, which looked like a carpet of peanut shells.

I remember that the stalls selling peanuts had large piles in those days, and although we already had electricity, the lighting was very dim. Each block had just one bulb, and in the square, although there were posts, each one only held a light bulb so weak it looked like a hanging orange. The entire town was powered by just one electric motor, owned by Don Pedro Castellanos, known as Pedro Chico.

The person in charge of the motor was called Maestro Masás. This motor not only provided electricity; it was also used to grind nixtamal to make dough and, with it, daily tortillas. Every morning, a long line of people formed, waiting their turn to grind their nixtamal, and at night, the motor was turned on again to provide electric light to the homes and the town.

A bulb was placed in the center of the four corners of each block. At 11:00 p.m., the light was turned off, announced first with a brief blackout fifteen minutes before. After this, people lit up with candles or oil lamps.

Posadas and Christmas

Returning to the Posadas and continuing with the peanut theme, I remember that at most stalls during the Posadas, vendors would spread out a petate; an indigenous word describing large mats made of tule. They would place handfuls of products on the petate, spreading them out carefully. Each carefully placed handful attracted customers with their calls: "Here are the golden ones!" "Come on, only twenty cents!" There was friendly competition among the vendors, but all managed to sell, constantly inviting passersby.

The Posadas began at the foot of the altar inside the church, representing Joseph and Mary's search for lodging before the birth of Jesus. Their pilgrimage through Bethlehem, seeking a place to stay, was represented. They were offered no lodging until they found a shelter on the city outskirts, where Mary would eventually give birth.

Continuing with traditions, during the Posadas, they carried figures of Joseph, Mary, cows, and lambs. These figures were not very large and were placed on platforms with handles to be carried on the shoulders. The procession began from the altar, and simultaneously, the choir inside the church began their hymns, marking the beginning of this beautiful tradition.

The Choir and La Chaparra: Musical Memories

At the top of the temple, there were several children accompanying the organist, whom we affectionately called "La Chaparra." She was an exceptionally kind person and was accompanied by an extraordinarily talented violinist, Jorge Venegas. His violin skill was marvelous, and his death at a not very advanced age was deeply mourned by the whole town. Jorge was not only a prodigious violinist but also a great person, just like La Chaparra. He never missed the rosary in the evenings and was present at all special events of the year, including elegant weddings and first communions.

On regular days, he dedicated himself to teaching singing to children. My brother Miguel, for example, was trained by him to sing in the choir. I was not taught, as I was quite mischievous.

Continuing with the Posadas, when they left the temple, they circled the square, singing praises in chorus. People joined in with voices that sounded wonderfully a cappella, intoning chants typical of Christmas Eve. We children almost always carried some noise-making instrument, imitating bird songs. These instruments were made of tin and were called "guajes de lata."

Song of the Güijolas

There was a craftsman in our town, a skilled maker of güijolas, whom everyone knew for his expertise. Güijolas were like round containers that were ten centimeters in diameter, whose lid was shaped like an inverted funnel, ending in a small hole, with the thickness of a pen cartridge. These instruments had a tube about five centimeters long and the thickness of a pencil. They were filled with water by blowing into them, producing a sound reminiscent of bird singing.

We were so many boys with güijolas that, when played together, the sound resembled a choir of birds. With these instruments, we accompanied the procession until returning to the temple. At the end of the procession, when Joseph and Mary, carried on a platform, approached a pomegranate hung like a piñata, the choir began to sing. At that moment, they opened the pomegranate into four parts, releasing a flurry of colored confetti and streamers, creating a magical and festive moment.

Mischief with Güijolas

Those times were beautiful. Among our mischief was also playing with the güijola. We filled it with water, which, when blown, produced a peculiar sound. Ingeniously, we would cover the hole where the air came out and, by tilting the güijola, we would launch a strong jet of water, drenching each other. We would leave the rosary completely soaked, always carrying a water bottle to refill the güijola when it was emptied.

Additionally, we used to play the güijola during each mystery of the rosary, coinciding with the choir and everyone's singing. Everything sounded so beautiful, as if they were songs from heaven. At the end of each mystery, instead of continuing to pray, we began to drench each other. We even wet the older people, acting as if, among so many people, they wouldn't know who had done it.

However, we once wet an older boy. When we sprayed him with the güijola, he turned around suddenly and saw us. We quickly hid when we saw him coming towards us, visibly angry. My friend, whom we called el Cisto, was with me. We both ran together to get away from his anger.

The Air of Peanuts

On that occasion, due to the large crowd, we had to run crouched among people's legs to escape. Almost reaching the exit of the temple, we stopped upon realizing we had evaded our pursuer. However, we found ourselves in a situation similar to a mouse that does not want cheese but to escape the trap. Right where we stopped, someone could not contain a fart, and as everyone had eaten peanuts, some had delicate stomachs.

Oh, dear! We almost asked for help from the strong smell surrounding us. The odors twisted us so much that we lost all orientation, not knowing where the exit was. We tried to hold our breath as long as we could, but it would have taken being a swimming champion to last long without breathing. And as we were crouched down, the smell hit us in the face. Finally, staggering like drunkards, we found the exit, thanking God for breathing fresh air again. Behind us, others who had also been affected by the peanut air followed. Thus ended those beautiful Posadas, followed by the Christmas celebration.

Christmas

On Christmas Eve, after the Posadas ended, the arrival of the holiday filled the town with joy and expectation. People gathered in larger numbers, and the markets enjoyed their moment of glory, selling toys on every corner. All of us eagerly awaited that day, imagining what gifts the Christ Child would bring.

In those days, an orchestra played in the plaza's kiosk, formed by local talents like Jorge Venegas and Zacarías, I think he was his relative, who played the trumpet. There was another, whom they called el Hory, and my grandfather Don Tachito played the baritone. The orchestra–directed by Jorge V., a magnificent violinist–delighted everyone with its music. The sale of peanuts was a source of joy, and the ground was covered with shells mixed with confetti and streamers, especially during the serenades.

After the rosary, the young women and men began to circle the plaza, while the housewives sat on the benches to watch all the exciting movement. When the ladies took a turn, the men did so in the opposite direction, creating a dance of glances and encounters.

Christmas and the Serenade

In the plaza, there were several stands at Christmas, and the stalls came alive. They sold confetti and streamers, and many offered carnations and gardenias. Women received these beautiful flowers with great joy, keeping alive a tradition that endures to this day. The sale of colorfully painted eggs filled with confetti, which were broken over people's heads, adding color and laughter to the festivities, was also popular. Christmas shone with fireworks, a spectacle that amazed us as we looked for new mischief to make.

Warrior Eggs and Other Mischief

I remember once, in the house my father had bought, I discovered a nest in a hole in the wall. A hen had abandoned about eight eggs there, already old. I thought about selling them at the store, but when I moved one, I heard the sound of its contents sloshing, a sign that it was rotten. Although the smell was almost unbearable, I decided to take them anyway. Along with my inseparable friend, el Cisto, who also loved mischief, we devised a plan together.

Mischief and Ingenuity

I took some of those eggs and, together with my grandfather Tachito in his carpentry workshop at his home, we found the perfect opportunity for one of our pranks. There, we painted some eggs with the paint my grandfather used daily and attached confetti to them so they would resemble those confetti-filled ones sold in the square. Our plan was to earn a few cents by selling them.

We waited until nightfall when people left the rosary and the serenade began. We met some older boys to whom we sold the eggs at half price. We didn't give the eggs away for free to avoid suspicion, as our real interest was the prank itself rather than the money we could make.

They believed the eggs contained confetti, and we even sold them some flowers we cut from my grandmother María's pots. I don't remember how much they gave us in total, but we soon hid to see what would happen with those eggs.

One of these boys, known for being a bully to the younger ones, had stolen marbles from us in the past. That night, as they roamed the square, they stopped to talk with two girls, about 13 to 15 years old, being a year or two older themselves. The bully, in particular, was someone we didn't care much for due to his past actions.

An Unforgettable Prank

I remember the day we decided to get back at a boy who had stolen our marbles one day while we were playing and had hit us. Our mischief was centered around the Christmas serenade. As the boys chatted with some girls, we seized the opportunity to break on their heads some foul-smelling spoiled eggs that we had prepared.

Screams ensued immediately. The stench was unbearable, so much so that the nearby boys covered their noses with their hands, leaving the girls alone, screaming and frantically cleaning themselves, even using their shawls to cover up.

Hidden and keeping an eye on the scene, we held back our laughter, witnessing the chaos we had caused. Soon, a policeman known as Pancho Pistolas came to investigate. Even he had to cover his nose from the bad smell. The girls, after explaining the situation, hurried off to bathe, seeing it as the only solution.

A Countryside Scheme

Later, Herminio Alcalá, the then long-standing commander known for his strictness, was looking to arrest the two boys involved in the hard egg incident. Upon finding out, they fled to their parents' ranch to avoid justice and waited for the issue to blow over, giving us a break from their annoyances.

Nevertheless, our paths crossed again. Whenever we saw them, we ran like champions, knowing they sought revenge. I remember one day while playing in the block where my friend Cisto lived, whose real name was Manuel Castellanos, son of the famous Chepillo. That time, the boys devised a plan to corner me: one appeared from one corner and the other from the opposite. They probably thought we couldn't escape.

Cisto, whose house was nearby, ran to take refuge inside out of fear and closed the door behind him, forgetting about me. I was paralyzed for a moment, watching the boys approach from each side. But then, recalling why they called me "el Zorrito," I reacted swiftly.

I dashed toward a window. It was one of my most memorable pranks, occurring in front of Cisto's house. His house had a railing, and right above the window, there was a quarry channel for rainwater drainage. Once, I climbed up this channel to reach the rooftop. The boys chasing me tried to follow, but from above, I threw a brick at them while they yelled that they had to catch me. They never succeeded; they were left wanting. After they left, I came down, and thus ended another of my many pranks.

CHAPTER 7

New Year and the Three Wise Men

After Christmas came the New Year. This celebration was quieter, generally marked by a midnight mass. Peanut sales continued, as people still gathered at night to wait for the mass. Back then, it was rare to see someone with a coat; the ranch folks never left their large hats at home. Then, on January 6, we celebrated the Day of the Three Wise Men. Sometimes we received gifts on this date, but other times there was nothing, as much had been spent during Christmas.

The purses were empty, and yet, this date was also celebrated with a mass, but during the day. The following day, people began to take down Christmas decorations and disassemble the nativity scenes. I especially remember the beautiful Nativity set up in front of the altar at the church, which was the most impressive of all those arranged in The Chapel.

We were fascinated to see how the church's Nativity recreated the entire village of Bethlehem with its small houses, many miniature figures, cows, donkeys, sheep, camels, and grape harvests. At the edge of this Bethlehem, they placed a portal with a manger, representing the birth of Jesus Christ, with Saint Joseph, the Virgin Mary, and the donkey. These figures were medium-sized, similar to those used in the Posadas pilgrimage. They also included cows, lambs, several shepherds, and, when placing Baby Jesus in the manger, they added the Three Wise Men with their camels and horses, creating a touching and detailed scene.

Tribute to Tomás Torres

I fondly remember the Nativity scene set up at the church's entrance. A star illuminated it, creating a truly beautiful scene. The second most impressive Nativity belonged to a lady named Aureliana, wife of a man known as Tomás Torres. Although there were rumors of him being selfish, my personal experience was always that he was a very good person.

Tomás was also famous for being an excellent hare hunter, never missing the hunting gatherings organized in the square every Wednesday, especially during the rainy season when the grass was tall. People eager to participate in the hunts would arrive with their dogs, and even the greyhounds that roamed the streets seemed to understand the excitement and approached the truck to be taken along.

Don Tomás Torres never rode in the truck. He had a medium-sized horse whose trot was so fast it was hard to find another that could match it, except perhaps for Don Felipe, the agrarist, who was also known for his good trot. Don Tomás would wake up early to go hunting, mount his horse, and by the time we arrived, he was already there.

Since childhood, I always enjoyed participating in the town's activities, one of which was going hunting with Don Tomás Torres. When we arrived in the truck, Don Tomás was already there, ready to start touring the pastures. His wife, Aureliana, whom I have already mentioned, was an exceptionally kind and beloved lady. The relationship between Don Tomás and her was evident; they got along very well and cared deeply for each other.

Speaking of the second most beautiful Nativity, Doña Aureliana set it up in her spacious living room facing the street. Every year, she arranged a large and beautiful Nativity that she kept open for public viewing. She would open the window facing the sidewalk so that anyone passing by could admire it, and she felt very happy when people stopped to look.

This couple never had children, as fate would have it. They lived with a godson, a very kind person who stayed with them until Don Tomás's death, assisting them in everything necessary. Don Tomás had pigs, and Lunis, the godson, took care of feeding them. They owned several pig feedlots with a large number of animals. We would see Lunis every day carrying water in his pair of buckets for the pigs.

Tomás Torres and Lunis

Don Tomás Torres had a peculiar relationship with his godson, Lunis. Although Lunis was dearly loved by Don Tomás, he was often treated almost like a slave, always hoping to inherit something when Don Tomás passed away. However, when Don Tomás died, Lunis stayed only a short while longer with Doña Aureliana before leaving to work in Guadalajara, realizing he had inherited nothing. Don Tomás, who hardly ever paid him, left Lunis in the same poverty, hoping vaguely that Doña Aureliana might recognize his nearly free labor over the years.

What happened next was sad for Lunis. When Doña Aureliana died, she took the young man's hopes with her. Before her death, the town priest, Father Vera, began visiting her daily to prepare her for the afterlife. Since Don Tomás Torres had been very wealthy and left everything to his wife, she was considered very pious and was said to go straight to heaven, just like her husband.

Father Vera and the Church Properties

Doña Mariquita de la Torre, wife of Don Felipe Navarro, managed the church properties. Upon her passing, she bequeathed numerous properties around and in front of the church for the benefit of the parishioners and the town. However, Father Vera, in charge of these assets, sold some of them, and it is unclear whether he respected the deceased's wishes. It remains a doubt whether he had the right to do so.

When Doña Mariquita died, she left all her properties to her youngest son, Vicente, who never married. Among these properties was the large house that her father, Don Felipe Navarro, had built, and a well known as "el Pozo de Adentro." Another well, located half a block north of the church, was known as "the pond." This completely stone-built well was impressive. I always wondered how they managed to extract so much rock to construct it. It would fill quickly when it rained, gathering water from the surrounding streets, but this water was not drinkable as it also collected runoff from nearby corrals and stables, turning dark.

Properties of the Temple

At the pond near the temple, all year round, a layer of greenery formed, like a carpet of miniature lilies, due to cattle manure. Sometimes, my grandmother María would send me to fetch water from this pond, carrying the jugs on a donkey, that is, a wooden pole over the shoulders. Over time, this pond was covered up and replaced by houses.

Indeed, it was no longer necessary, especially after Priest Vera sold the property. It was one of many he sold, something his predecessor, Father Morales, had not done. Of course, Priest Vera did it with a convincing pretext.

Another significant property was a temple located to the east of the main one, at the corner of La Capilla, known as the "New Temple." This temple, which was never completed, is the same one I have mentioned on previous occasions. It was initiated by my great-grandmother, Doña Mariquita de la Torre, after the assassination of her husband, Don Felipe

Navarro. Also, as I mentioned before, in that "New Temple," also called Alebo, was the first cemetery where the first founders of La Capilla were buried.

The New Temple

The New Temple, a project started by Doña Mariquita de la Torre, was a tribute to the town's founders and her ancestors. Among them was Don Antonio de Aceves, along with other prominent surnames like Navarro, González, de la Torre, and Franco, who were the first to arrive in the town originally called Guadalupe. Later, the name evolved to Capilla de Guadalupe, its official designation.

This temple was conceived by Doña Mariquita, not just as a place of worship but also as a monument in honor of her husband, Don Felipe Navarro, who died as a hero, and her grandfather, Amo Aceves. The idea was to build a temple around the cemetery to create a lasting memory of those who sacrificed to found our town, La Capilla.

I remember the New Temple as a grand brick structure, with all its walls already formed. It had beautiful arches, well-defined naves, and a tower that was already under construction. On the ground floor, you could still see the wooden crosses marking each of the graves. As a child, I used to explore these places freely and had great fun. I remember the first time I went; my cousin Ligo Ascencio, who lived near the New Temple, took me. We climbed up one of the walls where my cousin showed me an impressive view.

From there, we could clearly see the cemetery crosses, not realizing at that moment that our ancestors lay among those graves. I say "our" because Ligo also shared that same lineage. He was the son of a first cousin of my father, Don Eduardo Ascencio González, grandson of Don Eulogio González "el Plateado," also my father's grandfather, and together with his wife Doña Teodora Navarro, daughter of Don Felipe

Navarro, they rested in that cemetery. Doña Teodora, remembered as a saint for her patience and resignation in the face of a disease that took her in the prime of her life, was also there.

Doña Mariquita de la Torre had conceived the New Temple as a tribute to all these ancestors. However, bad luck would have it that she died when the construction was just halfway through. Sadly, the priest of la Mora, who had been in charge of the temple for many years and supported the New Temple's work, also passed away, and with his death, the construction stopped. I believe the heirs, facing problems in dividing the inheritance, showed no interest in continuing the work on the New Temple, leaving it unfinished.

The New Temple and the New Legacy

It narrates how the New Temple remained unfinished and, over time, was forgotten by the community, including the respect we owed to our ancestors buried there. It seems there was no one to take the initiative to continue the work, perhaps because the knowledge of the historical and familial value it represented was lost.

The successor of Father de la Mora, Father Morales, devoted himself entirely to the main temple, which still required much work to be completed and beautified. Under his leadership, the main temple transformed into a work of art, notable for its beautiful murals of the Virgin of Guadalupe. It is clear he invested much time and money in this project, which likely prevented him from attending to the New Temple. I cannot blame him, as being from Arandas, he was an exceptionally active and organized priest, distinguished by his humility, an essential quality for any representative of the church of Christ.

While I digress a bit from the main topic, it is important to acknowledge that, for one reason or another, we greatly appreciate Father Morales as a significant benefactor to our community and faith.

The townspeople, though not recognizing what the New Temple truly represented beyond mere ruins, always maintained a respect for the place. I believe the lack of an initiator among the descendants to organize cooperation for finishing the work was the main reason it was never completed. It was a very meaningful tribute, and it saddens me to have realized its importance too late.

What I relate now is the fruit of knowledge acquired over the years, memories stored in my memory of stories told by my grandparents and other elders of the town, even some older than them. I pieced all this together like a puzzle, and God has given me the patience and ability to remember and reflect to discern the truth.

I recall making mischief in the New Temple. When Ligo, my cousin, took me there for the first time, he also warned me not to come down from the walls. There were rumors that a feathered rattlesnake lived among the graves, keeping us alert. During our visits, we never dared to descend to the ground. Ligo was also given his own nickname, 'el Sopal.'

I vividly remember an anecdote with him. One day, his mother sent him to the store with 104 cents to buy noodle soup, made by Chepillo. It seems they gave him a generous amount for those 104 cents, and when he left the store, he showed us the large bundle of soup, shouting excitedly. From then on, we started calling him 'el Sopal.'

On another occasion at the New Temple, alongside Pillo, son of Elpidio Gonzales and my friend, we explored the great arches of the temple. We discovered a hole between the bricks of one of the arches and, seeing a dove emerge, I climbed up curiously, hoping to find squabs. Indeed, I found two. Each of us took one home. They were beautiful pigeons, blackish-blue with some white feathers and a distinctive white collar around the neck. They were special, though I never knew exactly what breed they were.

On another occasion, I went to the temple with another friend my age, Jesús Galván, whom we called 'Chu.' He and I decided to climb the higher walls of the temple, entirely made of brick. We did it because we saw, at the very top, a nest of barn swallows.

Despite the risk of falling, we proceeded carefully. We found a plank nearby and decided to use it as a bridge to cross. Chu, who lived nearby, brought it over, and we struggled to place it so we could cross.

Upon reaching the nest, I crouched down to pick up two small barn swallows, but suddenly, the mother swallow came flying toward us, attacking us with loud squawks. At that moment, I already had a small barn swallow in my hands. Chu started to throw clods of earth to drive away the mother swallow, and so we managed to escape, though with the danger of falling. I took the small barn swallow home; after a raffle, it fell to me. I fed it worms that I found in the flowerpots at home, where plants and flowers grew.

Such were my days of fun in the New Temple. We loved wandering among its walls. I am sure that if it had been completed, it would have been a beautiful place. But unfortunately, the project stopped with the death of mama Mariquita and the priest de la Mora.

With the arrival of Father Vera, a new chapter began in our town. Although he started with little knowledge about the history and founders of the town, his first steps were promising. He became involved in raising several material works, especially benefiting the school system. Thanks to certain influences and accumulated capital, as well as with the help of various town residents and the sale of some temple properties, he managed to renew the electric light system, a pressing need for the community.

With his character and leadership, he seemed to be a magnificent benefactor, but over time, his focus changed dramatically. He made the controversial decision to demolish the New Temple to build a Charro Field, a noble sport deeply rooted in our region and my town. The Charro team from La Capilla even became national champions twice.

However, this decision implied, perhaps unconsciously, a lack of respect for the sacred site of our ancestors. By transforming the space into a Charro Field, the traces of the sacred relics, including the consecration of the cemetery and the last sacrament given to each of those buried there, as well as the original consecration of the temple, were lost. I am convinced that there is no rite that can erase what has been consecrated; if there is, it is unknown to me.

In history and faith, there are deep mysteries, such as respect for the dead, who rest in anticipation of the resurrection promised by Christ. This respect is fundamental, as demonstrated by the biblical example of Jacob. When Jacob left the lands of Canaan, where he lived with his father Abraham, he went to Egypt with his son Joseph, a powerful and trusted man of Pharaoh. Joseph brought his entire family, totaling 70 people, including his brothers, wives, children, and father Jacob.

As the time of his death approached, Jacob made Joseph promise to bury him in the tomb where his father Isaac and grandfather Abraham had been buried. This property, purchased by Abraham, featured a cave turned into a family tomb. There, Abraham and his wife Sarah, Isaac and Rebecca rested. Jacob had already prepared his own burial place in that cave.

He asked Joseph that upon his death, he be taken to that tomb. And so it was. Upon Jacob's passing, Joseph organized a caravan with carts, horses, and camels, and with Pharaoh's permission, transported his father's body to fulfill his promise, respecting the sacred place and the memory of their ancestors.

Respect for the Dead

With Pharaoh's permission, Joseph undertook a long journey of hundreds of kilometers to Canaan to bury his father Jacob with all the solemnity and respect he deserved. This ceremony, full of mourning and honor, emphasized the importance of respect for ancestors.

Later, as his own death approached at age 110, Joseph spoke to his family about the future. He told them that a day would come when God would aid them in leaving Egypt and, when that moment arrived, he asked that they take his remains with them and bury him next to his father.

Centuries passed, and Joseph's descendants grew exponentially in Egypt. When they finally set out for the Promised Land, they numbered over half a million people, not counting women and children. Although Moses, who led the exodus, did not reach Canaan, Joseph's remains were carried to the family tomb after 40 years of sacrifices and journeying through the desert. Finally, they arrived in Canaan, east of the Jordan River.

This story illustrates the deep importance and love one should have for the will of the deceased. The decision to carry Joseph's remains to Canaan, fulfilling his last wish centuries later, demonstrates exemplary respect and devotion to family legacy.

The belief that bodies must rest in peace until the resurrection day holds a profound mystery. Why is it so crucial to respect the wishes of the deceased? It seems that there was greater knowledge of these matters in the past, knowledge that seems to be fading today. I often hear it said that, once dead, the body no longer matters and can be laid to rest anywhere. However, I firmly believe that, though the body is a temple of the Holy Spirit in life and the soul departs after death, the body remains sacred and deserving of respect.

Writing about this fills me with emotion, almost as if I had a lump in my throat. This might be a form of protest, and I feel I have the right to make it. My ancestors resting in the New Temple deserve our respect. Their silence does not mean they are unaware of what happens with their descendants. I believe that if spirits could weep, they would have shed many tears over how their remains and memory have been treated.

Regarding the desecrated sacred cemetery, I do not believe it means God will punish those who violated its consecration, perhaps unwittingly. I am sure this is the case because I know the charros in my town are people of great faith. Yet, there are aspects like this that we sometimes fail to fully understand, and we are all susceptible to making such mistakes. Occasionally, we are not taught to value the love and effort our ancestors put into creating a hereditary economy to improve their descendants' lives.

Those who managed to leverage this legacy did well; those who squandered it, what a pity. But it is undeniable that our ancestors made sacrifices, risking and even losing their lives in struggles, like don Felipe, who died heroically. They constantly faced dangers to preserve what they would eventually leave us, always combating bandits who wanted to snatch away what they had achieved through hard work.

It seems that, over time, those who live comfortably may easily forget the sacrifices and struggles of those who came before them.

The Forgotten Legacy

Many living comfortably in our town seem to have forgotten their roots, overlooking the significant sacrifices of their predecessors. The most distressing aspect is how the graves of our ancestors were handled. Sadly, they were removed from their resting places and transferred to what is known as the Common Grave, designated for the destitute unable to afford their burial. It's as if they were discarded, forgotten.

Mamá Mariquita's earnest effort to honor her loved ones and the founders of our Chapel of Guadalupe has faded, erasing the profound respect owed to them. Sometimes I wonder if there is any way to comprehend and redeem what happened. If my thoughts are mistaken, I ask for forgiveness and forgive those who may have erred, if there's something to forgive.

In our town, we are nearly all relatives in some way; some closer, others more distant. I cherish and have always felt their affection. I hope that one day, we can collectively rectify this mistake. I deliberated deeply before writing this chapter, seeking words to express these feelings and thoughts.

I felt a significant responsibility writing about the New Temple. While my ancestors cannot return to correct this mistake, I am honored that God gave me the opportunity to speak on their behalf, expressing the love and respect I hold for them. I firmly believe that the spirit of my ancestors, and all from the Los Altos region, endures in each place they lived, awaiting the day we reunite with them in eternal life.

Thus, I recount the story of the New Temple, a somewhat sorrowful tale I felt compelled to share. Some may disagree with my views on priest Vera and his mistake, but the facts speak for themselves. Conscious decisions, even when wrong, bear responsibility, and those in leadership and decision-making roles bear the most blame.

To ease the lump in my throat, I prefer to focus on the beauty of La Capilla, including its wonderful women, whose presence and beauty elevate every town event. Their loveliness is like flowers adorning the festivities, bringing joy and enhancing each moment.

CHAPTER 8

The Festival of My Town

In these festivities in honor of the Morenita Guadalupana, which were originally held in December in Mexico City and around the world, there was a significant change during Father Morales's time in my town. Under his leadership and with the community's consent, the celebration was moved to February.

This shift attracted not only residents from La Capilla but also visitors from other regions. In the festival's final days, the square would fill to the brim, and beyond the celebrations in the square, there were cockfights and thrilling horse races.

Before the first day of celebration began, the streets were adorned with elaborate ornaments made of colored paper strips. These decorations were attached to the walls with a special glue made from wheat flour and water, proving very effective. The sight of these colorfully decorated streets was a beautiful spectacle.

Moreover, some of our neighbors would hang lanterns on their door frames. These lanterns, equipped with candles, illuminated the night and added a special touch to the celebration. These details helped create a festive and enchanting atmosphere that everyone eagerly looked forward to.

The festivities in our beloved town were a true spectacle that filled our hearts with joy since we were children. The celebrations started with the posadas and extended through Christmas. From early on, anticipation would take over us, and our hearts would fill with joy knowing days of enjoyment and celebration awaited us.

One of the most exciting aspects was the fireworks that lit up the night sky. The charm of the fireworks became apparent with the magnificent powder castle that burst into bright colors. Additionally, the rockets of lights and the thunderous boom rockets, carefully aligned around the square and the church created a magical atmosphere.

The bulls of buscapiés, after their own display, would give way to the grand burning of the castle. The last two days of festivities were the climax with the parade of allegorical floats. These floats, designed with artistic mastery, depicted biblical passages and were true works of art.

The most colorful and anticipated parade was that of the Morenita Guadalupana, a tribute filled with fervor. Moreover, we cannot forget the parade of the brave local charros, riding their beautiful horses and proudly bearing the flags of the Vatican, Mexico, and H.S.A.

We all felt united in a spirit of community and neighborliness, sharing the joy of these festivities that enriched our lives and strengthened our bonds.

The Festival of My Town: The Dancers

The roar of drums and trumpets resonated in the air, heralding the festivity's arrival. Sometimes, the distinguished Charros of Tepatitlán would join the parade, accompanied by the melodious music of the Colegio Morelos Band. On special occasions, even the Municipal Band of Tepatitlán or Arandas was hired. Since the festivities took place in February, all this was possible.

But we must not forget the tireless Dancers, who expressed their love and gratitude to the Morenita Guadalupana for descending to Mexico, especially for our humble indigenous race, represented by the noble Juan Diego. The message and love they transmitted transcended skin color barriers, reaching everyone equally.

During the last two days of celebration, the Dancers, coming from various regions, would begin to dance in the church atrium. The constant clatter of their hooves and the sound of bells on their ankles created a unique symphony. Dressed identically to the ancient indigenous people, they wore multicolored costumes and headdresses adorned with long feathers swaying to the dance rhythm. Sometimes, to keep the beat, they brought along a violinist, whose violin had more history than Moctezuma himself.

In their hands, they held rattles that added cadence to their dance, and the ensemble was simply mesmerizing.

Amid the festivities, the Dancers stood out as an essential part of the celebration. One of them wore a spooky mask that reflected bravery and mystery, but also imposed a certain fear. He held a long whip that would crack now and then, maintaining the spectator line that crowded in large numbers.

For us, the daring young ones who used to stick our noses into everything, this figure was an enigma we had to solve. Particularly, my friend Cisto and I were inseparable, and we decided to team up to take that whip from him, as he constantly tried to lash us. We were two meddlers bent on changing the celebration's dynamic.

Our strategy was to distract him skillfully: one of us would entertain him while the other tried to snatch the whip. The task was not easy, but we had an ally in this mission, a young man known as la Carioca, who joined us. Among the three of us, we managed to surprise the Dancer and take the whip.

However, the scene became even more entertaining as, amidst the confusion, the Dancer lost his mask due to difficulty seeing clearly. As we could not advance with the whip in our hands, we decided to let it go. Laughter and amusement took over the crowd as they enjoyed our antics.

The Festival of My Town: The Carcamanes

At my town's celebration, one of the most thrilling attractions was the Carcamanes, and we, as daring youngsters, couldn't resist the challenge they posed. We ran like deer when chased but were determined to enjoy it to the fullest.

In that festivity that marked my childhood, we experienced something almost magical. Watching people from everywhere gather to set up their businesses and settle into their spots was a true spectacle. Within this context, the Carcamanes stood out as a particularly unique betting activity.

On a carefully prepared table, numbers from one to twenty were displayed, each marked with wire. Next to this, a row of numbered cards from one to twenty was placed. The Carcamanes' host was a skilled presenter who knew all the game's tricks. He would start the game with enthusiasm, inviting participants to place their bets.

The process was fascinating: the host spun the betting wheel and, upon stopping, announced that no more bets were accepted. With a composed gesture, he inserted an arrow into the wheel and blew on it. The arrow would stick into a specific number on the wheel, and excitement would flood the area as everyone eagerly awaited to see if they had won.

This Carcamanes game was a genuine challenge of skill and luck that kept everyone entertained for hours. Those moments, filled with camaraderie and thrill, left an indelible mark on my memory.

An Encounter with the Carcamanes

During my town's festivity, I ventured to participate in this activity that mixed the thrill of gambling with cunning. I carried a few coins in my bag— not many, but enough to join in the fun. Even though I was young, I began to develop an innate shrewdness that urged me to study the rules before betting.

Before diving into betting, I watched the game and its secrets closely. I did not want to risk the little I had without fully understanding how it worked. I realized that the game's host had his own tricks. He would blow on the roulette arrow, sometimes from one side of the table and other times from the opposite. This deceptive skill was his strategy to maintain the game's mystery.

With patience and cunning, I figured out his pattern. When I noticed the bets leaning toward even numbers, he would launch the dart from one end of the table. And when the bets favored odd numbers, he would switch sides. My ingenuity did not take long to pay off, and I began to bet and win.

I enjoyed a successful streak for a while, amassing about 5 pesos in earnings. I felt the thrill of victory, but my overconfidence betrayed me at a crucial moment. On my last bet, I wagered a considerable amount, but the host refused to pay out. The situation became tense, and I was not willing to walk away without what was due to me.

Just when things seemed to get complicated, unexpected help arrived. Alcalá, the commander, emerged from his own cantina, and there began an unexpected twist in this exciting episode of my life.

The Festival of My Town and an Unexpected Encounter

The celebration of my town always brings an air of excitement and surprises. During one of these festivities, I encountered Don Herminio, an imposing man who wore his 38 Super and its four magazines with a solemnity that commanded respect from those around him. His felt hat, always in place, added an authoritative touch to his appearance.

Without hesitation, I approached him before he vanished into the crowd. Don Herminio knew me and treated me kindly. I shared my situation with him and we decided to talk in private. Once we found a suitable place, I explained the situation and asked him to pay me what I was owed. My conversation with him was straightforward, and he soon rewarded me with more than five pesos.

Cinema at Home

In the midst of all the events, there was a detail I had overlooked to mention. My father was fortunate to discover something interesting in the house he had acquired. The house had a basement with a large window which, even on the brightest days, remained dim due to its location at the back and the solid door it had.

Interestingly, this solid door had a small round hole, about two centimeters in diameter, which paradoxically allowed the brightest daylight to penetrate and traverse the basement. The hole was about ten centimeters long and created a fascinating interplay of light and shadows inside. The house held secrets and surprises that were gradually revealed.

The light passing through the hole projected shadows and reflections on the white wall. Everything happening on the street and across the sidewalk was reflected clearly, resembling a cinematic projection of sorts. Carts, donkeys, people; everything was displayed on the wall as if we were spectators of our own open-air show.

During that time, there were numerous muleteers bringing their herds of donkeys loaded with wood and coal from the hill. Wood and coal were essential in a time when most kitchens operated with these fuels.

Petroleum and gas had not yet reached our kitchens, and the wall's reflection phenomenon became a constant source of entertainment for us.

A prominent figure in our community was "la Chona," whose real name we never knew. The Martínez family, who had migrated to La Capilla de Arandas, were very dear to the town. They had three children, hardworking and supportive people who helped their father in the business of transporting gasoline for the occasional vehicles passing through La Capilla. At that time, the arrival of vehicles was infrequent, and I believe the Martínez family only had two cargo trucks. One of the sons, whom we called "Probado," was in charge of driving one of the trucks.

The Legendary Car of "la Chona"

In my town, "la Chona" had become an endearing character. Although her real name was a mystery to most, everyone knew her as "la Chona." She was a kind and simple person, despite her apparent wealth. Her brother, affectionately called "Gordito," drove another van and was known simply as "Gordito." They also had another younger brother whose name I cannot remember, but I know that in his youth, he decided to enter the seminary and became a respected priest.

La Chona and her family were very beloved in the town, and their generosity was known to all. As a first-year teacher who treated children with great affection, we adored her. Her fame spread throughout La Capilla, and although they came from a well-to-do family, they never lost their simplicity, which earned them the love and respect of the community.

However, one day "la Chona" decided to do something that surprised everyone. Amid the festivities of La Capilla, she decided to travel to Guadalajara to buy a car and bring it to our town. No one in the town had a car at that time, and she wanted to be the first to own one. This happened during one of La Capilla's busiest festivities, and her aim was to show off her new vehicle to the crowd.

At that time, our community already had good dirt roads that allowed the passage of trucks and some cargo vans, which we called "trocas." But "la Chona" wanted to be the pioneer in bringing a car to our town and stand out during the celebration.

To ensure that her new car was driven with skill, she hired someone experienced in its driving.

This memory I share about "la Chona" is done with all the respect she deserves, as she was a person worthy of admiration. Although her story is curious and entertaining, it is important to highlight that her foray into the world of automobiles marked a milestone in our town.

Continuing with the famous festival of La Capilla, in one of these festivities, "la Chona" made her triumphant entry with her first car. This was not only memorable but, in my opinion, a unique event, as it was unlikely that anyone else would have arrived with a car of that magnitude to our town.

The Lottery: An Exciting Tradition at the Festivities

The celebration in La Capilla offered a wide range of activities, one of which was particularly eye-catching. It involved a raffle of various items displayed at the center of a tent on a platform. This raffle, known as "La Lotería," was held to raise funds for the church's aid.

In "La Lotería," they sold square cardboard sheets containing about sixteen cards with different figures like animals, insects, and characters engaging in various activities. Attendees could buy these sheets and then wait eagerly for the game to start.

One of the festival's most thrilling moments was when the announcer began to sing out the figures and their corresponding numbers on the cards. The tension was palpable, as everyone anticipated the chance to win a prize.

However, that particular year, "la Chona" decided to take things to another level. With her brand-new car present, she did something completely unexpected that left all attendees astounded.

Amid the excitement, one of the attendees, known as "el Valiente," stood out as he held a deck with the same figures present on the sheets. With surprising skill, he began to uncover the cards and shout the figures aloud: "¡la chalupa! ¡el borracho! ¡la Rana!", were some of the voices that resonated in the midst of the general expectation.

The tension increased until someone finally shouted "Lottery!" four times. At that moment, two or three lucky individuals became winners and shared the prize among them. The tent where the Lottery took place was always crowded, and sometimes it was necessary to wait for someone to leave their spot before participating.

The excitement grew even further thanks to the music that flooded the square throughout the day, with mariachis playing and enlivening the celebration. At night, the band took care of the serenade, while the youth threw streamers and confetti into the air, creating a festive and cheerful atmosphere.

One of the most tender moments of the evening was watching the young women with heaps of carnations and gardenias that the boys had given them. These gestures of affection helped make the festivities a joyful and lively event.

Our town's festivals were a celebration that united the community in a spirit of joy and camaraderie, where the Lottery and all the other activities were an essential part of the fun and tradition.

The exciting cockfights

The festivals in our town were a complete spectacle that offered entertainment both day and night. During the day, the square filled with music and joy thanks to magnificent bands like the Tepatitlán Municipal Band or the one from Arandas, which livened up the atmosphere with their captivating music. The music became the heartbeat of the celebration, bringing everyone into a festive and jubilant mood.

But the fun didn't end there, as the thrilling cockfights began in the afternoon. For me, this was a fascinating experience full of excitement, shouts, and music. Since I was young, I was drawn to this activity and couldn't resist the excitement it unleashed.

Back then, I didn't have the chance to be accompanied by an adult, as some children were brought by their relatives. However, I found an ingenious solution. There was a house adjacent to the cockfighting arena where a friend's family lived, nicknamed "Tolano," known as "the Camotero" for his talent in selling delicious sweet potatoes.

This family welcomed me kindly and treated me with affection, as if I were one of their own. Tolano and myself, along with some other friends devised mischief to dodge surveillance and sneak into the cockfighting arena. We knew we had to be discreet, taking advantage of moments when everyone was focused on the fights.

The cockfights were authentic duels of mixed emotions. The confrontations of the roosters triggered deafening shouts, while music and mariachis provided entertainment-filled interludes.

These moments became a welcome break between fights, and local artists delighted the audience with their songs. It was the perfect combination of emotions and entertainment amid the cockfights that lasted several days.

Our town's festivals were a complete celebration, where music, cockfights, and the festive atmosphere united the community in a spirit of joy and camaraderie.

During the festivals, intense passion was unleashed with the cockfights. Two teams representing different towns or cities faced off in exciting duels, like La Capilla against San Juan or La Capilla against Guadalajara. The atmosphere was so intense that a loud shout would start each fight: "Close the doors!" signaling that the bets were about to begin. The doors remained closed until all bets were agreed upon and confirmed.

In one of these thrilling fights, La Capilla and Arandas faced off. One of the roosters, known as "el Jiro," weighed one kilo and 700 grams, while its opponent from La Capilla, nicknamed "el Colorado," weighed one kilo and 750 grams. Both roosters were prepared for a clean fight, using half-inch blades. The bets rose to three thousand pesos, and enthusiasts began to shout their forecasts: "Who's for el Jiro!", or "Who bets on el Colorado!".

Amid the excitement, prizes were often raffled, with the most coveted being the fifty-peso gold centenarios. Once the blades were secured and everything was ready, the spectators and bettors left the ring area. Only those in charge of releasing the roosters and the judge remained, watching closely to ensure a fair fight without cheating.

The cockfights were a spectacle full of emotion and passion that brought the community together in an unforgettable celebration.

After each thrilling cockfight, the judge declared the winner, and there was a brief pause before the shout: "All is well! No complaints!" was heard. If no one raised any objections, it was excitedly announced: "Open the doors!" And so the celebration continued, accompanied by music, until the last fight of the commitment concluded.

Then, on occasion, extraordinary fights took place at night. Those wishing to stay enjoyed long tables where they shared jokes and anecdotes. Card games were also organized at another table, and sometimes, the mariachi continued playing for those who wished to enjoy the music by paying for it.

The night barely offered a break, as mariachis were often hired to perform romantic serenades. These musicians came from different places, like Guadalajara or northern bands with their guitars. Everywhere, one could hear serenades carried out by young men for their girlfriends, or suitors expressing their love. Sometimes, they were met with buckets of water thrown from the roofs, but this did not dampen the joy of the moment, and everyone enjoyed the fun.

These memories brought to mind a girl I liked very much, a beautiful young woman known as "la güerita de Victoria."

I admired her deeply, and she also thought highly of me.

An encounter at the cockfights with la güera de Victoria

Back then, during the exhilarating cockfights, something unexpected happened: la güerita de Victoria, a girl I was fond of, attended the fights. It was 1945, and I was about eleven or twelve years old. That day, when

I saw her among the crowd, my heart leaped with excitement. Her green eyes were simply beautiful, and her blond, curly hair made her even more charming. She looked at me with a smile that seemed to say, "How nice to see you." My heart was pounding.

I had the chance to talk to her, and I couldn't miss the opportunity. Despite my nerves, I approached her trembling and asked if she would be my girlfriend. Her reaction was instant: a delightful laugh that brightened her face even more.

At that moment, I felt fortunate and thrilled to have had the courage to approach her. La güerita de Victoria and I were young, but that encounter at the cockfights marked the beginning of a story that will endure in my memories.

The charm and sadness of la güerita de Victoria

Although our words were timid and our conversations few, we shared a special bond. We saw each other occasionally, but the last time I saw her was in the square of a store owned by Don Luis Gutiérrez, where she and a friend named Josefina Navarro Gutiérrez were.

During that meeting, I had the chance to chat with her for a while and received a portrait as a gift, a treasure I cherished dearly. However, the joy her company brought was fleeting, as she soon passed away. She suffered from heart problems, and her departure left a void in my heart. I was about thirteen or fourteen years old when she left us, and I no longer lived in La Capilla, as my father had taken me to San Luis Potosí. Despite the distance, I will always remember her with affection and gratitude.

Leaving these memories behind, I return to the festivities of La Capilla and its thrilling activities. Every morning, still in the dark, the pilgrimage began with the arrival of a crowd.

The early morning pilgrimage: An unforgettable celebration

The festival in La Capilla was a unique experience, full of traditions and emotions. One of the most outstanding activities was the pilgrimage that took place at dawn, accompanied by a live band or music group. From the moment they began to walk, the pealing of the bells announced the festivity that was approaching.

A pyrotechnician was in charge of launching rockets along the way, whose booms resonated like thunder in the sky. The pilgrimage traveled the streets of the town, singing beautiful praises to the rhythm of the orchestra and the explosions of the rockets. The combination of bell sounds and live music made it impossible to sleep. I remember one of the festivities I experienced in 1971 when I was near the square in the first block. It was impossible to sleep with the noise, so I preferred to join the pilgrimage and accompany it with songs in honor of the Morenita Guadalupana.

Upon returning to the temple, the first mass of the day was celebrated. The temple was magnificently decorated with a large number of flowers of various colors and types. This tradition continued for eight days, culminating on December 12. Each day, an individual or group assumed the costs of the festivity. Some of the luckiest had the honor of sponsoring the day of greatest splendor and expense.

The festivities were unforgettable, and the trucks from the Altos joined in the celebration, contributing to the festive and joyful atmosphere.

The Festivities in My Beloved Town: An Exciting Encounter

The festivities in my beloved town, La Capilla, were moments brimming with tradition and emotion. Various organizations and merchants came together to sponsor the celebration days, making each special day even more memorable. Undoubtedly, one of the most thrilling moments was when the "Hijos Ausentes" (Absent Children), those who resided in faraway places from La Capilla, had their special day.

This occasion was profoundly moving as a long procession took place from the town's outskirts to the church. The procession was led by a band or an orchestra, with most participants carrying a thick wax candle. For the "Hijos Ausentes," this day held a special meaning, as some had not visited their homeland for years. It was a moment of joy, reuniting with friends and, mostly, family members they had not seen in years.

Such were the festivities back then, and though the passion and vigor might have waned over time, they remain beautiful. The priest skillfully organized everything, yet there was a feeling that something was missing...

Continuing with my memories of childhood, the square transformed into a sea of tents, while the surrounding streets filled with itinerant vendors. It was delightful to see so many people gathered. Furthermore, tents functioning as mobile bars, all of considerable size, were erected. Throughout the day and night, norteño bands and mariachis played tunes, creating a festive atmosphere. Although there were drunks and occasional altercations, back then, the conflicts did not escalate to the violence we see today.

Festivities in La Capilla: A Time of Thrilling Shootouts

The festivities in La Capilla were undoubtedly a period full of emotions and astonishing events. At that time, most people carried pistols, and occasionally, when they drew them, gunshots echoed in the air. Individuals who had overindulged would trigger the gun carelessly, sometimes resulting in shots hitting shoes or legs. Personally, I remember witnessing one or two such incidents, as my friends and I were naturally curious and, instead of fleeing, we ran towards the event to see who was injured.

During the festivities, fights and shootouts were constant, especially among the ranchers, most of whom carried pistols. These confrontations were immediate, and gunshots thundered continuously in the air. For us, the youngsters of that time, this was perceived as a form of entertainment. When we arrived at the scene, the aggressor and their victim had already fled, while we watched, semi-hidden, yet continuing to cross the area. The police sometimes arrived and sometimes did not. When they did, they often chased the aggressor, who had a considerable head start, and we followed the scene with great interest.

It is curious how what might have been dangerous for some became a sort of amusement for us, though always with the intent to check if the police managed to catch the aggressor. However, sometimes, the police seemed to be a step behind in this kind of game.

The Serenade Party in La Capilla: A Battle of Emotions

The aggressor, feeling pursued, began to shoot at the police, and their ability to hide was remarkable, as most of the pastures were surrounded by large stones providing shelter. The police, for their part, would withdraw when this happened, and we found ourselves nearby, risking being hit by a stray bullet. When the pursuit ended, we quickly returned to avoid meeting with the police and instead headed towards the square, where the party continued unabated.

The night brought a new wave of emotions, as stalls selling confetti and streamers began to set up in the square. Piles of sacks filled with chopped paper and bags of colorful confetti flooded the area.

People enthusiastically bought confetti and threw it into the air, creating an atmosphere of joy. Additionally, various types of streamers were sold, joyfully thrown at the young women strolling around the square. Stands of carnations and gardenias were also set up, their fragrant aromas filling the air.

The cubes, small containers filled with assorted colored confetti, were an additional attraction. During this time, the festivity was at its peak, and everyone participated in the celebration with great enthusiasm.

The Serenade in the Square: A Dance of Emotions

As I mentioned earlier, after the rosary, the square came to life with the majestic music of the band. The melodies resonated in everyone's hearts, and I particularly loved listening to the "Marcha de Zacatecas." During this time, we took the opportunity to stroll around the square, which was covered in confetti.

We looked for paper bags on the ground and filled them with confetti to then throw at the girls. When I was interested in one of them, I would often visit my grandmother María's house, which had a spacious yard and a beautiful garden always full of flowers. I cut some of those flowers to give to the girls. Occasionally, my heart was gladdened seeing the fair-haired girl from Victoria walking around with her mother.

Another amusement we enjoyed at every party was the "volantín" and the "ferris wheel." The volantín had no motor, so it required people to turn it manually. It was surrounded by thick bars where youths would stand to spin it. When the spin got fast, the person in charge of the volantín would shout "up!," and instead of paying us to ride it, they charged us ten cents per bar. Despite this, we liked it so much that we looked for ways to pay the ten cents and enjoy this exciting experience.

The Volantín: A Game of Strategy and Mischief

The party continued, and when I didn't have the necessary ten cents to ride the volantín, which happened most of the time, I resorted to an ingenious strategy. My grandmother María was my accomplice in this mischief, as I used to spend a lot of time with her and even slept at her house to keep my two grandparents company. Most of their children had already married, which gave me the confidence to execute my plan.

My plan consisted of stealing some eggs from the hen nests at my grandmother's house. I knew exactly where the nests were, and once I had some eggs in my possession, I took them to sell at the local store. At that time, I remembered that eggs were paid for at five cents each. With the earnings from this little mischief, I could afford the fun that the volantín offered.

After enjoying the volantín, the anticipation grew while we waited for the exciting moment when they lit the fireworks castle. Sometimes, they even lit two castles, and the square was filled with gunpowder bursting in dazzling colors. After the castle, it was time for the "bulls of gunpowder," which were full of sparklers shot out like arrows, creating a scene full of fun and excitement as we tried to avoid being hit by them.

The Pyrotechnics Show at the Party

The party was in full swing, and the most awaited moment was the fireworks display that lit up the sky and attracted crowds of people, not just us youngsters, but also people of all ages. Before lighting the gunpowder bulls, the fireworks castle dazzled everyone present. The square was packed with spectators as hundreds of rockets lit up the sky with colorful lights, accompanied by loud explosions.

After the castle display, it was time for the gunpowder bulls, and to increase the excitement, a series of rockets and thunderclaps were placed around the church, on the atrium wall. These rockets soared into the sky, filling it with colored lights and creating an impressive spectacle. Among them was a rocket that didn't explode, which we called a "dud."

In a moment of curiosity, I approached the dud rocket that had fallen near me and tried to light it. However, I lacked a proper ignition source, so I asked for help from a friend of mine from the Gomez dam ranch, who appeared to have a lit cigarette. Unaware it was a thunder rocket, we attempted to light it innocently. Tragically, the rocket exploded in his hand, causing severe injuries to several fingers.

We stood astonished and silent, watching the blood spurt from his hand. First aid was quickly administered, his hand was wrapped in a rag, and he was taken to Dr. Isidro.

The Accident with the Sparklers at the Festivities

In those days, during the festivities, there were always certain risks, and one such incident involved a young man named Trujillo, who got burned by a sparkler. At that time, he was working at a pharmacy attended by Isidro, a very competent nurse known as "Chencho." It was Chencho who treated and healed him. Fortunately, fate willed that I was not injured in that incident.

During the festivities, accidents of this kind were unfortunately common. I recall another friend who suffered a similar mishap at the same party. He carried several sparklers in his pocket and, upon lighting one, carelessly caused all of them to ignite at once. He couldn't remove them in time, resulting in a burn that took years to heal. His wound, burned by gunpowder, remained open for a long time, and healing was a slow and painful process.

This young man was the son of a retired relative named Julio Martín, who had been one of the policemen of La Capilla. Julio Martín was a figure beloved by all the children and youth of the place. He was passionate about talking about soccer and carried a .38 Special with ornate grips and a holster full of bullets. Tragically, his life ended in an unfortunate encounter where bullets crossed at close range.

These incidents served as a constant reminder of the dangers that accompanied the festivities, and how fun could take an unexpected turn in the blink of an eye.

The Exchange of Bullets between Julio Martín and Santos Alcalá

On one occasion, we witnessed an exchange of bullets between two acquaintances: Julio Martín and Santos Alcalá. This happened in a barbershop of a friend of mine, also from La Capilla, whom everyone called "la Carioca." The other protagonist of this encounter was a descendant of La Capilla and belonged to the Alcalá family from Cacalote. We were very close friends and held each other in high regard. Both typically carried their firearms at their waists, as was common at that time.

Tragically, both lost their lives, like fine roosters in a fight. I cannot say who fell first, but the truth is that both lay on the ground because of a dispute that, in reality, no one knew exactly why it had erupted. However, the sadness we all felt was profound, as both were beloved friends.

Julio's absence in La Capilla left a void that was keenly felt, especially among the youth. But to lighten the mood a bit, let me continue with the serenade, a less sad story than the two deaths.

In the evening, while the girls dodged the confetti, the adults also had their fun. My father and his friends, like Padilla and Santiago, used to play among themselves, with nicknames like "el Diablito." They competed to catch the prettiest girls. There were many beautiful young women in the square, and throwing confetti at them was a form of entertainment. The square lit up with laughter and joy, and this was one of the most festive moments of the celebrations.

The Party in My Town and the Confetti Carpets

At the celebration of the festival in my beloved town, the creation of beautiful confetti carpets stood out. My parents and their friends, who were partners of the Red Trucks of the Altos, thoroughly enjoyed this festivity. In those days, business was going very well for them, allowing them to spend money joyfully and enjoy the fun healthily.

My mother also participated in the celebration, and the wives of my father's friends would gather in the square. They took a seat on a bench and watched eagerly as their husbands threw confetti and had fun. They also took the opportunity to catch up on the latest events and gossip of the town. As there was no local newspaper, they formed their own information circle until the time came for the fireworks and gunpowder bulls, at which point they would leave or move away, as it was dangerous for them. Those who stayed were the young people and men, ready to face the bulls and experience thrilling moments.

The serenade and the creation of these confetti carpets were part of the daily routine of the festivities. The housewives would designate someone to reserve the benches, and all my mother's friends and relatives, like Concha Martín, Tomasita Paredes, Angelina, Rogelia, Mariquita, María de Nina, and Concha, the one from Ángel Casillas, among others, were inseparable in these celebrations. They also actively participated in other important daily activities of the town's life.

The Festival - The Man Who Changed His Destiny

In the midst of the festive celebration in the square, a long table would sometimes be set up for playing word games after the cockfights, usually with the majority losing their bets. I vividly remember one of these nights in the square, around 10 p.m., when a shocking event occurred.

A man, who was the steward for a wealthy rancher, had received a significant sum of money to make an important payment. However, instead of fulfilling his task, he decided to enter the cockfighting arena and start betting. As he continued to lose, his hope of winning faded, and his desperation led him to drink more alcohol.

Eventually, he left the cockfighting arena and arrived at the square. On the sidewalk, right in front of Dr. Isidro's house, utterly desperate and under the influence of alcohol, he could not bear his misfortune. He pulled out his pistol in front of the crowd that had gathered at that moment and, without thinking, shot himself in the head. Dazed and without considering the consequences, he left behind his young children, his young wife, and all those who knew him.

This tragedy marked a turning point in the festival and in our lives. It was a reminder that the thrill of celebration could lead to impulsive and tragic decisions. The festivity continued, but the shadow of this event darkened the joy of that night.

CHAPTER 9

At School with Teacher Toña

After the intensity of the festivities, it was time to face the reality they left behind. Often, only the cockfights continued for about two or three more days, while everyone else focused on cleaning up and picking up the remnants of the celebration. For my part, I continued with my mischief, as I, being a child, was always thinking about what new prank I could play.

It was then that I started attending school with Miss Toña in the first or second grade. Although I felt comfortable in her class, my mind often wandered, distracted by the mischief that constantly swirled through my thoughts. Later, a teacher from Tepatitlán named Luis Camarena was brought in, an excellent educator and a great person.

I joined his classes along with many of my friends and relatives. I even have some photographs with the teacher and my classmates, although most of them, over time, got married. I enjoyed Professor Camarena's teachings very much, but at one point, I had a conflict with another student in the class. Since I was at fault, the teacher punished me and took me to Juanilla's house, where I lived.

The Punishment in the Big House and the Prank with the Curly Hairs

At that time, I was living in the big house that my great-grandfather Demetrio Estrado had built years before. My wise grandfather took me to a second floor and told me to stay there while he occupied the imposing residence of Don Jeranilly. He used to live on the San Antonio ranch, but circumstances led him to this house.

I spent quite some time punished in that place, I even ended up bald! I don't remember exactly why I was punished, but I believe it was related to some prank I had played. Back then, I was quite a mischievous child. Despite my small stature for my age, it seemed I was about four years old, but my development was delayed, and I started to grow properly when I was around eighteen years old.

One day, while at school, the older kids decided to play a prank on me. They asked me if I would like to have curly hair, and I, naively, thought curly hair would be great. They then told me I had to apply cow dung on my hair for two or three days until it dried, and afterward, you can imagine what happened; I had to pay for one of the many pranks I had played.

The Day They Smothered Pig Manure on Me

I remember one day, while at school, Lalo, who lived across from the school, took us to his large corral. At his house, they had a spacious yard where they milked cows and raised pigs. Lalo was determined to help me get curly hair, and for that, we needed a special ingredient: fresh cow dung.

However, we couldn't find any fresh cow dung in the corral. Instead, Lalo ventured into a fattening pen where there were many pigs. At that moment, I realized that this was not exactly pleasant, but I decided to ignore it since my desire to have curly hair was stronger.

Happy to have obtained the ingredient, I returned home without noticing my appearance. When I got home, my mother noticed something strange and covered her nose. I explained that they had smeared pig manure on my head to get curls in my hair. She told me, "Your curls are from the smell." My mother, with tearful eyes due to the strong aroma, even forgot to remove the quince branches she always carried with her because of the persistent smell.

That day, I received no beatings, but I was looked at with disgust when Lalo and I returned from the pig corral. Lalo told me to remove the pig manure from my head, warning me not to become conceited. With one hand, trying to cover her nose because of the bad smell, Maris told me to take a jug and a bucket and rinse myself completely after removing that filth.

Despite the lessons I received, my love for mischief persisted.

Mischief with El Cisto

Back then, when I was about six years old, El Cisto and I were inseparable. He was the same age as me and the son of the renowned Chepillo, who owned a store, a noodle factory, and even a bakery with a large team. His father, Don Emilio Castellanos, known as "Papoco," was a serious and respected man in the community.

I remember Chepillo's unforgettable laughter and smiles. He owned a noodle-making machine and spent all day producing this delightful food. It was a time when mischief and friendship were essential parts of our childhood.

At that time, I helped a boy they called Pedorrón to make noodles at El Cisto's noodle factory. Later on, I will tell the story of how he got that nickname. El Cisto's house had a very large yard, at the end of which was the bakery. I recall how El Cisto and I used to steal bread from there.

In that same yard, one day, we ventured to look for clay to make slingshots, and that's where we encountered a small turtle. We decided to take it with us, and at that moment, El Cisto's brother, named José, whom we nicknamed "Pepe la Cocorilla," was there.

While I was holding the turtle, Cocorilla warned us to be careful not to get bitten, as these turtles cling on once they bite. However, I didn't pay enough attention, and in a moment of carelessness, the turtle bit me. I screamed and struggled to get it off, but the turtle held firmly onto my finger.

Eventually, I managed to free myself by giving a strong pull, tearing off a piece of flesh in the process. To this day, I bear a scar on that finger as a memento of that episode. Everyone present laughed heartily, and I learned an important lesson that day.

Mischief with El Cisto - Sundays at the Square

Sundays at the town square were always special days. When we had little to do and were looking for exciting situations, we eagerly awaited Sundays. On those days, the square would become the stage for these extraordinary events.

The ranchers would come down to La Capilla to attend mass, a mandatory duty, and also to buy what they needed for the week. The square would be filled with ranchers who came joyfully and was full of market stalls. There was everything: fruits, seeds, and candy stalls of all kinds made by the people of La Capilla.

Among the special sweets were Charrascos, milk sweets, Jamoncillos (similar to nuts with cinnamon), Colaciones with anise inside, and many others. Early in the mornings, some ladies had stalls where they sold cinnamon water, coffee with milk, and upon request, would add a splash of alcohol for those who wished. They also offered Rompope with alcohol.

In the afternoons, a lady named "María Esqueda" would set up her stall with benches and large clay pots full of Pozole. She became famous for her delicious Pozole, and early in the morning, she also offered her specialty.

Mischief with El Cisto - Shootouts in the Square and Children's Games

In those days, shootouts in the square were an occasional occurrence that put everyone on alert. The sound of gunfire echoed, and people hurried to take refuge. The police would chase the shooter, we would follow the police, and Doctor Isidro Trujillo would come to attend to the injured, unless they were dead. The priests provided the Last Sacraments to aid those in their final moments. Meanwhile, El Cisto and I would sneak around, trying to understand what had happened. We didn't run out of fear but out of curiosity, thanking God that nothing happened to us despite being in the middle of the action. Once the Sunday incidents were over, Monday would come, and we had to return to school. After school, we amused ourselves with games like marbles and spinning tops. We also enjoyed a game called "Chollas," which involved creating three round holes, separated by about two meters each. The goal was to throw the marbles one by one and try to get them into the three holes in coordination.

When we managed to get a marble into all three holes, we could attack our opponents by throwing marbles at them. Whoever managed to hit their opponent won. This game could be played by two, three, or more people, and to determine who would go first, we ventured to put two marbles simultaneously into the holes.

In the streets, our games were our passion, but sometimes we were chased by the police. One of the popular games was marbles, where we drew a line in the dirt and each player threw their marble from the closest distance to the line. The one closest had the turn to throw first.

Another game we enjoyed was "Top." In the dirt, we marked a circle about a meter and a half in diameter. In the center of this circle, we each placed a coin. The challenge was to knock the coins out of the circle using the top. We threw the top with strength, making it spin and dance on the ground. Sometimes, with the first strike, we managed to knock out a coin.

If not, when the top hit the ground, we caught it between our fingers to bring it back to the palm of our hand. Then, with strength and skill, we approached our hand to the coins and threw the top skillfully. With experience, we hit the coin and made it fly. The coin we knocked out of the circle became our gain. It was an exciting and beautiful game.

Besides these games, we also entertained ourselves with "zumbas" and "balero." Despite our games, Commander Herminio Alcalá did not approve of our activities. He argued that we were gambling and sometimes sent his police to make us stop. Even occasionally, he himself would come to scold us. We were considered mischievous youths, can you believe it? However, all he detected in us was a passion for playing. I was only seven years old at that time.

Adventures with El Cisto - Childhood Feats

With my inseparable companion El Cisto, we used to spend our days playing and exploring. Often, we ventured to play baseball in the stream where Concha lived. We also played in other places, be it on the outskirts of town or in one of the streets. However, our fun often attracted attention and, consequently, the presence of the dreaded police.

The police chased us as if we were criminals, armed with their formidable quince sticks or riding crops. When they discovered us, a frantic race began in the escape of their reach. Some of our friends were not so lucky and were caught by the police, who punished them harshly. I, on the other hand, was very fast and agile like a fox, allowing me to dodge them and escape unharmed. El Cisto was also not far behind in skill, and we always looked out for each other.

Once, we decided to venture near La Capilla, in the south of town, next to the lagoon. There, we found a corral belonging to an uncle of El Cisto, who also raised cows and pigs. This place had a peculiarity: the walls of the corral were full of "purriches" nests, as they are also called. These small birds were experts at jumping from one wall to another and had a unique and beautiful song.

Without thinking twice, we climbed onto the corral wall. As it was made of adobe to withstand the rain, we could jump from nest to nest. The purriches surrounded us, singing their characteristic melody. It was an unforgettable and exciting experience, exploring and enjoying nature in its splendor. Nothing could stop our thirst for adventure and discovery in those days of our childhood.

Adventures with El Cisto - The Tile-Breaking Incident

In our mischief, we often ventured to explore and discover new thrills. One day, we came across a nest that caught our attention. This nest was surrounded by a path that, instead of facilitating our passage, only seemed to hinder it. To overcome this challenge, we decided to jump from one tiled roof to another, even though these tiles broke easily due to their baked clay nature. Despite this, each of our jumps emitted a charming and resonant sound.

Finally, we reached the nest and discovered it contained small brown-toned eggs, similar to those of the purriches. Without thinking twice, we committed the mischief of taking the eggs and breaking the tiles that guarded them. It was an impulsive and mischievous action, but at that moment, we felt satisfied and free of remorse. No one reprimanded us for our actions, but some discreet glances surely had observed us.

Later, we learned that someone had shared our mischief with Don Elidio Novaure, a respected man in the town who usually carried a hook for pigs. He was known for his skill in this task. Don Elidio had a sister nicknamed "Cista la muda," and her reaction was entirely understandable.

One day, by chance, we were near his house. Although I didn't even look at him, he grabbed me by the arm and confronted me, asking if I had been the one who broke his tiles. Despite my denial, Don Elidio was determined to teach me a lesson about the importance of responsibility and maturity. That day, I experienced a lesson I would never forget.

Mischief with El Cisto: The Encounter with Don Elidio's Hook

In one of our most daring escapades, I encountered Don Elidio's feared hook. The story began when I got involved in a mischievous game with my friend El Cisto. In a moment of carelessness, Don Elidio surprised us and quickly caught me with his hook. My instinctive reaction was to scream in fright, which I did, while he firmly held the hook. I felt like a frightened animal trying to break free.

Finally, after a series of screams, I managed to slip away from his grasp and run off, feeling like a scared fox fleeing from a predator. Don Elidio, who watched me with his hook open, probably only wanted to scare me. In retrospect, I admit that our pranks deserved a lesson, and that was the way Don Elidio chose to teach it to me.

CHAPTER 10

The Horse of Don Filojio

On one occasion, I encountered a peculiar horse in the life of Don Filojio. This horse was an imposing chestnut stallion, large and potbellied. Don Filojio owned a ranch in El Espino, about six kilometers east of La Capilla. Though I did not know him well, I remember his tall figure and robust appearance, which commanded respect from all of us.

Don Filojio lived in the house that would later be inherited by his son Chepillo. He was a solemn man and, after his wife's death, he often visited his ranch on his chestnut horse. Though he had little to do with our mischief, his presence in El Espino and his unique horse were part of the stories told in our town.

Don Filojio, dressed in the fashion of the well-off ranchers of that time, looked like a genuine charro, albeit in simple style. He wore a large, yet not exaggerated, palm hat that complemented his outfit. He regularly visited El Espino, and when he did not stay there, he would arrive in the town by evenings, almost at dusk, riding his faithful horse Panzón. Although both he and his horse showed signs of the years they had passed, they remained a respected presence in the community.

It is also worth mentioning that Don Filojio had children, Chepillo and la Canaleja, though I cannot precisely recall the latter's name. Both were considered as the "Fres o Cuatro Mujeres" by their mother, aunt Lupe. My aunt Lupe, an exceptional and devout woman who married my uncle Felipe González, was a person deserving of all respect. Her marriage was exemplary and noted for its sanctity.

In the same family, we had Trina, a good friend of mine, who became a widow at a young age due to the revolution. Her husband, Thomas Carranza, was related to President Venustiano Carranza. The story goes that Thomas's father arrived in La Capilla fleeing the revolution and married a local lady there.

In summary, Don Filojio and his horse Panzón were significant parts of our community, and the Carranza family had deep ties with La Capilla.

The Horse of Don Eulogio and His Family Legacy

The horse of Don Eulogio was a notable figure in the community, but it was not the only remarkable aspect of his life. Besides being a horse lover, Don Eulogio was a caring father and an affectionate grandfather. He had two children, Juan and Trina, and lived to nearly a hundred years, passing away in 2000 while still vital and youthful in spirit. It was said that Don Eulogio did not dismiss the idea of remarrying, but he always mentioned it jokingly, stating that if so, his wife should be just like the previous one.

He was known for his sense of humor and zest for life. He referred to his son Thomas as a handsome and attractive man, joking about his flirtations before he died. He often mentioned that he would soon reunite with his "doll," referring to his son Thomas. His wish was for them to be together in the afterlife.

Don Eulogio's family included other notable figures. He had a sister named Mariquilla who never married and another sister who moved to Guadalajara after getting married, though, unfortunately, I do not remember her name.

Regarding his son Chepillo's family, he and his wife lived in the same house as Don Eulogio, caring for him lovingly in his final years. Chepillo had two sons; my friend Cisto and Pepe, nicknamed "la Cocorilla."

Thus, Don Eulogio shared his home with his loved ones and enjoyed the company of his family, keeping alive the tradition of horses he cherished so much. Each time he arrived home on his horse, he dismounted with a smile on his face, ready to share stories and experiences with his family.

Don Eulogio's Horse: A Trustworthy Friend

Don Eulogio had a special relationship with his horse, and their bond was truly unique. Every day, a trusted man cared for and tended to the horse, preparing it for Don Eulogio's arrival. When Don Eulogio approached on horseback, the man would assist him in dismounting and removing his spurs, especially considering Don Eulogio's prominent belly, which made bending over difficult.

The man skillfully and carefully placed Don Eulogio's feet on his own legs to help him remove the spurs. He also took care of the horse after its journey, helping it cool down and recover from sweat. Afterwards, the horse was led to the stable to eat and rest, preparing for the next day.

This relationship between Don Eulogio, his horse, and the man who looked after it was an example of mutual trust and respect between humans and animals. The horse was not just a mode of transport for Don Eulogio, but also a loyal friend receiving the utmost care from its owner and the caretakers. This scene reflects the love and appreciation Don Eulogio had for his horse, a faithful companion in his daily life.

The Unforgettable Journey to Ranch "El Espino"

On a sunny day brimming with expectations, Don Eulogio decided to send Cabo del Cisto on his trusty horse Panzón to his ranch, "El Espino." Though he had never ridden a horse before, the exciting opportunity enticed him, and he didn't hesitate to accept the invitation. However, with short legs, mounting the imposing horse was no easy task.

Once atop the horse, Cisto noticed two holes in the saddle, specifically designed to hold leather cords known as "tientos." These tientos, firmly tied to the saddle's vaqueta, provided a secure grip point. They were also handy for securing items, such as a blanket or a raincoat, preventing them from shifting during the ride.

As they progressed through a long pasture, Cisto heard Don Eulogio's words: "Anchor yourself well; I'm going to run." With no time to react, horse Panzón began to gallop vigorously. With short legs and unable to use the stirrups, Cisto clung to the tientos determinedly.

The horse's speed and lack of leg control made the situation challenging. He tried to scream for them to stop, but the wind silenced him. His arms grew tired from the effort to remain clung to the tientos.

Finally, as they were about to arrive at "El Espino," Cisto longed to be freed from the relentless race. His adventure on horse Panzón was an experience he would never forget, filled with emotions and challenges that left him an indelible memory of his journey to Don Eulogio's ranch.

The Unforgettable Adventure at El Espino

The excursion to the "El Espino" ranch was expected to be thrilling, but for Cisto, it turned into an unforgettable and challenging experience. As they made their way along the dusty road, Cisto realized that horseback riding was not as easy as it seemed.

Cisto's short legs and lack of riding experience made him feel uncomfortable in the saddle. As Panzón, the horse, sped up its gallop, Cisto clung tightly to the reins, but soon felt pain throughout his body. The journey became increasingly exhausting, and he was unable to utter a word due to tiredness.

Upon finally arriving at "El Espino," Cisto dismounted with difficulty, feeling unable to control his legs. He was completely exhausted and sore, with blisters on his hands from the effort to stay attached to the reins. His walk was clumsy and wobbly, like that of a weary duck.

A kind man working at the ranch noticed Cisto's plight and approached him with concern. He asked what had happened, and Cisto, still recovering, recounted the experience. Initially, Cisto had tried to downplay the situation, but the man could see his distress. His only reply was: "I thought they were well secured." Cisto, stuttering, responded that he would have clung on with all his strength if possible.

Cisto asked to get back on the horse, but the man refused, fearing he might repeat the thrilling experience. Instead, they prepared donkeys, and Cisto was loaded onto one of them.

Later, when they returned to La Capilla, Cisto was covered in blisters and with numb legs. He approached his mother, who, upon seeing him in that state, asked what had happened. He told her about the experience, and his mother, instead of showing concern, told him that this is how one learns. With tenderness, she invited him to take off his pants to examine him and apply a remedy.

Cisto, with his buttocks sore and blistered, lay down in bed while his mother prepared a bottle of "Tintura Mertiolate," known for its effectiveness in healing wounds.

The application of Tintura Mertiolate was painful, and Cisto screamed loudly as his mother removed the blisters with determination to heal him. Despite the pain, by the next day, Cisto was noticeably better and ready to face new thrills. Although the experience was intense, it left an indelible lesson in Cisto's memory, who felt a mix of excitement and pride for having ridden a horse for the first time, despite the consequences.

The Muleteers and Don Chuy the Charcoal Burner

After the thrilling experience of riding Don Eulogio's Horse Panzón, Cisto and I embarked on another escapade, this time involving donkeys that transported charcoal and firewood from the hill.

When the muleteers released the donkeys into the corral after selling their load, they headed to the stores to buy what they needed. We took this opportunity to each take a donkey and passionately ride all over town on them. When we got tired, we simply left them anywhere in town.

The poor muleteer, realizing his donkeys had disappeared, began an exhaustive search throughout the town to find them. There was a man known as Don Chuy, nicknamed "the Charcoal Burner," because he exclusively sold charcoal. Don Chuy had a special donkey named "Tranquilino." This donkey was his favorite and not used for carrying charcoal; instead, he rode it daily.

Tranquilino was a herd donkey, and as is often the case with these, he was strong and stubborn. Even though Cisto had knocked him down two or three times, Don Chuy held him in high regard. He had managed to train this donkey uniquely, holding it in high esteem. Don Chuy had a whole group of donkeys, including Tranquilino, whom he considered a loyal companion.

This mischief with the donkeys provided us with moments of fun and adventure as we explored the town on their backs. Although the poor muleteer struggled to find his animals, we enjoyed our pranks with the donkeys, especially with Don Chuy's beloved Tranquilino.

Don Chuy, nicknamed "the Charcoal Burner," was a memorable figure in our town. His relationship with his favorite donkey, Tranquilino, was unique and amusing. Don Chuy used to sell charcoal in La Capilla and then buy what he needed before returning to his ranch. Curiously, he tied his purchases to Tranquilino's saddle, his inseparable companion.

One peculiarity of Don Chuy was his fondness for beer. When he arrived in La Capilla after selling his charcoal, he headed to a local tavern. There, he began to enjoy beers, and surprisingly, he also shared them with Tranquilino, who enjoyed his own share. On the way back to the ranch, both of them swayed along the road, with Don Chuy singing and Tranquilino braying, always wanting more beer. Sometimes, due to our pranks, Don Chuy would forget about the other donkeys and not find them when he returned.

Don Chuy owned land on Cerro Gordo, filled with oaks, redwood, and oak trees, which he used to produce charcoal. When he came down from the hill, he always passed by Guerrero Street, which was in front of a tavern owned by my uncle Eulogio, my father's brother. My uncle loved entertaining his customers with tales and anecdotes, some real and others fabricated. Sometimes, he claimed that Tranquilino was related to the donkey ridden by Sancho "Panza." When Don Chuy and Tranquilino passed in front of my uncle Eulogio's tavern, fun and stories ensued, creating a lively atmosphere in the town.

The visits from Don Chuy and Tranquilino always aroused curiosity and laughter among the attendees. In return, many offered him a beer, creating a jovial atmosphere.

We took advantage of these entertaining moments to explore the town and wandered the streets until we were tired. Later, when Don Chuy continued his journey, he often had trouble locating us, as we had dispersed in different directions. On one occasion, they passed by my uncle Eulogio's tavern, and both were in a good mood. My uncle said he didn't know how they had gotten home because even the other donkeys had been left to roam the streets freely until the next day.

Sometimes, they even grazed on the cobblestone streets, eating the grass that had grown between the stones.

A memorable day came when they returned from their ranch, and both Don Chuy and Tranquilino were hungover. Known for his stubbornness, Tranquilino tripped with Don Chuy and made him fall to the ground. It was a comical scene that made everyone laugh, including Don Chuy.

The adventures of Don Chuy with Tranquilino brought laughter and joy to our town, and their visits to the tavern were eagerly awaited by all.

When they entered the Llanito Pasture, where the Lagoon was located, Tranquilino showed a great desire to drink water from the Lagoon. Although Don Chuy was dealing with a hangover, he too craved the water. Tranquilino began to run to reach the shore quickly, but Don Chuy, without malice due to his condition, tried to stop him, spanking him. However, Tranquilino didn't care about being hit, but when they reached the lagoon's shore, he began to get angry.

To everyone's surprise, Tranquilino stopped abruptly, and in the blink of an eye, Don Chuy was thrown into the air like a bird and landed flat in the mud. He could barely utter a few words as he recovered from the fall, muttering something like "damn donkey."

Tranquilino, paying him no mind, entered the lagoon, where the water reached his ribs, to cool his belly. Don Chuy also benefited from the dip, as the immersion in the water helped lessen the hangover effects. After a while, Don Chuy came out completely soaked and headed to the square to enjoy a delicious menudo, prepared by María Esqueda, which she made exquisite with her very spicy sauce to alleviate the hangover. He paired it with a good cold beer, knowing this would be a balm for his discomfort, especially when the beers are ice cold. This was one of the things Don Chuy liked to do to overcome a hangover.

On Sundays, Don Chuy used to pass through the square with his donkeys loaded with charcoal, taking advantage of the animation characteristic of that day, with the square and streets full of fruit, vegetable, and other merchandise vendors. The ranchers congregated as usual, creating a festive atmosphere with so many people gathered. Don Chuy saw this as an opportunity to sell his charcoal and buy what he needed.

After finishing selling his charcoal and acquiring his provisions in large bags, which he filled with things he had bought, he tied them to Tranquilino's saddle. He never put a pack saddle on Tranquilino, his spoiled donkey. Then, he quickly headed to Rafael's tavern, as if he had a concern that day. He began to consume beers like a champion, leaving Tranquilino outside.

In the tavern, they began to play the gramophone, which charged twenty cents for each song that played. My uncle Eulogio used to watch everything related to Don Chuy. That day, Don Chuy only selected two songs he repeated over and over: "Me importa poco que tú ya no me quieras" and "Viva mis desgracias." It seemed as if he had had a disagreement with Doña Chepa, his wife, whose full name was Josefa, but whom they affectionately called that. That day, something had upset Don Chuy, and the music reflected his mood.

While they were in the tavern, Don Chuy, as usual, forgot about Tranquilino. He forgot to give him his deserved beer, something that usually brought a smile to his face. At that time, Corona was the most popular brand. Don Chuy used to put the beer on the curb, and I had taught Tranquilino to pick it up with his snout, which was usually a funny act from the donkey. However, that day, Don Chuy completely forgot about Tranquilino.

After a while, Tranquilino began to get restless, knocking on the wall. I think he was upset because he had inhaled too much air when hitting the wall, and this made him bray. Finally, Tranquilino decided to enter the tavern. Don Chuy, who had already had a few drinks, was surprised when he saw Tranquilino inside. When he saw him, he exclaimed: "Chepa! What are you doing here?" He then realized his mistake and apologized again because he had forgotten about him. He gave him his beer, and they both continued drinking like champions.

Don Chuy shouted: "Long live my misfortunes!" and "I don't care that you don't love me anymore." Tranquilino brayed in response, as if he felt offended by Don Chuy's neglect. The scene continued with laughter and jokes, demonstrating the peculiar relationship between Don Chuy and his donkey Tranquilino.

After their visit to the tavern, Don Chuy and Tranquilino headed back to the ranch. Both were laughing and bumping all over the street, even on the cobblestoned parts. When they arrived in front of my uncle Eulogio's tavern, Don Chuy, still a bit affected by the spicy food, felt the urge to drink more beer at the well-known tavern.

Don Chuy had a great friendship with my uncle Eulogio and often went to chat with him and enjoy some beers. In one of those conversations, Don Chuy shared how much he appreciated Tranquilino and told my uncle why he started giving beer to the donkey. He said that once, Tranquilino had ventured inside the tavern because he got desperate not seeing Don Chuy come out.

Don Chuy, who was somewhat affected by the alcohol at that time, decided to share his beer with Tranquilino. He forcibly opened the donkey's mouth and gave him a beer, then another and another. By the third beer, Tranquilino was already excited for more. After spending a good time chatting with my uncle Eulogio, Don Chuy decided it was time to leave, as it was late and both he and Tranquilino were swaying like a pendulum due to the effects of the drink.

After their visit to my uncle Eulogio's tavern, Don Chuy and Tranquilino continued on their way to the ranch. As was common when Don Chuy got drunk, he forgot the other donkeys, but they knew that in the end, they would earn their deserved rest in the Laguna pasture.

They left through Guerrero Street, and my uncle, who came out to watch them, told me that Don Chuy was singing joyfully: "Long live my misfortune, I don't care that you don't love me anymore!" while Tranquilino brayed nonstop, eager for more beer. This is how Don Chuy turned the donkey Tranquilino into a booze enthusiast.

My uncle always opened his tavern early, where he prepared excellent cinnamon drinks with alcohol for those early risers who arrived. The tavern was filled with people enjoying these cinnamon drinks laced with alcohol, and my uncle entertained them with his stories.

Elpidio González's Horses

Allow me to share another true story recounted by my uncle Eulogio about Elpidio González, who had long maintained exceptional racehorses that were the envy of the region. These horses were highly valued and respected for their elegance and performance in races. In those days, Elpidio González stood out in the horse racing world with his nationally renowned pairs of horses. They competed against jockeys who brought their horses from various parts of Mexico to challenge Elpidio's. The venue for these thrilling competitions was an excellent long track located in a pasture known as "Potrero de Triángulo," adjacent to El Lavadero Ranch and north of Gómez Dam, near La Capilla.

I particularly remember one race when I was about eight years old. This race had become extremely popular, drawing people from all over. Elpidio had an exceptionally fast horse named "Canelo," known for its beauty and great stride. Its rival was a horse named "Kilómetro," and the race was to be contested over a thousand meters, suitable for these two long-distance sprinters.

The last time Kilómetro had competed in a similar race was in Piedras Negras, Chihuahua, where it had won. That day, the square was filled with people excited about these races, with vendor tents and traveling taverns. As a curious child, I stealthily approached and listened to people discussing and placing their bets before the main race. Betting was an important part of these competitions, and I keenly observed how bettors evaluated the horses and their jockeys. The excitement in the air was palpable.

That was my first experience at a horse race, and I must admit that I felt somewhat overwhelmed by the large number of horses and people gathered along the track. The hustle and bustle and the crowd's shouts increased my nervousness. However, amid that throng, I was fortunate to encounter Elpidio's son, whom we called "Pillo." We were friends, although at that moment he didn't seem to notice my presence, as he was absorbed in concern for the race.

Pillo was riding a beautiful horse that also belonged to his father, the renowned "Canelo." I continued to explore the place and soon joined a group of friends my age. Together, we curiously looked around, trying to soak up the event's excitement.

It was then that we noticed a young boy our age who had just arrived in La Capilla. His name was Barbarito Gutiérrez, and for some reason, he had decided to move here. Being a stranger to us, some of my companions sought to pick a fight with him. I, not one to back down from challenges, found myself involved in a scuffle with him.

The situation escalated quickly, and we began to exchange blows on the ground. Barbarito, realizing he couldn't beat me, picked up a stone and hit me. I was injured in the confrontation, and after that incident, I retreated home without knowing what had happened afterward or who won the fight.

After the fight at the horse race, I returned home with several wounds and bruises. It was almost night, and my mother was alarmed to see me arrive in that state, with tattered clothes and bleeding. She asked me worriedly what had happened, and I explained that I had had an altercation with another boy who had left me injured.

My mother, seeing my condition, was frightened and began to care for my wounds. With the love that only a mother can provide, she took care of cleaning and disinfecting my injuries. I remember she pulled out the bandages and quince ointments she always had at home. Her loving hands placed the purple bandages over my wounds.

Despite the discomfort, I felt a great sense of relief and love at that moment. Even though the wounds still hurt, I knew my mother was there to care for me. The memory of that night stays with me, my mother's tenderness amid adversity.

As for the boy who had injured me, he was nicknamed "Caña Bofa" at the races. After that incident, we became good friends and shared mischiefs together.

Returning to Elpidio's fine horses, my uncle Eulogio used to tell a story about two of his most outstanding horses. These horses were accustomed to eating green alfalfa every day, in addition to the excellent pasture they had at their disposal. However, on one occasion, they ran out of alfalfa due to supply problems from Arandas and Tepatitlán. In La Capilla, alfalfa was not grown during drought periods due to the lack of water for irrigation, so it was brought in from outside. This episode posed a challenge to keep the horses in optimal condition.

These were the finest horses of all, and this dietary habit was taking its toll. Their bodies began to thin, which worried Elpidio greatly. He did not know what to do to solve the problem, as he could not get alfalfa at that time.

One day, while walking on the sidewalk where my uncle Eulogio's tavern was located, Elpidio was surprised by my uncle's greeting, who shouted: "Elpidio! I want to ask you something." Elpidio, intrigued, replied: "Tell me, Eulogio, what's up?" My uncle explained the situation of the two horses that refused to eat and suggested an idea he considered effective.

My uncle Eulogio proposed that Elpidio buy some green glasses and put them on the horses. According to him, this would make the horses eat everything that was offered to them. Elpidio, willing to try any solution, agreed to the idea and put green glasses on the horses.

The result was astonishing. The horses began to eat everything within their reach, even the pasture they had previously rejected. The sight of the green pasture through the green glasses encouraged them to feed enthusiastically. The solution had worked perfectly.

This anecdote became a humorous story that my uncle Eulogio shared with people to entertain them. Moreover, it showed that sometimes the most unusual solutions can solve unexpected problems.

CHAPTER 11

Tacho, My Cousin and His Nickname

Tacho, or Tachín, as we used to call him, was christened Anastasio Gutiérrez, just like my grandfather. Tacho was my first cousin and, beyond that, one of my best childhood friends, just like Cisto. Even though the three of us didn't usually get up to mischief together, Tachín and I were inseparable for a time.

Tacho wasn't much of a fan of pranks; it was more me who used to play jokes and pull pranks on him. My uncle Eulogio, Tacho's father, had a large family, with three sons and six daughters. Rafael was the eldest, followed by Concha, and then came Tacho, both born in H. S. A. The rest of the siblings were born in La Capilla, in Mexico.

As Tacho and I were the same age, we spent a season being inseparable. Although Cisto was still my friend, we didn't hang out as much as before. I was always a lone soul and bonded with those who adapted to my style and mischiefs and felt comfortable with me. That's why Tachín became one of my best friends, just like Cisto.

My bond with Tachín strengthened when he came to visit his mom, my aunt Magdalena, along with another first cousin named Gamaliel, who lived in Guadalajara. These family gatherings and our shared pranks made our friendship grow even more.

Tachín and My Cousin Gamaliel: Family Reunion and Mischief

A few days after the arrival of my aunt Elisa and her two daughters, Elisa and Ester, at my grandmother María's house, my cousin Gamaliel, whom we affectionately called "Gama," also arrived. I used to spend a lot of time at my grandmother's house, and when Gama arrived, it was a joyful moment for both of us. I remember that on that occasion, he even brought me a gift: a dagger with a chromed eagle head on the hilt, a popular item in Mexico. To prevent it from being taken away at home, I hid the dagger in one of the corners of the corral, in the adobe wall. It remained hidden for a long time until I finally sold it.

The three of us, Gama, Tachín, and I, would often meet to play in the square along with other village children. The departure of my aunt Magdalena to Guadalajara and her taking Gamaliel with her left us sad, as he had perfectly adapted to our games and pranks. Gamaliel's father, whom we called "Chuy," bore the surname Castellanos and was a very kind person. He was known for having successful dairies, as was typical of the Castellanos. Despite Gamaliel's departure, we continued to meet and share adventures.

From my time with Gama, I have some interesting anecdotes that also form part of my memories. We called my mom "Emilia," and her surname was Torrez. She was very close to me, and her father, Martín Torrez, owned the best butcher shop in La Capilla, standing out as a renowned merchant in the locality.

Tachín, My Uncle Eulogio, and Don Martín Torrez: A Special Relationship

Don Martín Torrez, whose wife was named Doña Conchita Barba, was a respected man in our town. Sadly, Doña Conchita passed away early, leaving him widowed. Don Martín was left alone with his two children, and it was then that my aunt Emilia, part of my uncle Eulogio's family, took on the responsibility of caring for him and his children. This generous action allowed all of my uncle Eulogio's children to be raised with Don Martín's support.

My uncle Eulogio, as I mentioned earlier, used to travel to the north of the United States to work. During his prolonged absences, Don Martín took care of the family. Rafa and Tacho, my cousins, helped him with the slaughtering and in the butcher shop. Don Martín found satisfaction in the fact that, with his daughter and grandchildren, he felt like he was in his own home.

However, Don Martín knew he could count on the support of his son-in-law, my uncle Eulogio, when he found himself in financial straits. When my uncle needed money, he would travel to the United States, where he already had a stable job on a cattle ranch in Palo Alto, California.

He was highly valued by the owners for his dedication and quick learning ability; he even came to master Portuguese and speak English fluently. Although he was cheerful, the only drawback was his long absence from La Capilla, during which he sometimes neglected his family. But in those moments, Don Martín became a fundamental pillar for his daughter and grandchildren.

Tachín and the Death of My Uncle Liborio

Continuing with my family's story, I recall my Uncle Liborio, who worked at the Palo Alto stable before my Uncle Eulogio. Like Uncle Eulogio, the Portuguese owners held him in high esteem for he was a tireless worker with extensive knowledge gained from his time in La Capilla about cattle and their handling.

Once, while working in the stable, a tragic incident occurred. A large bull, considered a high genetic value breeder, grew furious because Liborio wouldn't let it join an agitated cow. Despite the bull wearing a nose ring with a chain, it didn't stop. It furiously charged at Liborio, pinning him against a wall and killing him instantly.

This tragic event deeply affected my grandfather Tacho and Uncle Eulogio, who were in Palo Alto, California, at the time. Tacho returned to La Capilla after his brother Liborio's death, carrying profound sorrow.

Liborio was known for his seriousness and responsibility, and his departure was a harsh blow for the family. It was then that Uncle Eulogio began working at the stable with the Portuguese, marking a new phase in his working life.

Let me continue the story about my Uncle Liborio and my cousin Tachín. My father wanted me to take his place in San José, California, about fifteen kilometers from Palo Alto. I thank God for being christened Liborio. I am profoundly proud of it, among other reasons, because Liborio stands for "Freedom." And it is true; throughout my life, I have felt a great sense of freedom inside.

I have always tried to share this sense of freedom with those around me, despite, as is natural, some people trying to make us feel imprisoned throughout life. I have faced obstacles, but they will never knock me down. If I am removed from my path, I always return to my road, called "Freedom."

But let's leave the sad things aside for now and continue with the story of my cousin Tachín. We were inseparable for a while. We were around seven or eight years old and used to gather in the square with many other children in the evenings. We made so much noise that the merchants around the square complained, and sometimes, the local commander would appear to calm things down.

The Hot Spanking

Recalling our childhood days in the square, we used to run like mad when Commander Herminio Alcalá and his policemen with quince sticks and cardboards appeared. Some of us were caught by their sticks, but when they didn't bother us, we played in many ways. We shared jokes, like those about Pepito and others we knew.

A popular game at that time was called "The Hot Spanking." It involved a larger child sitting on a bench in the square with a shirt or jacket over their legs. The person to receive the spanking would crouch down to cover their eyes and not see who would spank them. Many other children would gather around, eager to watch the game.

The child would stand up and have to guess who had spanked them. If they failed, they had to crouch again and keep guessing. Sometimes, this could go on for quite a while, and those who hit the hardest even removed a sandal or shoe to make it more thrilling. If they guessed who had hit them, that person had to take their turn, and the spanking could be so intense it left buttocks bruised.

Tachín and His Hat

Allow me to share the story of Tachín's famous hat. Back in those days, his grandfather Don Martín bought him a Charro-style wheat straw hat with a simple design. This hat almost completely covered his head, shielding him from the scorching Californian sun. Don Martín would send him to work on nearby ranches to La Capilla, where they sometimes needed to transport cattle or pigs for slaughter. The hat became his faithful companion under the blazing sun.

I enjoyed playing with him, occasionally snatching the hat off his head. Tachín always reacted with determination, chasing me tirelessly. Although I was more agile, he had astonishing stamina and strength, making him seem like a real bull.

Day after day, he would catch me and reclaim his beloved hat. I admit it gave me anxiety, but he wore it with pride, becoming a sort of living portrait with his cherished hat.

Tachín, His Hat, and His Colt

Tachín's hat, though sturdy, couldn't withstand the test of time. With the rains and wear, the brim of the hat, originally reaching almost to his shoulders and covering his sight, began to deteriorate. But I couldn't resist the temptation to snatch it off repeatedly, causing it to get shorter and shorter.

What truly made this period special in Tachín's life was his relationship with a colt. This colt was the offspring of a mare Don Martín had for many years and had never been ridden by a rider. Until one day, Tachín decided to tame it and establish a unique bond with it.

From a young age, Tachín began working with the colt, quickly earning its affection and respect. Breaking it in wasn't necessary, as the colt accepted Tachín as its rider without resistance. However, I tried to ride it once, and the colt reacted violently, trying to bite me and kicking towards me. Tachín, always donning his iconic chin-strapped hat, was always ready to protect me from the colt's mischief.

Tachín and his colt became an inseparable pair. When he mounted the colt, he looked like a revolutionary with his characteristic hat, nearly covering his eyes. If Pancho Villa had seen him, he surely would have invited him to join his cause; he just lacked the uniform.

Tachín, His Colt, and Our Friend Juven

Tachín, with his distinctive hat and colt, became quite a character in our community. He boasted of his colt's skills as if he were a true revolutionary, following in Emiliano Zapata's footsteps. He rode with skill and agility, flaunting the good training he had given the animal. He could gallop at great speed down the cobblestone streets, sparking flames in his wake.

But not just that, Tachín also made his colt walk sideways elegantly, as if they were part of a show. His prowess in handling the colt filled him with pride, and sometimes he seemed more an experienced rider than a boy his age.

Tachín and his colt became a common sight in the community, and his defiant and proud demeanor recalled the revolutionaries of old, especially Emiliano Zapata.

Yet the story continues, as Tachín and I began to drift apart somewhat because of the friendship he established with a mutual friend, Juven, our same age. Juven had the advantage of having his own colt, while I had not even a donkey to ride and had to settle for the mules of the muleteers descending from the hill. The difference in possessions led us to separate paths in our adventures.

Tachín and Our Friend Juven: An Encounter with Wealth and Adventures

As I was saying, amidst our pranks and adventures, a new character emerged: our friend Juven, who belonged to one of the wealthiest families in La Capilla, led by his father, Don Juventino Aceves. Beyond his wealth, Don Juventino was an extraordinary person, very sociable and kind to everyone. He had several children, all equally beautiful, with fair skin, light hair, and eyes, typical of Castilian descent. At that time, the origin of our genealogy had fallen into oblivion, as very few people cared to trace it in detail.

But returning to our adventures, I apologize for the brief digression about our roots. I'm here to share the exciting story of Tachín and our friend Juven, who owned a beautiful mare, and Tachín pretended to have acquired a mare from Don Juventino. Together, they would head to the pastures of his ranch, supposedly to learn roping, but in reality, to train with any animal they found, be it cows, calves, or donkeys. On the streets, they spent their time practicing their roping skills.

For Juven, this experience proved beneficial, as one day Don Juventino decided to move to Guadalajara for reasons unknown to us. Juven and his brother joined the Jalisco Charro Association, and rumor has it that they became excellent riders, even winning the championship at some point.

Tachín and Our Friend Juven: A Wild Race

Let me return to La Capilla, where on one occasion, I was invited to visit my friends' ranch. They intended to teach me to throw, and excitedly, I joined them. I mounted Juven's mare, a docile horse on which I settled at the back. We headed towards a pasture known as "El Potrero del Triángulo," which I mentioned before and served as a crossing toward Mirandilla.

We were moving at a good pace, both riders on their respective horses when suddenly, they got the idea for a race. Without a second thought, they sped up, and I, eager for competition, followed them determinedly. At that time, I was older and had experience in riding, so there was no reason to worry.

However, the situation took an unexpected turn when Juven's mare, seemingly calm, suddenly bolted. As any rider knows, a runaway horse is hard to control, unresponsive to reins or brakes, and continuing to run until it tires. I tried to brake and Juven pulled the reins, but the mare wouldn't respond.

We were near a wire gate leading to the Potrero del Triángulo, but the mare couldn't stop in time due to speed and crashed into the gate, which was high and sturdy. The impact threw us all from its back. At that moment, we were left stunned and somewhat dazed by the unexpected incident.

Tachín and Our Friend Juven: A Challenging Adventure

Let me continue with the story of Tachín, Juven, and me, as after the wild race, we decided to abandon the idea of practicing lassoing cattle.

Yet, six months later in the same Potrero del Triángulo, another incident occurred that would leave its mark on our memory.

One afternoon, as usual, we ventured into the pasture. The previous experience didn't deter us from enjoying nature and the company of livestock. However, this time, tragedy lurked in the shadows.

We strolled carefree, watching the cows and savoring the cool breeze. But life had another challenge in store for us. In the blink of an eye, as if we were birds, we flew and landed on the other side of the fence.

I can't explain how I managed it, but fortunately, I was unharmed. Juven suffered a scratch on his leg, and Tachín, my cousin, initially ran over, fearful of what had happened, but soon burst into laughter with the joy of having escaped imminent danger. We, puzzled by his contagious laughter, eventually joined him. However, after a while, we stopped him, and instead of laughing, we started playfully throwing stones at him.

This was our second adventure in the Potrero del Triángulo, and after this episode, we decided it might be better to stop exploring that place. However, this wouldn't be the last incident we'd experience together in that corner of La Capilla.

One Day in the Triangle: An Unexpected Accident

I want to share an incident that occurred while we were heading to a party organized by Father Morales and Professor Rafael Camarena from Tepatitlán. They decided to rent a van to take us to the celebration, and although I don't remember who was driving, the route took us through the same terrain where we had the encounter with the mare in the Triangle, a large and steep pasture.

The van had to cross the Triangle Pasture and continue until reaching Mirandilla. The pasture was vast and steep, and as we moved forward, we made a mistake. Some of the boys decided to climb onto the back of the van and sit on the railings. There were about six or seven of us, young people, all singing and having fun. The van was full of people, mostly young, with some older ones, but no one was concerned about looking after us or telling us not to climb on the railings.

As we progressed through the pasture, the unexpected happened. The van drove over a hole in the road, and because of our weight, the rear railings broke. The van lurched, and I, miraculously, was not injured. I performed a kind of somersault in the air but landed sitting. The van kept moving, which prevented a more serious accident.

This incident, though a scare, reminded us of the importance of caution and safety in our adventures. It also brought to mind two other previous incidents: the famous day of Canelo's race and the encounter with Kilómetro the horse, as well as the incident when I was hit by a stone in the face a few years ago.

These episodes, although full of challenges and dangers, are part of the stories that bind us to La Capilla and the people we met there, like Don Gregorio, the respected baker who prepared the best picones in Jalisco. Each of these incidents left its mark on our memory and taught us valuable lessons about life and adventure.

Don Gregorio Trujillo and His Excellence in Baking

I want to talk about a prominent figure in La Capilla, known to everyone as Don Gregorio, and to his friends simply as Gregorio. He was the brother of Doctor Isi Roy de Teodoro and had an impeccable reputation in the community.

Don Gregorio was a person of great prosperity and gentle character, as were many inhabitants of La Capilla. He was also known for his brother who lived in the same town. Both were recognized for their integrity and contributions to the community.

After returning from the United States, Don Gregorio chose not to go back north and instead decided to set up a bakery. I am amazed at the mastery he had in this profession, as he produced bread of the highest quality that, in my opinion, surpassed any other in the state. His picones, in particular, were a unique delicacy that attracted people from Guadalajara and elsewhere to buy them.

Don Gregorio was not only an exceptional Baker, but also a very hard-working person. His dedication and skill were reflected in the excellence of his bakery, which became a landmark in La Capilla. His legacy in the community endures through his unmatched artistry in baking and his contribution to the local culinary tradition.

Don Gregorio Trujillo and His Illustrious Bakery

I wish to share a memorable facet of La Capilla involving Don Gregorio Trujillo and his renowned bakery. Don Gregorio was an early riser, starting his day at three in the morning when he lit the oven and began kneading the dough.

I vividly remember his characteristic palm hat, considerably sized but not overly large, with a round design and slightly raised sides. Don Gregorio used to buy large amounts of firewood from the local muleteers and was undoubtedly one of their most distinguished customers. Each day, as the muleteers unloaded the firewood on the cobblestone street in front of his house, we, the local children, watched eagerly and waited for them to go to the stores to buy what they needed. We seized the opportunity to climb onto the donkeys and take a ride, as we often did. They frequently lost sight of their animals and had to ask if anyone had seen their donkeys.

After these episodes, Don Gregorio hired us to transport the firewood to the back, where a corral and the bakery's oven were located. There, the bakery's magic happened daily. After completing the task, he rewarded us with twenty pesos each and gave us a generous portion of bread. Despite the scratches on our arms from carrying the firewood, we were happy with our task and the reward.

I also recall that during the corn season, my mother used to prepare "tacachotas" for those who did not have mills to grind the corn. Don Gregorio Trujillo and his bakery were not only a landmark in La Capilla, but also a testament to the generosity and community connection that prevailed in our beloved town.

Gregorio Trujillo and His Bakery: A Delight for the Palate

I'd like to share a charming aspect related to Don Gregorio Trujillo and his famous bakery. Don Gregorio was a generous man who contributed to the community in unforgettable ways. One of his most notable kindnesses was his involvement in making "tacachotas," a type of semi-tender cornbread that was ground without leavening to prevent it from puffing up.

Don Gregorio volunteered to bake these delicacies, which turned out as tasty as they were peculiar. Sweetened with piloncillo and kneaded with milk before being carefully browned in the oven, the result was a uniquely delicious flavor.

In addition to "tacachotas," we would bring him pumpkins, which he also baked to transform them into "atoladas," another very tasty treat. These roasted pumpkins were served on a plate with milk and sugar, affectionately called "Taninole." This combination was beloved and always a pleasure to savor.

During Lent, my mother prepared a popular and delicious dessert known as "capirotada." It consisted of toasted bread, similar to French toast but golden in color. To prepare it, my mother or grandmother would cut the bread into slices and let them dry in the sun until they were quite hard. Then, they fried the slices until they turned an appetizing golden color. In a clay pot, they prepared a thick piloncillo syrup and also toasted tortilla pieces. Later, they immersed the golden bread slices in the pot with the piloncillo syrup and served them as a delightful capirotada.

Thus, Don Gregorio Trujillo and his bakery were not only a landmark in La Capilla, but also a constant source of joy and flavor in our lives, leaving a culinary legacy that endures in our memories and taste buds.

Gregorio Trujillo and His Bakery: The Delicious Capirotada Recipe

Now, let me share a recipe that evokes delicious memories of Lent in La Capilla, thanks to Don Gregorio Trujillo and his bakery. Capirotada, a traditional dessert, was a delicacy prepared with mastery and affection.

To make it, slices of bread were first toasted until they turned an attractive golden color. Then, in a clay pot, a piloncillo syrup was prepared and poured over the toasted bread. Carefully, raisins were added in abundance, and crumbled cheese was generously sprinkled over the mix. To prevent the bread from burning, tortillas were placed at the bottom of the pot before pouring the hot syrup.

The capirotada was further enriched with nuts and almonds mixed with the raisins. A touch of cinnamon stick and a few cloves completed the combination. After ensuring everything was well distributed and allowing the ingredients to blend and soften in the heat of the syrup, the pot was covered. The result was a delicious dessert, perfect for Lent, though enjoyable any time of the year.

So here is the capirotada recipe for those who wish to try this delicacy at home! Now, without further ado, I'll proceed with another of my adventures, as I can't resist the temptation to share them with you.

CHAPTER 12

Carmen, the Sacristan: A Man of the Church with Firm Hands and a Rough Heart

Allow me to tell you about Carmen, the sacristan, who was the brother of Santos, the bell ringer. These two men played a fundamental role in the church's life. Although they were brothers, their personalities were entirely different.

Carmen, so to speak, was Father Morales's right-hand man. Despite his blood relation with Santos, his temperament and character were noticeably different. Carmen leaned towards severity, especially when dealing with the community's children.

Carmen often experienced a series of frustrations, and it's possible he was dealing with mental health issues at the time. Sometimes, his treatment of the children was harsh, and he often became enraged. He might have felt relieved from the burden of these tensions when he left us at a young age, and God called him to a better place, free from the concerns that plagued him.

I remember when we saw him in the church; we stayed alert and, if possible, discreetly withdrew. Carmen had the habit of catching the naughty ones by surprise, and in his fury, he sometimes gave us knocks that left us momentarily dazed. Although we were mischievous, his reaction often seemed excessive.

However, it's important to point out that he had his reasons, as sometimes, we used the temple as a place of amusement. I personally loved climbing up to the belfry to ring the bells alongside Santos. He enjoyed this activity and taught us how to do it. When he needed our help, he left the ground floor door open so we could ascend the spiral staircase to the top of the belfry.

That's how I remember Carmen, the sacristan, a man of the church with firm hands and a rough heart, who left an indelible mark on our community, both for his dedication and his inflexible ways.

The Sacristan: Adventures in the Temple and the Creation Courtyard

The temple has always been a mysterious and appealing place for daring youths, and I was no exception. During my childhood, I often climbed up to the temple's belfry, sometimes out of duty, other times for sheer pleasure. When I felt the urge to explore, I headed to the temple to see if the spiral door leading to the belfry was open. If it wasn't, I sought another entry.

On the temple's left side, during the day, a door opened to an inner courtyard. This courtyard housed large tar deposits that burned continuously, releasing their characteristic smoke into the air. The primary function of these deposits was to keep the tar hot for various purposes, and this task required a constant water supply to maintain the tar at the proper temperature.

The sound of hammering and shaping resonated incessantly in that courtyard, as artisans worked tirelessly to sculpt and shape the quarry and stone that would be used in the temple's construction. This painstaking masonry work was a true masterpiece, and the results were evident in every temple detail.

In that same courtyard, there was also a large roller, akin to those used in rope-making, but much larger. This roller was connected to strong ropes that easily lifted large quarry blocks. Stairs and scaffolds were strategically placed to facilitate access to different levels.

Whenever we had the chance, we ventured up there secretly. We loved the feeling of exploration and the thrill of being in a place where we usually had no access. The mischief in the temple and the creation courtyard was an unforgettable part of our childhood, filling our days with fun and curiosity.

Carmen, the sacristan, and the magical pendulum clock on the temple's roof

The temple always attracted us like a magnet, and although Carmen, the sacristan, was not exactly a saint, that did not prevent us from exploring its heights. Climbing the temple's roof offered us a panoramic view of La Capilla's surroundings, allowing us to see every ranch and the majestic mountains surrounding the area. From that perspective, everything seemed closer and within reach.

In addition to enjoying the views, we were entertained by a fascinating object: the pendulum clock at the top of the temple. It had been placed there with great skill and experience by someone who perfectly understood its workings. The clock was connected to heavy ropes that held stones, and these ropes had to be lifted periodically to keep it running correctly.

The pendulum clock, with its astonishing precision, continued its steady march. The ticking echoed in the surroundings, marking the half-hours and hours with chimes that still endure from seven in the morning until noon.

In one of my adventures, I joined my friend, nicknamed "Cama Bofa," with whom I had had a clash in the past. However, over time, we had become friends. He knew how to climb the temple's courtyard stairs, even when the spiral door was locked. I told him, "Come with me, I know how to get there." It was a special day, a national date that inspired us to explore and discover new wonders in our beloved temple.

Carmen, the sacristan: Guardian of the temple and the bells

On those special days when we waved the Mexican flag at the temple, we decided to venture to the heights. Carmen, the sacristan, watched our daring climb and joined us.

Santos, the bell ringer, also appeared on the scene, asking from below how we had reached there. We showed him the way we had taken, and he warned us to be careful not to fall, sharing a tragic story of someone who had been careless and had suffered a deadly fall from that same height. His story served as a constant reminder of the importance of caution.

We spent time up there, enjoying the view and sharing anecdotes with Santos, who was always willing to chat with the youth. When it was time to ring the bells in the temple, we always volunteered to help, especially when long, resonant rings were required.

However, upon returning, we realized that the door leading to the spiral stairs was locked. We did not know how Carmen, the sacristan, had realized our presence, but suddenly, he emerged from the shadows and surprised us. With a serious face and a lantern in hand, he scolded us for our antics.

Carmen, the sacristan, and my Grandpa Tacho: An Unexpected Encounter

On one occasion, while venturing near my Grandma María's house, close to the temple, I was accompanied by my grandmother. Suddenly, Carmen, the sacristan, appeared behind me and called out. Recognizing his face, I felt nervous, and he beckoned me closer, foreboding that something was amiss.

However, Carmen had a warning for me. He said he would give me a couple of "whacks." Alarmed, I started running, but Carmen was hot on my heels. With no escape, I sought refuge in my Grandpa Tacho's house. To the left in the hallway was a room that had been my birthplace but now served as Grandpa Tacho's carpentry workshop.

I dashed into that room to evade Carmen, who seemed intent on punishing me. The tranquility there offered me protection.

In a panic, I bolted toward safety. My grandmother followed, concerned, asking what was happening. I barely managed to say, "They want to hit me". I continued to flee, seeking refuge and a way out.

Quickly, I found a wall leading to a pen, with an open room. In a corner, there were holes in the wall, familiar to me. I climbed swiftly, using a nook where the adobe walls met. Carmen couldn't catch me, and I soon reached the rooftop.

From there, I saw Grandpa stopping Carmen, who had intruded into the house without permission, regardless of his intentions toward me. Grandpa, never seen so angry before, was furious. Despite his gentle nature, seeing Carmen threatening me stripped him of his usual kindness.

Grandpa yelled at Carmen, "You better not touch that boy, or you'll regret it if you do. What did he do?" Carmen, taken aback by Grandpa's assertiveness, began to explain.

Grandpa, staring down Carmen, heard him say, "They made the church dome, as you know, and recently broke one of the window panes with a slingshot." To which Grandpa retorted, "Carmen, listen to me. Did you see who did it?" Carmen, hesitating, said, "I didn't see it, but I was told it was him." Grandpa responded, "What you were told doesn't prove it was him. And let me warn you, if you touch that boy again, you'll see what happens. Understand?" Carmen, struck by Grandpa's firmness, could only nod and withdraw.

Meanwhile, I listened from my hideout on the rooftop, grateful for Grandpa's vigorous defense. After that, Carmen wouldn't dare harm me, and I felt safe. Grandpa, always affectionate and generous, would sometimes gift me small wooden crafts as trophies and gave me piloncillo every day, which he was fond of, and even sometimes three onions, as he loved them too. Our shared culinary tastes, I believe, contributed to his affection for me.

My relationship with Grandpa Tacho lasted many years and was unique. It was said that those who consumed raw onions rarely suffered from heart issues, crucial for a healthy heart (here's a free recipe). I think this helped him, as he lived to be ninety one. When the incident with Carmen occurred, Grandpa was about seventy five and still robust, continuing to be a strong presence in our lives.

Life in La Capilla: Connection with the Outside World

Grandpa Tacho was a restless and curious man, always up-to-date with happenings in Mexico and the world. He had a habit that captivated us: gathering in the square with locals, fostering a learning and discussion environment. The square would buzz with people eager to hear his stories and insights.

Besides his varied knowledge, Grandpa treasured an interesting book collection, most of which I inherited. When he came to La Capilla, he'd stay for days. In the evenings, the square was the perfect venue for sharing his stories and wisdom with eager listeners.

In La Capilla, a unique tradition prevailed: people gathered in the square to discuss various topics and conduct business. Often, benches were filled with conversationalists. On Sundays, the square buzzed all day, and with no local newspaper, an improvised "newspaper" relayed local and regional events, gossip, and anecdotes.

I recall a nearby outdoor theater by the temple, on the northeast corner, oddly part of the properties the priest donated to the temple. This open-air theater was a special venue for community cultural events and plays, enriching La Capilla's cultural life.

The Enchantment of the Open-Air Theater

In a village as small as ours, having an open-air theater was a true treasure. This venue, with a proper stage and dressing rooms, was the epicenter of local culture back then. It hosted theatrical performances that enriched our community life.

The theater boasted an impressive seating area and dressing rooms where actors readied themselves. Stands were arranged like boxes on the sides of the stage, about a meter above the ground and three meters long. Each attendee brought their own chair from home and set it up in these improvised boxes during comedies.

Though I was young then, the theater had established its place in the community, but its exact construction date eludes me. I distinctly remember one comedy in which my father performed alongside his good friends, one being Ángel Cacillas, my father's compadre, and Santiago Padilla.

This comedy was a humorous drama that had the audience roaring with laughter. Ángel and my father delivered their roles masterfully, creating an unforgettable spectacle at that magical open-air theater.

The Magic of Traveling Cinemas

In those times, life had a special flavor, and one of the events that brought the most joy and entertainment to the community was the arrival of traveling cinemas. This happened around the years 1943 and 1944, when these unique cinemas began to reach our beloved Chapel.

Traveling cinemas were quite a spectacle. They brought all the necessary equipment in a truck and set up their functions in a suitable space. For this, they usually rented a large corral, generally owned by a man named Pablo González or his brother Maximino. These gentlemen stood out for carrying impressive firearms, with their belts adorned with bullets or their six-bullet magazines. It gave the impression that they were licensed to carry weapons, which gave them an even more mysterious air.

The corral where the movies were projected was quite large and could accommodate many people. It was located north of The Chapel, and the tall poles on which the screen was installed were erected with great care. On those magical nights, the atmosphere was filled with anticipation and excitement, as we all eagerly awaited the start of the projection.

The traveling cinemas brought one or two movies, and the audience settled into chairs arranged in the corral. As night fell and the projectors were turned on, the screen was filled with fascinating images that transported us to distant worlds and exciting stories. It was a true spectacle that allowed us escape the daily routine and immerse ourselves in the magic of cinema.

Those outdoor movie nights were etched in our memory as special moments of our childhood. The arrival of the traveling cinemas was a gift that reminded us that, despite the simplicity of our life at that time, magic and fun were always within our reach.

In the streets of The Chapel, there was one that led in the direction of the temple in the square and headed north. A couple of blocks away, was the place where the magic of the traveling cinema unfolded. This show was quite an event for our small community.

The traveling cinemas' teams traveled from town to town, and their truck was a true traveling treasure. With great skill and dedication, they set up their screen, made of a thick blanket and white canvas. In addition, they prepared the projector and strategically placed their powerful speakers. They also had a car that became their promotion vehicle during the afternoons. A town crier was in charge of touring the town's corners, announcing with a large hand-held horn the details of the two films that would be projected and the time the function would begin.

I vividly remember the excitement I felt the first time the traveling cinema came to our town. My father had promised to take us, and that filled us with joy. As night fell, he ordered us to take a chair each, which we carefully placed on our heads. We walked with light steps, completely excited about the prospect of seeing a movie that promised to be unforgettable.

The movie was called "El Charro Negro", starring figures like Paul de Anda, Carlos López Moctezuma, and Miguel Inclán, who played two memorable villains. That night, the story unfolded before us, and the film captivated us entirely. It was a time when happiness was found in simple things, and those moments at the traveling cinema were true treasures of childhood.

Other films also left their mark on our memories, like "¡Ay Jalisco, no te rajes!", with the immortal Jorge Negrete, the Singing Cowboy, who made us vibrate with his performances. The traveling cinema not only gave us entertainment but also the opportunity to immerse ourselves in stories that were etched in our hearts. It was a time when the simplicity of life was filled with emotions and shared joys in the community.

The End of the Traveling Cinema and the Arrival of Television

The traveling cinema was a beloved part of our life in The Chapel during those years. We remember with special affection the films "Chaflán" and "El Chicote", which captivated us and left a mark on our memory. These screenings became an anticipated and exciting event every time the traveling cinema visited our town.

However, over time, The Chapel saw the construction of a more permanent cinema in the form of a simple large shack. It was decided not to spend too much money on its construction, despite the principle that the cheap sometimes turns out to be expensive. Despite its simplicity, this new cinema became a meeting place for the community, where we enjoyed movies and shared special moments.

Unfortunately, a fierce storm, which seemed like a hurricane, struck The Chapel one early morning. The wind knocked down the cinema's roof, and although fortunately, there were no injuries since it occurred at night, the cinema was left in ruins. People did not want or could repair it, and the idea of building a new one was forgotten.

Over time, television made its entrance into our lives. It became a new means of entertainment and communication that gradually eclipsed the cinema. The construction of a new cinema was no longer a priority, and to this day, we still do not have one in The Chapel. Despite the absence of cinema, life continued in our town, and I, for my part, continued to enjoy my daily mischief and adventures.

CHAPTER 13

Talayotes: An Adventure in the Forest

I vividly remember a day in September when adventure beckoned me from the forest. I had discovered a special place in some pastures where talayote plants grew. Upon arriving, I found all the plants laden with talayotes, large and juicy. It felt as though I had stumbled upon a treasure amidst nature.

As I explored the plants and collected the talayotes, I became wrapped in a sort of frenzy. There were so many that I no longer knew where to place them. In my mind, I thought of how delighted my mother would be to see the vast amount I had gathered. I remembered how she used to prepare them, wrapping them with beaten cheese and stuffing them with ground meat or more cheese. The result was a delight, very similar to stuffed peppers, though with their own unique and delicious flavor.

However, my enthusiasm made me lose track of time. I forgot I had to be home at a certain hour for lunch. It was then when I heard the church bells ringing at two in the afternoon, their sound reaching from the distance. But at that moment, I didn't even heed the call of the bells, engrossed in my fascination with the talayotes.

Talayotes Adventure: An Unexpected Return

That day, thrilled by the abundant harvest of talayotes in the forest, I arrived home past three in the afternoon, carrying a treasure trove of these natural delights. I was eager to share my find with my mother, thinking she would be overjoyed to see how many talayotes I had managed to collect.

However, upon arriving home, I realized my mother was anxious and worried, thinking something bad had happened due to my delay. Before I could say anything, I saw the expression on her face, which indicated she was about to scold me. To prevent her from fetching the punishment rods and disciplining me, I quickly exclaimed, "Look, I brought many talayotes!"

She looked at me, surprised and relieved at the same time, and walked toward me to bring the punishment rods. Although she didn't physically discipline me, she scolded me with her words and gestures, as was her custom. This habit of getting the punishment rods out due to fright and worry never completely disappeared in my mother, even when the only reason for my delay was the excitement of collecting talayotes.

On another occasion, during the same season when wild fruits like prickly pears and white sapotes were abundant, I enjoyed these natural delights. I loved participating in the collection of these fruits along with others, experiencing the joy and freedom of childhood to the fullest.

Adventures in the Field: A Dangerous Game with the Rods

As a child, when I had the chance to go out into the fields, I would take advantage of those moments when my father was not around. We feared him more, as he was stronger, and his punishments were more severe. However, when he removed his belt, I knew the storm was about to start, and that was when I would escape his scoldings.

Sometimes, I would go out to the field with my mother, feeling freer and safer. We took advantage of my father's absence since he was the one we struggled with the most. Although I didn't understand why, I knew he would hit me anyway, so I preferred to enjoy my time outdoors. Once, while in a pasture, I lost track of time and realized it had passed the hour to return home for lunch. For some reason, I decided not to go home.

Instead, I chose to stay where I was, having already eaten prickly pears and talayotes. I was afraid of the punishment rods, knowing that sooner or later, I would face them. I was at a ranch to the west of The Chapel, known as "Coleto." There was a granary there where straw was stored, and I had the chance to hide because the door bars were detached.

I decided to stay and eat more prickly pears, as there were many cacti with ripe "Chamacuera" and "Negrita" varieties. It was a dangerous game, as I knew that sooner or later, I would have to face the consequences of my disobedience.

Trapped in the Granary and a Dangerous Encounter

Having decided not to return home, more worried about the possible consequences of my tardiness than my own safety, I headed to the granary seeking refuge. Being a small child, I managed to squeeze through the slightly detached bars of the door. I found myself settling inside, not contemplating the repercussions I would face later for my disobedience.

It was there, in that shelter, when I heard the howl of a coyote nearby. My thoughts shifted toward the fear of being discovered by this predator. I decided to leave the granary quickly and started running toward The Chapel. However, the path was nearly blocked by vegetation, with sunflowers and cockleburs filling the way and spider webs spun by giant spiders covering it.

In my hurried flight, I spotted a snake on the path and stopped abruptly, looking around for the coyote. Acting cautiously, I cut a cocklebur stick, knowing it was the best weapon against snakes. I had killed vipers this way before, aware that a good strike would leave them numbed and dazed. A hit on the head was best, but this time, I faced a potentially dangerous situation.

Encounter in the Cemetery

With the stick in hand, I quickly made my way through the path, but luck was not on my side. In the blink of an eye, my stick was gone, likely lost in my hasty escape.

My path took me near the cemetery, and at that moment, a sense of urgency overcame me. I did not want to be near when it struck eight, as it was said that at that hour, the dead rose from their graves to pray. Although I generally wasn't afraid of the cemetery, once I arrived home late, around five in the afternoon, my mother had sent some older boys to look for me and bring me back. But on that occasion, instead of heading home, I ran toward the cemetery.

I ventured into the burial ground, hiding in one of the freshly dug graves while waiting for the danger to pass. I stayed there for a while, waiting patiently until the situation calmed down. Eventually, I emerged when I realized the boys hadn't found where I was.

The night was beginning to fall, and the full moon lit the path. However, this strange encounter in the cemetery still left many unanswered questions.

As I crossed the cemetery, surrounded by graves and crosses extending in all directions, I began to hear the clock chime marking eight o'clock at night. Suddenly, a disturbing thought seized me: "Eight o'clock!"

Popular belief claimed that at this hour, the dead left their graves to pray, and at that moment, strange sensations began to course through my body. My hair stood on end like a frightened cat, and my skin was covered in goosebumps. I turned abruptly in all directions, scrutinizing every corner of the cemetery with paranoia.

Shadows seemed to come to life, and my hair remained bristled as I ran toward the exit. However, when I arrived where the door should have been, it seemed to have vanished. Fear completely overtook me. My heart rate accelerated, and my senses were heightened to the extreme. I felt trapped in a nightmare where the world around me twisted and darkened.

With my hair on end and my heart racing, I ran frantically, stumbling and bumping into everything in my path. My mind was flooded with panic as I imagined someone or something chasing me. My hair felt so alive, and my ears seemed to want to leave my head. I ran and ran until I finally escaped the cemetery.

Trembling like a leaf and with my heart pounding wildly, I realized my pants were soaked, likely from panic. But at that moment, nothing mattered except putting distance between that place and myself. I knew my grandmother, my father's mother, attended the rosary every night at eight o'clock in the church, and I headed there as if my life depended on it.

A Refuge in the Church and Meeting My Grandmother

My heart was still pounding after my rushed escape from the cemetery. I knew the spot where my grandmother would sit in the church every day, a sturdy wooden bench with round crossbars. It was her corner of reflection, and I headed there seeking comfort.

Upon arriving at the church, I looked for my grandmother among the worshippers. There she was, in her usual seat. Though terrified and with my heart still in my throat, I knelt behind her, hoping her presence would shield me, as if she could intercede for me against any impending punishment.

My grandmother had always been kind and affectionate toward me, sharing a special bond. She often kept me company, and this was one of those times. After all, she had been my constant refuge since I had arrived running, my hair bristled with fear.

She noticed me and turned around, concerned. "Where have you been, child?" she asked. I explained that my mother was worried and that I feared going home because I thought I would be reprimanded. With her usual sweetness, my grandmother comforted me and invited me to her home.

In her humble abode, I prepared something to eat and enjoyed a comforting meal. After dinner, she suggested we go back to my house to ease my mother's worries. Though I initially resisted, I eventually agreed, knowing her presence would soothe any difficult situation at home.

My Grandmother's Comforting Advice

"Don't worry, don't rush," were the first comforting words I received from my grandmother when I returned home, tail between my legs, after my unexpected cemetery adventure. She had found me there, and her mere presence filled me with calm and relief. My mother was concerned, but my grandmother, with her wisdom and understanding, reassured me.

She told me that once things had settled down, my mother had left, and upon her return, she had explained the situation. She had assured that no harm would come to me. It was then I realized the special bond I shared with my grandmother, Maria.

I trusted her completely, and her wisdom gave me the confidence to face my parents. Though I entered the house with my head bowed, feeling like I had defied my parents' authority, they did not punish me. They simply asked where I had been, to which I responded with a guilty expression. But that was all; they did nothing more.

My parents were good people, though sometimes I challenged them and caused them distress. Fortunately, on that occasion, love and understanding prevailed, and I received no punishment. My grandmother Maria had been my refuge in times of trouble, and I am deeply grateful for her support that day. My adventurous spirit would not cease, but I had learned a valuable lesson from that episode. Now, I will share another of my favorite adventures: hunting doves on the ranches.

Dove Hunting: A Regional Pastime

In our region, what we call "spying" referred to an activity we especially enjoyed during the dove hunting season, or "huilotas" as we knew them in our town. We knew it was time to hunt these birds when they started to arrive at the nopales to rest and sleep at night. We carefully observed the nopales with the most droppings underneath, as this indicated where many doves gathered at night.

The dove hunting season was particularly exciting in mid-September when these birds migrated from the north, even from Canada. I vividly remember the day we killed a dove that wore a Canadian band, demonstrating the distances they traveled. During this time, thousands of doves came to our region seeking quality grass and seeds.

Our hunting technique was simple but effective: we used slingshots and black mud balls instead of stones. We collected these mud balls from the Laguna, near El Tajo, where this resource was abundant. Once the mud balls dried, they became as hard as stones and were ideal for use in our slingshots.

We often made these mud balls in large quantities, sometimes even to sell to other hunters. Luis Galván was one of the most notable hunters in our region and bought our mud balls at twenty cents per hundred. I often saw him loading large quantities of them into his cart as he prepared for his hunting day.

The dove hunting was a pastime that united the community during the migration season of these birds. It gave us the opportunity to enjoy nature, learn to observe, and work together to procure this prized resource. It was an exciting time we looked forward to each year.

The hunting of "Tortolitas" and the preparation

The dove hunting season, or "espiar", was a highly anticipated moment in our region. It was an activity that involved both young and old alike. In the days leading up to the arrival of the doves, excitement filled the air. People began preparing for this thrilling activity.

In homes, mud balls were made in large quantities, sometimes weighing as much as a ton. When the mourning doves finally arrived, this whole heap of balls was ready and waiting. Both adults and children planning to participate in the hunt without mud balls would go to Luis Galván to buy them. Each person carried a bag slung over their shoulder, crossing over the chest, and filled the bag with more than a hundred balls.

Armed with our slingshots, which we made ourselves, we headed to different hunting areas in groups of three or four. The slingshots were specially designed and prepared for the occasion. We looked for bushes, which were abundant on the ranch, specifically a bush called "granjenos," known for its durability. We looked for forked branches, cut them, and shaped them according to our preferences. Once the slingshot was ready, we added strips from truck tire inner tubes, which were more resistant than those from cars. This made our slingshots effective and durable.

After carefully shaping the slingshot and securing the bands, we were ready for action. Each of us prepared with determination for the exciting dove hunt. It was a time when the community came together around a tradition that brought excitement and camaraderie into our lives.

The experience of going dove hunting, or "espía", was truly wonderful. Every moment was filled with beauty and wonder. As we walked through nature, we could enjoy the symphony of sounds emanating from the gently flowing streams and brooks, while tall grass surrounded us and flowers of various colors adorned the landscape. We ventured into vast prickly pear cactus fields, exploring for places where streams turned into small brooks. We knew these were the favorite spots of the doves, as they would come there to drink water before heading to the cactus fields to rest.

Our strategy was to wait patiently for the doves to arrive, ready to strike them down with our slingshots. Some of our companions had exceptional skill and could knock down several doves in one shot. I, for one, was not as adept at hunting and sometimes only managed to take down a few doves. Although my skill was limited, each catch filled me with joy and satisfaction.

One of the most beautiful experiences during the hunt was when the night was clear, and the moon shone in all its splendor. The moonlight illuminated the landscape and created a magical atmosphere. I felt like I was immersed in an enchanted dream, surrounded by the scent of flowers, the sound of frogs, crickets, and fireflies, and the characteristic murmur of the doves. Their song had a unique and distinctive sound that made them recognizable among all other sounds of nature.

We crouched under the prickly pear cactus, ready and excited for the impending hunt. The anticipation and connection with nature made every moment memorable.

Our adventures in searching for the doves, affectionately known as "espía", were moments of excitement and anticipation. We delved into nature with our slingshots and black mud balls ready in their leather pouches, moving stealthily and making as little noise as possible. Accompanied by an expert in dove hunting, we learned the tricks and strategies necessary for success in this thrilling venture.

The arrival of the doves was a moment of great joy. The birds, taking flight or diving down, were a spectacle that filled us with excitement. Despite my inexperience, I endeavored to take down these agile birds, though I often missed due to the excitement that overwhelmed me. The more skilled hunters always encouraged me, gifting me some of their catches, in the hope that I would improve with practice. Every dove I managed to bring down filled me with deep pride.

Once at home, my mother took care of plucking and cleaning the doves, preparing them deliciously. The taste of her dishes was simply exquisite, and we enjoyed a meal I will never forget. Such was the exciting "espía" of doves, an activity that made me lose track of time and fully enjoy nature.

Today, as I relive these memories and share them, I feel thrilled about those moments of childhood that, unfortunately, will never return. Although those times are gone, the beautiful memories endure in my mind and fill me with gratitude for the experiences lived.

Hare hunting and the greyhound tradition in my town

In my beloved town, mi Capilla, there exists a unique tradition that endures to this day. Approximately seventy percent of the dogs in the locality are greyhounds, a breed specialized in hare hunting. Allow me to recount how this tradition took shape and the reason behind the prominent presence of these noble dogs in our community.

It all began in the era when families from Castile arrived and settled in the region. As they organized agriculture and livestock, they encountered a persistent problem: wolves. These predators constantly threatened livestock, particularly the sheep and goats of those who owned herds. The locals found themselves needing to confront the wolves and protect their animals, turning it into a challenging battle.

The first dogs used for this task were Danes, effective in their role but somewhat clumsy in catching the cunning wolves. However, as the 19th century progressed, by the late 1800s, the situation changed. Knowledgeable hunting individuals like my Uncle Silviano, who had a deep understanding of this tradition, shared valuable stories with me.

That was when greyhounds, specifically trained to face wolves, began to be imported. The greyhounds proved to be an exceptional choice, as their agility and speed allowed them to efficiently catch up with the wolves. The arrival of these dogs marked the beginning of a new era in wolf hunting in our region.

The greyhound tradition became deeply rooted in our community. Over time, the need to protect livestock from wolves decreased, but the passion for hunting persisted. The greyhounds found a new purpose: hare hunting. This activity became an integral part of our culture, and the greyhounds became inseparable companions for those who enjoyed the thrill of the hunt.

Thus, in mi Capilla, hare hunting and the presence of greyhounds have become a fundamental part of our identity. Each greyhound that runs across our lands is a living testament to a tradition that has been kept alive for generations, continuing to enrich our lives and our community.

Hare Hunting and the Era of Russian Greyhounds

During the time when hare hunting became a passion in our community, Russian greyhounds emerged as the main protagonists. These elegant, long-haired dogs proved exceptional in wolf hunting, thanks to their speed and stamina. When facing a wolf, they stood their ground, and with determination, they managed to catch up and neutralize the threat. Besides their considerable size, they were notably strong, comparable even to the robust racetrack greyhounds, albeit slightly smaller than the imposing Russian breeds.

The battle against wolves was a communal effort across the region. Ranchers united and coordinated their endeavors to eradicate this menace. Initially, they conducted advanced incursions into vast fields and hills, often spanning several days. They rode horses, brought dogs, and traversed on foot, meticulously scouring the area for wolf traces. At the most remote ranches, they awaited with dogs and shotguns ready for confrontation.

With resolve, they managed to kill significant numbers of wolves. Yet, this struggle took a toll on the Russian greyhounds, who wore out and, regrettably, started to perish in the battle. That led to the introduction of racetrack dogs, known for their prowess in racing but less resilient compared to the Russian greyhounds.

Despite transitioning to racetrack dogs, the advanced incursions against wolves persisted until the 1940s. As time progressed, strategies became more sophisticated, and wolves grew tamer. Nevertheless, the legacy of the Russian greyhounds in our hare hunting history remains indelible, reminding us of their bravery and commitment to protecting our lands.

The Tradition of Hare Hunting on Holy Thursday

In bygone days, our hills came alive with excitement on a special occasion: Holy Thursday. It was when hunting enthusiasts gathered to partake in a deeply rooted regional tradition. Gordo and Carnicero hills were the favored venues for this festivity, and at night, bonfires flickered in the darkness, spaced apart, signaling the presence of those seeking to hunt wolves.

It's crucial to note that by then, wolves were scarce in the area, but the tradition persisted, and the bonfires lit up Holy Thursday night. Over time, wolf hunting transitioned into a different pursuit: hare hunting.

This change was seamless, as hunters needed the thrill of the chase, and hares became an ideal target.

I recall my youth, fondly engaging in these hare hunts. The season kicked off about a month post-rainfall onset, when lush, green grass provided a perfect backdrop. Additionally, hare offspring were sufficiently grown and agile.

Tradition mandated that all hunting aficionados assemble at the plaza every Wednesday morning, early. Each brought their dogs, leashed to collars. This scene set the stage for our thrilling hare hunting ventures.

The Excitement of Hare Hunting in the Region

The tradition of Holy Thursday hare hunting resonated with immense enthusiasm in our area. The plaza's atmosphere was unique, brimming with anticipation and zest, especially at dawn's early light, with a truck ready to transport people. Soon, the square filled with hunters and their dogs, all tethered by cords to their collars.

Upon reaching the western meadow, we were greeted by arriving horses and a truckload of folks, along with neighboring ranchers bringing their dogs. It was a grand event, featuring nearly a hundred individuals, each with their dogs.

The meadow itself was an expansive area, long and bordered by stone walls, characteristic of the region. Its vastness was akin to a football field. The initial task was to "ripiar" the entire meadow—clearing and removing tall, dense vegetation that could hinder the hunt's progress, a critical step before embarking on the exciting hare hunting journey.

In these gatherings, a variety of dogs were seen, from graceful greyhounds to small, bobtailed terriers. The latter, often multicolored and diminutive, were adept at tracking rabbits and badgers hidden in burrows and tunnels. Their presence added a picturesque element to the scene.

Hare hunting did not involve firearms; instead, hunters armed themselves with stones, sticks, and occasionally rode horses to follow the dogs. Enthusiasts like Don Tomás Torres and Felipe the agrarian ventured into the fields on their steeds, carrying an unparalleled passion for the hunt.

Despite the dogs' bravery, they were wary of the abundant rattlesnakes. Encountering one, they crouched, bending knees to shield their necks from venomous bites and displaying an instinctual understanding of the peril.

Once, I ventured into the pig meadow, east of La Capilla, a vast expanse akin to the hog pen. Its name derived from introducing pigs to curb the viper population. Hare hunting there was an exhilarating, joyful experience for all participants.

Hare Hunting: A Vivid and Thrilling Tradition

Hare hunting was an activity brimming with excitement and meticulous preparations. Before starting, we had to ensure all holes in the fences around the pasture were covered to prevent hares from escaping during the chase. This was crucial to keep the hunt controlled and prevent the hares from dispersing.

Once everything was set, hunters lined up along the fence, spaced evenly like the teeth of a comb, ready to initiate the thrilling hunt. This process, known as "combing," involved moving along the fence while holding the dogs by a thin leash on their collars, ready to release them at the sight of a hare.

When the hunt finally began, the excitement filled the pasture. Hares leaped and fled, with hunters releasing one or several dogs in pursuit.

The pasture became a hub of action, with dogs tirelessly chasing the agile hares, and riders on horseback following.

The atmosphere was charged with enthusiasm, some hunters running after the hares, and others waiting strategically for their chance. At times, hares would change direction, igniting excitement with shouts of "Here it comes!" or "Oralé!" as everyone followed the chase's frenetic pace. It was a vibrant and passionate tradition in our region.

Hare Hunting: Thrills and Competition

In the midst of hare hunting, excitement and competition were tangible. Pancho, ever vigilant and ready, alerted the others when he spotted a hare. Adrenaline surged through the hunters' veins as they prepared to snatch the prey from the dogs.

The tension in the air broke with an excited shout of "Here we go!" while other hunters rushed towards the action.

The scene resembled a frenetic race, with dogs chasing the hare as if they were motorcycles, all vying to snatch the prey. The excitement extended throughout the day, with tireless dogs, the crowd, and horsemen maintaining the frantic pace of the hunt.

There was fierce competition to take the hare, and the victor earned bragging rights. In this competitive spirit, every hunter yearned to capture their hare, bringing it home as a trophy. Up to fifty hares were caught in a single day, evidencing the participants' skill and passion.

At day's end, tired yet content, they returned to La Capilla. They arrived home with pride, showcasing the hares they had captured. Their mothers cooked it with rice and potatoes, rendering the meal exceptionally flavorful and delicious. These memories were cherished treasures.

Among the notable hunters was Luis Muñoz, beloved by all and passionate about hunting throughout his life. He never missed these adventures, especially when accompanied by his exceptional dog, "El Tiro," famed throughout the region.

Another esteemed dog was "El Venado," owned by Don Pancho Paredes and Manuel Navarro, son of the local grocery store's proprietor, José María Navarro. These dogs were champion hare hunters, revered by all.

Fondly remembered too was Javier Paredes' dog, affectionately called "la Cochonena," another outstanding hunter known for its persistence.

"El Tiro" often roamed the streets freely, endearing himself to the local children. Tragically, he was poisoned. Despite efforts to save him, including inducing vomiting, he did not survive, a loss that saddened the community. "El Tiro" was a loyal, beloved companion.

Thus were the thrilling hare hunts of my Capilla, a shared passion that united people in exciting adventures. Though these stories only scratch the surface of lived experiences, they reflect the love and dedication the community held for this age-old tradition.

CHAPTER 14

National Holidays: A Fairy Tale

The month of September, as the National Holidays approached, was a magical time in my childhood. The celebrations around September 15th and 16th seemed straight out of a fairy tale. I wish to share some memories of those National Holidays, which felt even more splendid during my youth than they do today. Without diminishing the value of current celebrations, I believe there was a spirit and passion back then that made them extra special.

Long before September 15th, preparations began. A beautiful parade float was crafted; parading around the square, carrying the Fiestas queen–which was chosen by popular vote–at its center. Flanking her were the princesses who hadn't won, and I assure you, all three were absolutely charming.

The parade took place on the 16th and was a sight to behold. Yet, the real magic started on the 15th, with streets adorned with colorful paper garlands, affixed with paste and stretching from one side to the other, like stepping into a fantasy world.

Homes were also decked with flags, streamers, and lanterns, with lights illuminating the night, creating an unforgettable festive ambiance. However, that wasn't all. Traditional music and dances filled the air, and people gathered in the square to enjoy cultural performances.

Carnival rides were a special treat for the children, and the fairs with their food stalls offered culinary delights eagerly anticipated. Plus, the surprises added excitement to the celebration.

I fondly recall those September days of my childhood when the National Holidays were like a fairy tale come to life. Every detail, from the decorations to the smiles on people's faces, made that time truly special. Though times have changed, these memories remain vivid in my mind as a beautiful legacy of tradition and celebration.

National Holidays: Tachín, Gamaliel, and Me; Aunt Magdalena

The National Holidays kicked off with competitive and entertaining activities in the square. From the day before, the Greased Barrel and the Greased Pole were set up. Prizes were placed atop the pole for anyone who could climb to the top and claim the reward. Following these games, a large tent was erected for family bingo, Carcamanes, and pun-laden games, starting in the evening. Yet, we had to pause them around eleven or twelve at night, sometimes earlier, to count the princesses' votes and determine the queen.

I remember being in the square with my cousins Tachín and Gamaliel, the latter visiting from Guadalajara. Tachín and I were inseparable, and with Gamaliel's arrival, he joined in our fun. I recall Gamaliel's laughter as he snatched Tachín's famed hat, prompting me to run and him to chase. Tachín only removed that persistent hat when I managed to grab it, and without it, he seemed like another person; believe me, he wore that hat for years until he finally caught me and reclaimed it.

During the National Holidays, Tachín, Gamaliel, and I longed to buy treats from the plaza, yet we were penniless. Suddenly, I had an idea. We decided to check if any eggs had been laid at mother María's house, knowing where they were kept.

We three stealthily approached the coop. Aunt Magdalena, Gamaliel's mother visiting her mother (my grandmother María), was there but didn't see us. We reached the coop and started checking the nests, luckily finding several eggs and taking two or three each. As we opened the old, large door, which I believe my great-grandfather Felipe Navarro installed around 1850, it creaked loudly, betraying its age, perhaps a hundred years. This creak alerted Aunt Magdalena.

She, being in a room with my grandfather, realized we were coming from the coop. As we headed to the street, she called out, "Where are you going? Wait!" "To the square," we replied. She suspiciously asked, "What's in those bags?"

All I could think of was to claim they were balls for playing. Yet, upon revealing their true contents, we were speechless to show they were eggs. Aunt Magdalena, mixing surprise and authority, took the eggs from us, leaving us embarrassed and without the coveted treats.

Disheartened but not defeated, we returned to the plaza, immersing ourselves in the joy and various activities. We continued our mischief like stealing Tachín's hat and evading him, relishing the festive atmosphere that lingered into the late afternoon.

At one point, we hurried past Luis Gutiérrez's store. There, on the porch, Doña Cleta, an elderly lady, usually sold golden pumpkin seeds. However, in our haste, we didn't notice her and accidentally scattered some seeds on the street.

As we ran, unaware that the fireworks were about to start—a tradition involving striking a small packet with a mallet (marro) to produce a loud bang—I was nearly hit by the mallet, adding a dash of danger and excitement to our National Holiday adventures.

During these vibrant National Holidays, we braved the thunderous booms, which we called the blasts, resonating like dynamite. I vividly remember one such blast going off near my feet, sending my hat flying. The shock was immense, and the noise so loud I was temporarily deafened.

Tachín, ever-present during these escapades, noticed the impending explosion but didn't warn me. Following the blast, I had to sit on a bench, waiting for the ringing in my ears to subside. These booms, made from a mixture of chlorate and sulfur wrapped in paper, were deafening when struck with the mallet. It took nearly three days for my hearing to fully recover.

After this event, we each returned home for dinner. Later, around six in the evening, the festivity resumed with a serenade. We strolled around the square, gifting flowers and tossing confetti and streamers to the music's rhythm. It was truly beautiful. Everything paused around nine-thirty at night, the moment to prepare for the vote count.

At the heart of the National Holidays, a pivotal moment unfolded: casting votes for the queen candidates. Watching the setup of three ballot boxes at strategic locations was fascinating: one near local merchants, another in the town center, and the third, always lively, near the Los Altos trucks. The latter were known for their tendency to win the vote count.

Vote selling began around two weeks before September 15th. But the real hustle happened on the 15th, just before ten p.m., when the boxes closed. Political parties hurried to bring in huge bundles of money to deposit. The exact amount remained unknown until they began counting these bundles.

In the closing seconds, parties clustered, extending their arms with money packets, eager and determined to win. After the boxes closed, anticipation hung in the air, everyone hoping their favorite candidate would win. Almost invariably, the Los Altos truck party surprised everyone. They used to insert smaller packets to mislead other parties, but these contained thousand-peso bills, astonishing everyone with their strategy.

Immediately following the closure, the counting began, and soon everything was tallied, marking a climactic moment of the National Holidays.

The Cry in the Square

During the vibrant National Holidays, the climax arrived with the announcement of the vote winners. Those victorious were engulfed in overwhelming joy, while the defeated briefly saddened, all knowing that on the following day, September 16, everyone would joyfully partake from dawn, leaving the vote competition behind.

On September 15, right after the vote count concluded, everyone prepared for the speech and the traditional Cry of Independence. I remember, at that time, the municipal delegate was Don José María Navarro, a very respected and kind man, assisted by many children in his store. Located right in front of the square, he ascended to the kiosk with his entourage that significant night.

Though it was his duty to deliver the speech and the Cry, Don José María, a humble man aware of his oratorical limits, had his secretary, believed to be his compadre, by his side. I was just a child, but I recall my uncle Eulogio recounting how the secretary had to deliver the speech because Don José María preferred a supporting role.

The secretary, somewhat clumsy with words, began the address. Don José María, beside him, watched with a mix of support and nervousness. The plaza, filled with eager citizens, hung on every word, every announcement, especially the heartfelt Cry that echoed in every present heart.

National Holidays: The Cry and the Gunfire in the Square

It was the night of September 15th, when amid the National Holidays, everyone was gearing up for the most anticipated moment: the Cry of

Independence. The square brimmed with expectation. The speech began with a memorable "Beloved People!", but then a humorous misunderstanding occurred. The speaker, Don José María, in his zeal, proclaimed: "When the sun shone brightly!", to which his compadre, reacting quickly, corrected: "It must be the moon!". Don José María, regaining his composure, continued: "Yes, the sun of our liberty! Just as when Priest Hidalgo, in the town of Dolores, rang the bells to issue the Cry of Independence! Long live Mexico! Long live Priest Hidalgo! Long live Morelos!".

However, just as he was about to proceed, an unexpected gunfire outbreak began. The compadre, taken aback, exclaimed: "Long live those who can survive!". At that moment, people began to scatter, some jumping off the bandstand and others seeking refuge in a nearby basement.

Despite the police being deployed throughout the square to prevent any shooting, it seemed everyone had agreed to bring out their hidden pistols from home. What started as a ceremonial act turned into chaos resembling a revolution. Gunshots echoed everywhere, so much so that even the police, observing the intensity, opted to retreat. Amid that pandemonium, I was the only one who remained steadfast.

Julio Martín, a police officer cherished by all, got swept up in the night's fervor and drew his revered .38 special revolver, joining the fray. Those nearby encouraged him with cries of "Up, long live Mexico!"

Don Herminio Alcalá, for his part, wasn't in the square that night; he preferred to be in his tavern enjoying his fondness for poker. Despite the tumult of gunfire and revelry, he stayed aside, perhaps thinking, "I should join the fun on this momentous day, but I cannot, I must not."

Thus passed that September 15th, with us collecting bullet casings, plentiful from the countless shots. The next day, we inserted match heads into them and, with a stone, crushed them to make them pop, simulating gunfire.

The festivities of September 16th continued with the same fervor. Activities like the lottery moved to the first street off the square, making room for the Barrilito and the Greased Pole. The surrounding streets had to be clear for the anticipated Cape Fight, a tradition that also specially adorned the day.

National Holidays: The Combat of September 16th

The National Holidays focus on the thrilling "Combat" of September 16th, starting around 4:30 or 5:00 p.m. On this special occasion, I vividly remember a photograph taken by my mother. She, with her well-known camera, captured the moment when the queen and the two princesses settled into the parade float.

That year, the queen was a beautiful daughter of Don José Aceves May, and the princesses were Mariquilla, known for her radiant youth and beauty, and Concha Navarro, equally enchanting. The chambelanes, numerous in number, and the drivers, including José Paredes and José Gutiérrez (my father), played a vital role in organizing the event.

The parade float, a pickup truck without a body for better visibility, began the Combat. Filled with color and joy, the queen and her entourage threw bunches of Santa María and streamers. Interestingly, only the queen's truck was allowed to throw Santa Marías, creating a uniquely festive atmosphere.

The trucks, moving in opposite directions, met and engaged in a friendly joust, tossing tied bunches of Santa María at each other. The rooftops too were crowded, joining in the celebration with confetti and streamers. As night fell, the ambiance filled with a special magic, reflecting the jubilant spirit of the National Holidays.

National Holidays: Serenade and Fire Bull

The Combat left the square's streets adorned with remnants of Santa María, confetti, and streamers, and the air was imbued with the distinctive and pleasant aroma of Santa María. The band, set up in the kiosk, began to play, and youthful joy overflowed. The young men, in a gesture of chivalry, gifted carnations to the beautiful young ladies they encountered, accompanied by compliments like, "Place a carnation in your lovely hair so it matches your beautiful red cheeks." The scented gardenias were also a must.

Meanwhile, adults and women enjoyed the colorful atmosphere while sitting on the benches, savoring the revelry and taking the opportunity to chat or form social gatherings. The square was so filled that, besides the Combat and the serenade, many emotions were experienced.

Around 10:30 p.m., the fire bull show began, usually featuring two bulls. People, especially women, started to run upon seeing the bull being lit, looking for a safe place away from the square. Many climbed onto sidewalks, balconies, or rooftops to enjoy the spectacle from a safe distance. From there, they watched the young "bullfighters" challenging the bull and dodging the fireworks it launched, in a display of bravery and skill.

During the National Holidays, the spectacle of the fire bulls and fireworks was a highlight. These bulls, filled with fireworks, spun aimlessly, emitting sparks in all directions. The courageous and skilled youth jumped and dodged the fireworks, which occasionally hit someone, burning their clothes in an exciting and risky game.

The fun continued until the last bull was extinguished. Then, attention turned to the fireworks. Some sold and bought them in large quantities, creating an atmosphere reminiscent of authentic bullrings. Those who acquired them started lighting them one after another, throwing them at the group of eager youth waiting to "fight" them. Even the adults caught the excitement and joined in. I, following my mother's instructions, stayed on the sidelines, watching from the porch. But the excitement was so contagious that sometimes I couldn't resist and ended up joining the revelry.

These two days of thrilling celebrations adorned the month of September, culminating the National Holidays. Now, I will continue recounting what happened after these festivities in my Chapel and its surroundings. At that time, we began harvesting corn in October, marking the start of my autumnal mischief.

Flocks of Grackles and the Harvest

Grackles are small birds, slightly larger than a sparrow, with shiny black plumage. During harvest time, when the grass seeds ripen, these birds arrive in September by the thousands, forming flocks so large they darken the sky. The males of this species are particularly striking, some with yellow and others with red chests, while the females are smaller and of a duller hue. The male, with its intense, almost bluish-black plumage and distinctive, though not very loud, song, is a notable presence in the landscape.

These grackles, along with the brown mourning doves, set the rhythm of life in my picturesque and fragrant town. Surrounded by flowers, the air was filled with scents that lingered until late October. With the ripening of the seeds, all kinds of birds, including the grackles, gathered in the corn and wheat fields.

It was a time when, along with my friends, I continued with my mischief. The temptation to venture out was too strong in such a beautiful and lively place. Hunting grackles became a common activity. Armed with shotguns, we chased after these abundant birds.

The flocks of grackles, these black birds larger than a sparrow, were an impressive sight in our fields. When they fell under shotgun fire, the large flock swirled in the air, trying to lift the fallen and take them along. While we reloaded our shotguns, the sky darkened with them all. We also used pebbles and even rods to push down the shotgun wads, managing to knock down a few more.

These birds were cooked fried or with rice, just like the doves. Interestingly, even shooting at them, we could not deter them from the corn fields. My friend and relative, Rubén, who owned a large ranch in the clay lands, discovered an effective tactic against the flocks invading his corn and wheat fields. He began launching fireworks; the booming and noise of the rockets made the birds retreat and not return.

Thus, in my entire region, the corn fields, looking so beautiful during the harvest, were safeguarded. The cornfield had been harvested a month earlier, and during the harvest season, heaps called "monos" were formed in the fields, and the flocks of grackles and the "harvests" created a lively and colorful tableau. The cornfield, once ripe, transformed its ears into dry cobs, which then were known as stubble after removing the cobs. The sight of fields full of people harvesting and transporting these corn cobs in baskets or sacks to the carts, pulled by oxen, was worthy of a song. The joy and bustle of the harvest filled those fields, especially beautiful at dusk.

Twilight, tinged with flocks of grackles eager to eat the corn, heralded the moment when these birds withdrew to sleep. The trees filled with their chatter before nightfall. Speaking of the harvest, each "mono" of corn harvested left behind the stubble, those dry leaves later gathered in bunches. The farmers, with great skill, braided a long and flexible grass, similar to that used for brooms but more pliable, to create efficient ties for transporting the harvest.

Grackles, Harvesting, and Magpie Nests

The narrative focuses on the "harvesting" and the grackles, as well as the practice of making grabbers to collect the stubble leaves. These leaves, once piled up in large heaps, were stored during the dry season to feed the animals until the rains returned.

Magpies, birds as black as grackles but larger and with longer tails that seemed to fan out, were less numerous in the fields and are related to crows, though smaller. These birds mainly build their nests in eucalyptus trees.

I remember a time when climbing these trees to explore magpie nests became our favorite adventure. The eggs, which I will never forget, were a picturesque blue. Along with my friend "Cisto" and another equally daring peer, we ventured in search of these nests. Magpies built them at the top of the eucalyptus trees, and we, full of bravery and curiosity, strived to reach them.

In this chapter, I recall our adventures looking for magpie nests. We delved into the eucalyptus trees with a dexterity only youth allows. Chuy was the most skilled and daring among us, always eager to be the first to climb. The branches, though thin, bore our weight as we were still children. Sometimes, we found small eggs or butterflies in the nests.

I remember convincing my brother Miguel to join us on this quest. I promised him some magpie eggs, and, gullible, he joined the expedition. However, my true intention was to keep him busy and away from home, where he was usually scolded.

That day, even my father joined the search. Miguel, who feared my father, did not expect his arrival. As we climbed the eucalyptus trees, my father, from the base, warned us about the dangers of our risky endeavor. "You'll kill yourselves if you're not careful!" he exclaimed worriedly. Hearing him, we quickly descended, only to find him waiting, belt in hand. You can imagine what happened next...

The Linos Stream in Saltillo

Saltillo, a modest ranch located east of La Capilla and about three or four kilometers away, was a place of great adventure for us boys. Although not very large, it represented a world to explore for us. The Linos Stream flowed through it, where we used to swim in its pools. The surroundings were full of grass and bushes, from which we cut the forks to make our slingshots.

In those bushes and cacti, abundant in the area, we found the ideal place for hunting mourning doves and brown doves. The birds would come to the stream to drink water and then head to sleep, where we awaited them with our slingshots. Additionally, cacti growing in the area bore sour prickly pears and other varieties. When there were no doves, we hunted other small birds known as "Sititos," which we later fried.

The terrain was very varied, with rocky areas and pronounced unevenness, probably giving rise to the name "Saltillo." Near the stream was a ruined house, of which only the walls remained, a testament to bygone times. This place, with its multiple bird nests and eggs of various colors, was a paradise for us, full of adventure and discovery.

In Saltillo, we also enjoyed nature in an abandoned orchard. There, a pear and a capulin tree still grew; we liked the fruits of the latter, similar to cherries but a bit smaller, black, and with a sweet and exquisite flavor. During the fruit season, we loved climbing the trees to collect the capulins.

Moreover, in this area grew tame cacti, producing large red or yellow prickly pears. Among the cacti lived the "torcacitas," birds similar to doves or pigeons but slightly smaller and of a lighter, mottled color.

These native birds did not migrate and built their nests in the orchard to breed.

It was curious that these "torcacitas" seemed exclusive to our region; I don't remember seeing them in other states. Another characteristic bird of the area was the "purriche," also known as "jump wall." This bird, common on walls and recognizable by its unique and distinctive song, was somewhat larger than a hummingbird, with a long beak and a mottled brown tail. I've only seen it in my Altense region.

El Saltillo and the Jicotes

In El Saltillo, one of our most memorable adventures was confronting the jicotes, bees known for building their holes and tunnels in the walls. These nests were filled with honey, and our curiosity led us to try extracting it, despite the jicotes' fierce defense. They were wild bees that did not hesitate to attack us, making us run as if we were track champions, while the persistent jicotes followed us tirelessly, stinging us relentlessly.

Armed only with our hands or whatever we could find, we desperately tried to shoo them away, but they clung to us, even at long distances. Sometimes, they wouldn't give up until they managed to sting us. However, our determination was such that we returned the next day, not so much for the honey, but for the challenge of facing the jicotes. We even carried long sticks to defend ourselves or fend them off during these encounters.

I remember one day, after having eaten capulines until we were full, we approached the jicote nests. We provoked the bees by poking their holes with a straw. It seemed they communicated with each other because they emerged en masse, ready to attack us. And so the chase began once more, until one day I arrived home with my face and an arm swollen. Seeing me, my mother exclaimed alarmingly, asking what had happened to me. "Don't worry, mom, it was just the jicotes," I replied. When she asked where I had been, I simply said, "At El Saltillo."

My mother, seeing my condition, quickly prepared a home remedy. She crushed the heads of some matches and mixed them with saliva, applying the paste to the stings. She explained that this would neutralize the poison, although it was somewhat late, and it might burn a bit. "It should be applied immediately after the sting," she advised.

The next day, I woke up still swollen, but the remedy had helped. My mother taught me that the phosphorus from the matches was useful for neutralizing the poison from various venomous insects. In the case of ant stings, I prepared the matchhead mixture myself. Additionally, I found out that garlic was another effective remedy. Peeling and crushing the garlic cloves, I would take them with plenty of water, or even better, with milk, which also provided significant relief.

However, in cases of more severe stings, like those from a scorpion, it was crucial to suck out the venom as quickly as possible and then apply the crushed matches. This knowledge and these home remedies were an essential part of our lives in El Saltillo, where every day was an adventure and a chance to learn.

In El Saltillo, we learned to deal with the stings and poisons of various creatures. With scorpion stings, for example, speed is crucial to prevent the venom from spreading through the blood. Some people react very badly to this venom. In such cases, the garlic remedy I mentioned earlier is used, or one should drink plenty of milk. These solutions are known in natural medicine, and I share them here for free.

The Arlomos and Their Traditional Antidote

A particular case involves the "arlomos." This small worm, which glows in the dark like fireflies, is a unique creature in my region of Los Altos de Jalisco, or at least it seems so to me, as I have not heard of it elsewhere. The capulina spider or black widow is another being whose bite is feared for its potent venom.

The venom of the arlomo, though less known, is equally dangerous. The sting of this worm doesn't cause initial pain, but over time, a sore forms and begins to spread, consuming the flesh around the bite site. Those unaware of its danger and who do not seek medical attention in time can face severe consequences. Even doctors may struggle to treat these stings due to the unusual nature of the arlomo's venom.

Thanks to wisdom passed down from generation to generation, likely since pre-Hispanic times, we have learned to identify and use an effective remedy.

The "arlomo herb" is the only known cure for these stings. There are two varieties of this plant: the female "arloma" and the male "arlomo." Interestingly, the type of herb used depends on the gender of the arlomo that caused the sting. If the male herb doesn't provide relief, it's known that the sting was from a female arlomo, and the corresponding herb is sought. The people in my region can easily distinguish them.

The treatment involves boiling the herb and applying the warm water to the sting, which provides almost immediate relief. While I have never suffered an arlomo sting myself, I have witnessed how this traditional remedy effectively cures those affected. I have also observed these small worms lighting up the night with their glow.

Now, I continue with more tales of my mischief and experiences in the region.

CHAPTER 15

María Esqueda and Her Pozole Recipe

María Esqueda was a very popular lady in our town. Daily, and especially on weekends, she set up her food stall in the square, near the portico. Early in the morning, she prepared an exquisitely tasty menudo, accompanied by a red sauce made with tree chili, perfect for hangovers when added to the menudo.

In the afternoons, her famous pozole was a must. This dish was made with nixtamalized and desilked corn, a process only pozole experts know how to perform correctly. The pozole's base was pork, but the key ingredient was the pork feet, which gave it a gelatinous texture and an incomparable richness. It was said to be a fantastic vitamin source, ideal also for hangovers.

The pork feet had to be cooked at least an hour before the rest of the meat, due to their toughness. The head of the pig was added, deboned, including the tongue, snout, ears, and even the eyes and brains, which I personally loved. While the meat cooked, after about two hours, the desilked corn was added. The proportion was crucial: two-thirds corn to one-third meat, to achieve the perfect balance of pozole.

For a good pozole, the corn proportion is crucial: it must be plentiful. Besides the pork feet meat, lean meat is added to enrich the flavor. As for the chilies, I personally prefer to use California Chili, which is mild and adds flavor without spiciness, and also New Mexico Chili, which is spicy. Sometimes, I add pasilla chili, either powdered or whole, which darkens the broth but makes it deliciously tasty.

The meat's cooking should be slow and careful, approximately three to four hours on medium heat, stirring constantly to prevent sticking.

Once the meat is tender and the corn cooked, the pozole is ready to serve.

To complement the dish, an assortment of accompaniments is prepared: chopped lettuce, onion, grated radishes, lemons to add juice to taste, and a very spicy sauce for those who enjoy spiciness. All this is added to the pozole just before serving it, in deep and large bowls, creating a feast for the palate.

In California, where I prepare this recipe, I buy all the ingredients at large markets, where I find everything necessary to recreate this traditional dish.

María Esqueda, Her Diner, and Her House

María Esqueda was not only famous for her pozole but also for her diner in the square. I am excited to recall the recipe I shared with you, especially useful for relieving hangovers with its hot broth and a good dose of spicy sauce.

Besides pozole, María sold exquisite tostadas and fried tacos, accompanied by her spicy sauce and a bottle of "Chile Chiflador," so strong that it made those who tasted it whistle. María lived on the outskirts of La Capilla, in an area known as "Las Colonias," although at that time there were only about ten houses there.

I remember one day, upon leaving school without knowing what to do to entertain myself, I headed towards Las Colonias. In that place, there were often many lizards sunbathing on the stone fences. While I entertained myself by throwing stones at them with my slingshot, without realizing it, I arrived at María Esqueda's house's kitchen. At that time, I did not know whose house it was. Curious, I peered in and saw that the door was only closed with a latch.

María Esqueda and the Pots I Broke

In those days, María Esqueda's house, made of adobe and with a tiled roof, was the place where she prepared her famous pozole. One afternoon, driven by curiosity, I peeked into her kitchen through a half-open door. Inside, I saw large clay pots used to cook the pozole and menudo.

That day, motivated by childish mischief, I thought breaking those pots would result in a very appealing crash. Ensuring no one was around, I untied the rope that kept the door shut and entered. Inside, I found bags of granulated salt and dried tree chilies. Looking for something to eat and finding only a chili with salt, I tasted it, but its spiciness made me desperately seek water.

In my desperation and still with a burning mouth from the chili, I decided to break the large clay pots. The resulting noise was so thunderous and satisfying, it became my revenge for the spiciness. With a sense of triumph, I watched as the pots shattered, creating a noise that echoed in the kitchen like the rumbling of a drum.

María Esqueda and the Pot Incident

After my mischief in María Esqueda's kitchen, I left satisfied yet aware of my wrongdoing. Just as I was leaving, I ran into María face-to-face. She had heard the crash and, worried, was heading towards her kitchen. When she saw me, she asked what I had done, to which I responded with an innocent "Nothing, nothing!" and then, I took off running like a cunning fox. María followed me, but I quickly outpaced her, even hearing her skirt flapping behind me. Though I escaped, she shouted a warning that she knew who I was.

As I jumped a fence and moved away, I wondered if she had really recognized me and if she would talk to my father. Indeed, my father had to pay for the broken pots, but curiously, I was not punished on that occasion. I felt lucky to have avoided punishment.

Don Pedro Chico's Mules and the Electric Motor

Don Pedro Chico, as he was called because his father's name was Pedro Castellanos. Don Pedro was the brother of Don Eulogio Castellanos, father of Chepillo and grandfather of Cisto, my friend.

Don Pedro Chico, a respected man in La Capilla, was known for his seriousness and imposing stature. He and his brother, Don Eulogio, owned properties near the picturesque town of Mezcala, belonging to the municipality of Tepatitlán, located to the northwest near the Río Verde.

Don Pedro was one of the wealthiest men in the area. He owned a string of about fifty mules used for trade, transporting goods from Guadalajara and neighboring towns. He had a huge corral where he housed the mules, located in the first block southwest of the square. He was also a pioneer in bringing electric light to the town, installing a huge motor that ran on gasoline. This motor drove a dynamo to generate electricity, connected by a thick canvas belt. Though the light it provided was weak, making the bulbs look like hanging oranges, it was a significant advancement for the community.

In the mornings, Don Pedro would start the motor to grind the nixtamal, necessary for making masa for tortillas. People lined up waiting their turn to get fresh masa, an essential service in the town's daily life.

Don Pedro Chico's Mules and the Masa Master

Continuing the story of Don Pedro Chico's mules, they were indeed numerous and an essential part of his business. Before motor vehicles arrived, mules were crucial for transport, making them very profitable. However, with the advent of trucks, Don Pedro had to sell them. When he still had them, their arrival through the town's streets created a great commotion. The noise of the mules was so imposing that it often scared us, forcing us to take refuge at home or to climb onto window railings.

The mules were taken to the corral to be unloaded, right where the electric motor was operated by a very popular figure in town, known as the Masa Master. His nickname surely came from his skill in making masa for tortillas. He was a beloved person, originally from Arandas, also known as "the Arandense."

The Masa Master also had a special talent for curing tonsillitis. I, who frequently suffered from this discomfort, was treated by him at my mother's request. Despite the pain his arm massages caused, relief was almost immediate. He also recommended eating ripe red tomatoes as part of the treatment. Most admirably, he never charged for his services.

Don Pedro Chico's mules were a constant presence in our town. In exchange for his healing services, the Masa Master only asked for a candle for the Virgin of Guadalupe. However, despite his abilities, he couldn't cure the craters in my tonsils that appeared with white spots. I frequently fell ill because I had a very resistant virus that could affect the heart, lungs, or liver. Fortunately, I never suffered serious complications and finally cured myself with penicillin and an operation to remove the tonsils.

Continuing with the story of Don Pedro's mules, I remember once almost getting caught in the street. I lived near the mill and the electric motor in the corral, where Don Pedro kept his string of mules. I used to hang out with Cisto and sometimes another friend named Rubén Castellanos, whom we nicknamed "Patolo." He was a peaceful and kind boy from an early age. We liked to play marbles near the corral, and it was there that the mules, accustomed to galloping to their final destination because they knew they would be fed, nearly caught us in one of their frenetic races to the corral.

I remember Don Pedro Chico as a gallant figure of the era. He used to dress in the charro style, with tight pants, a short jacket, and a round hat, not too big but elegant. His brother, Don Eulogio, whom his family called "Papoco," shared his imposing stature and fair complexion, both very Castilian, as indicated by their surname.

On his ranch "El Espino," which I have already mentioned, a tragic accident occurred that I will never forget. Two young girls, known as "las güeras" for their blonde hair and beauty, tragically drowned. They were about fifteen years old, in the prime of youth, as beautiful as freshly cut gardenias in the morning, covered with dew. Their beauty and tragic end remain in my memory as a bittersweet recollection of those times.

CHAPTER 16

The Tragic Fate of the Güeras

I remember it was in September, a month of abundant rains, when the tragedy of the güeras occurred. One of them was the daughter of Chepillo and granddaughter of Don Eulogio, while the other was the daughter of my uncle Felipe González and my aunt Lupe, also a descendant of Don Eulogio. Irene Brimo Castellanos, daughter of Trina Castellanos and another descendant of Don Eulogio, was also with them, along with Altagracia González, known as "Gacho."

The unfortunate event took place at "El Espino," a beautiful ranch owned by Don Eulogio. The girls had gone there to enjoy a few days in nature. At that time of the year, the place was especially beautiful, with lots of fertile land where delicious products such as fresh cheese and prickly pears were abundant. Don Eulogio also had a large orchard of various types of peaches next to his big house and a cow stable, always ensuring fresh and frothy milk for cheese making.

The ranch's wells and waterholes were brimming with water, and it was precisely this excess that triggered the misfortune. The girls, in a moment of carelessness, found themselves in a situation they could not escape from.

The incident occurred at a well, a pond about ten meters in diameter. Although it seemed harmless, it was actually a deadly trap. The well had a depth of about four meters, and next to it was a smaller circular area, slightly less wide, about two meters across and just over one meter deep. I assume it was designed to collect water when the main well overflowed.

That morning, after breakfast, the young women spent their time in the peach orchard, picking fruits to eat and to take with them. I believe it was around noon when they decided to go to the pond to bathe. The two fair-haired girls and Gacho entered the water, while the cousin stayed on the edge, fearful of the water. They confidently started walking toward the center of the well, oblivious to the depth that awaited them.

Suddenly, one of the fair-haired girls sank into the deepest part, struggling desperately to stay afloat. She tried to reach the surface, but the depth, and perhaps panic, prevented her. It was a moment of terror and confusion, marked by the desperation of that fateful day. The fair-haired girls, despite their courage, faced a life-or-death situation: neither of them knew how to swim. Seeing one of them in trouble, the other jumped in to try to save her, but without knowing how to swim, they both ended up in the same desperate plight. Gacho, although she was close and also desperate, decided to join them in the water, and thus all three sank.

Irene, the daughter of Trina, witnessed everything and recounted the story to me. She said that seeing them disappear under the water, she was paralyzed at the edge, not knowing what to do. She knew if she went in, she would face the same fate. Instinctively, she ran to the house to look for help and encountered Papoco's foreman on horseback. She quickly explained the situation, and together they hurried back to the well.

Upon arrival, they saw Gacho floating in the water. With skill, the foreman threw his lasso into the well, managing to hook Gacho by the foot and dragged her out. They took her to the house while alerting everyone in town. Many people came to the well, but no one knew how to swim. Someone was sent running to La Capilla to look for someone who could. Meanwhile, Gacho, who was unconscious, finally woke up.

A young man who found the foreman ran off in search of more help. I remember this event with a mix of sadness and shock.

That day, I was bathing at La Grifa pond with several friends when a boy ran by on the path leading to El Espino. He was heading to La Capilla to give notice of what had happened. He quickly shared the news with us, and we ran toward El Espino. The boy reached La Capilla, and the first to learn of it was Panchillo, son of Don Pancho González, a tailor and excellent swimmer. Panchillo was also a blood uncle, brother of Chepillo's wife, and grandfather to one of the fair-haired girls.

With palpable desperation and impressive swimming agility, Panchillo arrived almost at the same time we did, even though we had a head start. It's about three kilometers from La Capilla to the pond. When we arrived, there was already a large crowd around the well, but no one dared to enter. Some suggested that I should dive in, knowing I was a good swimmer, but being still a child, I hesitated, fearing the same fate as the fair-haired girls. However, Panchillo didn't hesitate for a moment and dove into the water to look for them.

After Panchillo and other brave individuals arrived at the accident scene, the search for the fair-haired girls began, clinging to a thread of hope. Unfortunately, by the time they brought the first one out, it was too late. She still had a peach in her mouth, a poignant reminder of their carefree moments before the tragedy. Later, Panchillo managed to retrieve the second girl, who had gotten stuck among the rocks.

That day, it seemed the entire village had gathered at the scene. As people began to return to the village, they took the road of the under-construction, unpaved highway. I remember seeing my uncle Felipe and Chepillo walking with bowed heads, surrounded by people offering their condolences.

Later, the fair-haired girls were laid out in my uncle Felipe González's house. That night, I could not sleep, replaying the events in my mind. I was with Cisto, and one of the girls was his sister. She resembled him greatly: blonde, fair-skinned, and blue-eyed. Pepe "la Cocorilla," another brother, was also there, deeply affected by the loss.

After the tragic drowning of the fair-haired girls, I remember overhearing a conversation among people of Pepe's age, my uncle, which I'll never forget. They discussed a popular belief that kissing the feet of the deceased would ward off fear and their apparitions. Influenced by my innocence and credulity at the time, I went to the room where the girls were being watched and secretly kissed their feet. They were dressed in white cotton stockings, a detail that still resonates with me.

Gacho González, for her part, miraculously survived the incident. After the event, she participated in a contest and became a rider. Irene, who also survived, moved to the United States with her mother and son Juan Carranza, who had been born there. Irene married a kind man named Amado Pérez, and together they had three sons and two daughters, enjoying a full and happy life.

On the other hand, my uncle Felipe and the mothers of the deceased were plunged into sadness over the loss of their daughters. My uncle Felipe was named in honor of my great-great-grandfather, his great-grandfather, whose memory lived on through the generations.

The fair-haired girls who drowned and Aunt Cristina's family

The story of my Aunt Cuca, mother to my Uncle Felipe and sister to my grandmother Maris, is remarkable. She married a wealthy man from the González family of La Loma, known as "Los gorditos de La Loma." Sadly, she became a widow at a young age, inheriting considerable wealth from both her husband and her own family after her mother, Mamá Mariquita, passed away.

Of Aunt Cuca's children, only one was a boy, and he had three sisters. One of them, Lupe, married a relative from the same González of La Loma but also died young. Another sister went to Spain, where she lived and died in a convent. The third sister, tragically, suffered from mental health issues, particularly during the Cristera War.

As an adult, Uncle Felipe took over the family estate from both his father and mother, Aunt Cuca. Aunt Cristina, on her part, fell ill young. She had a boyfriend but never married. After Aunt Cuca became a widow, she devoted her life to caring for Cristina during her years of illness.

Aunt Cristina's story is one of mixed emotions. She was confined to a room facing the street, likely the living room, with a window and railing. I believe she was placed there to find distraction in watching the street, an attempt to soothe her nerves. Sometimes, Aunt Cristina became agitated, and Aunt Cuca would call for help, especially to change her clothes.

For us, the children of that era, Aunt Cristina was a source of curiosity. We would climb the railing to look into her room. Sometimes we saw her pacing back and forth like a caged animal. Aunt Cuca always kept a chamber pot ready in a corner of the room. Initially, Aunt Cristina liked seeing us, but then we would start yelling things, sometimes even shouting, "Cristina is crazy!" which upset her greatly.

Once, we were shocked and ashamed when, in a fit of anger, she threw the chamber pot's contents at us. In hindsight, it was a deserved reaction to our disrespect. Thus concludes the story of the fair-haired girls and my Aunt Cristina, a tale reflecting the complexity of human condition and the challenges of those times.

Chapter 17

Tacho Burras, a unique character

Continuing with our series of stories and antics, the figure of Tacho Burras, a peculiar bachelor, comes to mind. He was a mature man, between thirty five and forty years old, who sometimes seemed to lose his mental composure. He owned a small plot near the Gómez dam and often sat on the park benches, wrapped in a checkered blanket, wearing a large hat and sandals. He was not very keen on personal hygiene and rarely spoke to anyone due to his episodes of confusion.

Tacho Burras was observant and had a particular fondness for beautiful women. He noticed the young women leaving the rosary in the evenings or on Sundays. He always found a seat on a bench in front of the church, where he could admire the girls, most of whom were truly beautiful. Among them, Irene Carra, known as "la Chata," daughter of Trina Castellanos and cousin of the fair-haired girls who drowned in El Espino, caught his attention especially.

Tacho Burras and his infatuation with "la Chata"

Tacho Burras, a peculiar character in our town, had set his sights on Irene, affectionately known as "la Chata." She was one of the survivors of the tragic incident in which the fair-haired girls drowned. Irene stood out not only for her beauty but also for her friendliness and sociability. She was, without exaggeration, one of the most beautiful young women in the place.

I remember one day, while playing with other boys in the square, Tacho Burras approached me. Apparently, he had noticed my presence and thought I could act as an intermediary in his courtship attempt. He approached and asked me for a favor, offering me two twenty-cent coins, a considerable sum for a boy my age. His request was for me to deliver a note to La Chata, Trina's daughter. The reward and curiosity drove me to accept the task.

Tacho Burras instructed me to tell La Chata to send a reply with me after reading the note. He promised me two more coins if I completed the task. At ten years old, this seemed like a golden opportunity, though I wondered how La Chata would react. Deep down, I knew it was unlikely that she would reciprocate Tacho Burras's feelings, but the hope and innocence of youth led me to accept the challenge.

Armed with Tacho Burras's message, I was in a dilemma about how to proceed. I didn't want to miss out on those coins. While pondering what to do, I ran into Pepe "la Cocorilla," Cisto's brother, and decided to share the matter with him, especially since La Chata was his cousin.

Upon telling him about the task assigned by Tacho, la Cocorilla laughed, and together we devised a plan to reply to the letter as if it were La Chata. Since he had better handwriting, I gave him one of the twenties Tacho had given me, and we went to his house to draft the response. Tacho's original message was full of love, so our reply had to be equally sentimental to continue the game and perhaps get more money from Tacho.

The next day, I found Tacho sitting on the bench in the square, wrapped in his blanket and with his hat, the very image of expectation. I told la Cocorilla to hide while I delivered the response we had created, full of loving words. La Cocorilla could barely contain his laughter at the situation.

Tacho Burras and the imaginary infatuation

I delivered the fictitious letter we had composed to Tacho Burras. His face lit up with joy upon reading it; had he been a dog, he surely would have howled and wagged his tail in delight. After finishing, he handed me two more twenty-cent coins and asked me to return the next day with another letter and more money. The scheme worked so well that we repeated it a few more times.

Our operation lasted for a couple more instances. The fictitious love we conveyed to Tacho in each letter seemed to bolster his spirits so much that he decided to seek out La Chata in person. One evening, draped in his blanket and hat, he stood outside La Chata's house, who was unaware of his affections. That night, Celina, my Uncle Felipe's daughter of the same age as La Chata and her usual companion at the rosary, also came out. Tacho, believing he was close to his "heaven," approached them with a mix of hope and nervousness.

Startled by a shadowy figure nearing them, La Chata and Celina screamed. Chepillo, the uncle of both girls, came out to confront the situation. Recognizing Tacho even in the dark and despite having his gun, Chepillo halted when Tacho pleaded not to shoot. La Cocorilla, hidden yet fully aware of the scheme, watched anxiously.

Chepillo sternly warned Tacho to stay away from his family. Unaware of the unfolding drama, I was startled to witness the altercation. Despite the tension, I pondered the potential benefits from the situation. However, when Tacho noticed me, his frustration erupted, and he started throwing stones. I had to run to avoid getting hit.

After that incident, I always kept my distance whenever I saw Tacho Burras on the street. Despite my mischief, I learned a valuable lesson about the consequences of toying with people's emotions.

Chilindrín, the Barber of La Capilla

Chilindrín was among the most renowned and beloved figures in La Capilla. By the time I got to know him, he was already an elderly man, highly popular as a barber. His barbershop, situated across my home, served as a significant gathering spot in the village. Despite suffering from cataracts, Chilindrín continued to dedicate himself to his craft every Sunday, when his shop would brim with ranchers attending mass and doing their weekly shopping.

Chilindrín's barbershop was modest, featuring just one chair, but this did not deter his customers. "Chilindrín, I'll come back later; you're too busy," they would say, aware of his poor vision and the outdated state of his tools. His scissors resembled sheep shears, and his razor, though constantly sharpened, no longer cut as it once did.

Nevertheless, the ranchers left his shop content, even if their haircuts looked as if they were done with a rough blade or as though a donkey had nibbled on their heads. Despite the occasional uneven results and the stray long hairs Chilindrín might leave behind, everyone enjoyed his engaging conversations and left with a smile.

Chilindrín, with his cataracts and not always accurate hands, had become an emblematic figure in La Capilla. Despite the imperfect haircuts and occasional minor injuries—which he would treat with alcohol and powder to prevent infection—there was even a local saying: "Fear Chilindrín more than the razor," referring to his unique shaving style.

Despite his clouded vision and advanced age, Chilindrín retained a youthful spirit and was in good physical shape. We, the village children, would sometimes target him for our pranks. With nothing better to do, we would approach his barbershop and shout: "Chilindrín, where's your rough blade?" Knowing he would chase us, his agile and nimble response provided us with exhilarating chases. Occasionally, he would emerge with the razor he used for shaving, adding excitement to our escapes. At heart, Chilindrín was a kind and tolerant person, though our antics could sometimes be over the top.

El Mocono, a Beloved Character in La Capilla

El Mocono was another well-known figure in La Capilla, particularly for his connection to Chilindrín's barbershop. He lived in what is now the Smurfs' house. A humble man, he had a wife, a sister, and a niece named Enedina, who was around twenty years older than me and very friendly with everyone. El Mocono, older and somewhat portly, ran a small business from his home, selling candies and toys.

I remember he would display his goods in a room facing the street, opening a window without a railing to showcase his merchandise. Like with Chilindrín, we kids played similar pranks on El Mocono. Shouting "Mocono!" from the street annoyed him. Though he tried to chase us, his bulk made it difficult, and we could easily run and hide in the quarries near the temple.

Our antics in the square sometimes caught the attention of Herminio Alcalá, the police chief, and his officers. Brandishing their quince sticks, they occasionally gave unsuspecting boys a scare. Thankfully, I never experienced a beating or capture. There was a time when the police began detaining mischievous children, taking them to the station as a corrective measure.

Chuy from Tiburcio, a Baseball Afternoon

Chuy, whom I've previously mentioned when talking about taking down magpie nests with Cisto and myself, was known as "Chuy from Tiburcio." His father's name was Tiburcio, and they lived at the edge of La Capilla, just three blocks east of the square, on the same street as my grandmother's house.

Opposite the New Temple to the north, the land stretched to their home and beyond, there were only pastures. One day, seeking amusement, we decided to play baseball. About fifteen boys gathered, and taking advantage of a suitable field, we improvised a baseball diamond. We used balls made of cord and bats from pieces of log, lacking real bats. We were enjoying the game, amidst laughter and shouts, when suddenly Herminio, the police chief, appeared with his officers, some even on bicycles.

I vividly remember that moment: Chuy and I were together when we saw Herminio and the policemen approaching. Instantly, all of us, frightened, started to run. I didn't learn what exactly happened until later that night. "We ran as if we were bullets," I would recall, reminiscing about the adrenaline rush and the fear that engulfed us then.

Chuy from Tiburcio and the Police Escape

That day's adventure intensified with Chuy from Tiburcio when we had to hide from the police. At his house, we found two or three large baskets used for carrying corn cobs, big enough for us, as children, to hide inside. Terrified, we concealed ourselves in the baskets, watching the officers search fruitlessly.

From our makeshift hideout, we could see the officers roaming the streets and sidewalks, relentlessly looking for us. Fortunately, they decided to leave without finding us. My brother Miguel was also there that day. He opted to run towards a field with furrows and corn stalk remnants. Herminio followed him on a bike but couldn't navigate the furrows, so he shouted at Miguel to come out, claiming it would be easier to catch him in the open field.

Miguel, as cunning as a mouse evading a snake, stayed vigilant. He knew Herminio often carried his pistol and feared he might use it. It was a moment filled with tension and fear, blending child's play with the real dread of potential repercussions.

Chuy from Tiburcio and the Encounter with the Law

The adventure with Chuy from Tiburcio took an unexpected turn when authorities decided to apprehend the village's mischievous boys. They managed to capture almost all, except for Chuy, me, and a few others. We prided ourselves on our ability to elude capture, with the frustrated police often remarking, "That fox is slippery; we can't catch him."

Those captured ended up in jail, merely a room with a dirt floor. Among them were Herminio's son, known as "el Guarro," and another boy named Chime, whose family had recently moved to La Capilla for a state government job transfer.

The boys spent about three or four hours in jail, yet it turned into a chance for them to jest and play, making so much noise that eventually, the police decided to release them. This incident provided us with entertainment for many days, reminiscing and exaggerating the story with laughter.

Mischief on the Buses: The Feats of the Trucks in Los Altos

It was around the year 1942 or 1944, and I would have been about ten years old. At that time, in those days, in Los Altos, two remarkable passenger trucks were manufactured in Tepatitlán. Originally, the chassis were brought from the U.S.A., and an extraordinarily skilled bodywork master in Tepa, whom I personally knew, was in charge of their finishing. He was called "Maestro Tonila," and he was so close to being a genius that he turned those chassis into true works of art, practically indistinguishable from mass-produced ones.

These trucks, which operated daily between Guadalajara and Arandas, had earned their own names: one was called "el Plating" and the other "la Catrina." Their names were proudly displayed on the front windows, a common and allowed practice at that time before the transit government banned this custom.

The trucks had a distinctive dark, somewhat opaque red color, reflecting the typical red soil of the Los Altos region of Jalisco. Back then, the route between Guadalajara and Arandas was merely a trail, full of cattle guards that, at that time, Chuy el de Tiburcio, I, and another friend of our age named Salvador, affectionately nicknamed "la Rana," shared adventures. La Rana, coming from a humble family, was a brave boy and a prominent soccer player on the "El Nacional" team, the only one in town.

In the afternoons, we used to gather in the square to plan our mischief. One day, we decided to go to Rancho de Coleto with our slingshots to hunt doves and enjoy the delicious chamachera prickly pears, abundant in that area. We always walked along the trail that came from Guadalajara, passing through Tepa and following the royal road to Thanacasco, from where it deviated directly to La Capilla, passing by Cerro Carnicero, near Rancho de Coleto.

In the afternoons, around five or six, the passenger truck from Camiones de Los Altos used to pass by there, dropping off people going to La Capilla and then continuing towards Arandas. That day, while we were in Coleto, we saw the red truck approaching, and at that time, Chuy, La Rana, and I agreed to go to La Capilla on one of the trucks. These vehicles had to slow down for each cattle guard, structures placed at the edge of each pasture. A cattle guard, for those who do not know, consists of a square hole about one meter deep, slightly more than one meter wide, and two meters long, with several wooden beams arranged at certain distances to prevent livestock from escaping.

That afternoon, we took advantage of the truck's sturdy rear ladder, leading to a rack where luggage was usually loaded. Running, we got on the truck and traveled as stowaways to the square. This game became a custom for us for a while. We used to go early, armed with our slingshots, and delighted in eating prickly pears. Sometimes we would climb a nearby white sapote tree that bore very sweet sapotes, or we looked for wild cucumbers or passion fruits.

When we saw the truck approaching, someone would give the signal, and we all ran to hide. These trucks were large, resembling turtles with the engine at the front and a broad rack on top for luggage. It was a time of mischief and adventures, a testament to the innocence and daring of our youth.

Our adventures on the trucks became a routine part of our life in La Capilla. The trucks, always packed full, carried all kinds of cargo on the rack: people, chickens, pigs, goats, turkeys, in short, a bit of everything.

We took advantage of the wide ladder and the truck's bumper to climb and travel hidden.

But the day came when I decided to leave these mischiefs behind, especially after an incident that gave me a great scare. One day, trying to get off the truck while it was moving slowly, my foot got stuck in a cattle guard. Fortunately, I only lost a sandal, but the scare was such that I decided not to continue playing with my luck. Chuy and La Rana, seeing me fall and lie on the ground, yelled at me to run, but my ankle was slightly injured, making me limp.

Moreover, the townspeople began to notice our daily escapades on the trucks, hanging like monkeys. Even our getaways reached the ears of Don Juan Casillas, the ticket office owner, whom we affectionately called "Don Juan Casillas's hotel" for the rooms he had built. That's when we began to moderate our mischief.

Don Juan Casillas and His Hotel

Don Juan Casillas was a very generous and helpful man in La Capilla. He was also a partner in the Camiones de Los Altos and most of the partners actively participated in the business. Don Juan had his own office where he sold tickets for public transport. At that time, two buses operated regularly: one went to Arandas and the other, which arrived later, stayed in La Capilla, leaving early the next day.

The drivers and collectors from La Capilla, like my father, Jesús "el Diablito" or Eusebio Paredes, had no problems since they had their families and homes in the town. However, those who were not from La Capilla often had to sleep in the buses. Realizing the difficulties they faced and being someone who always sought to help, Don Juan decided to create a solution.

With his usual spirit of service, Don Juan devised the construction of a small hotel. Thus, the truck workers who were not from the place had a comfortable site to spend the night. This gesture reflected the solidarity and considerate character of Don Juan Casillas, always ready to assist others and contribute to the community's well-being.

Always attentive to solving problems, Don Juan transformed part of his spacious office into a small hotel to address the accommodation needs of drivers not from La Capilla. Although I do not remember exactly, I think he built about six rooms. They were narrow, with just enough space for a small bed and little else.

Once, a tall and burly driver, not from the town, was sent to La Capilla to spend the night and leave early the next day. Don Juan, always kind and hospitable, offered him one of his rooms, assuring him he would sleep comfortably. The driver, fully trusting Don Juan, did not check the room beforehand and went off confidently to have dinner.

He went to have dinner with María Esqueda, famous for making the best pozole and delicious pork loin tostadas with pickled onion, lemon, and tomato slices. Given his appetite and size, he enjoyed two large bowls of pozole, delighted with the food. However, after enjoying a hearty dinner of pork loin tostadas and pozole at María Esqueda's stand, the burly driver headed to Don Juan Casillas's hotel to rest. To his surprise, he found that the room Don Juan had assigned him was so small that he barely fit in the bed. Moreover, Don Juan had not yet installed electric light in the rooms, so he left him a candlestick with a candle.

Tired, the driver managed to lie down and fell asleep quickly. But after a while, the heavy dinner started to take effect. He began to have nightmares, probably caused by the pozole, and woke up in a state of confusion. He began to stretch his arms in the narrowness of the room, which seemed more like a coffin than a place to sleep. Lost in the darkness and trapped in his nightmare, he started to scream desperately: "Get me out of here!"

His cries alarmed the family of Don José Navarro, whose house was attached to the office and the hotel rooms.

An Unforgettable Night at Don Juan Casillas's Hotel

That incident at Don Juan Casillas's hotel became a memorable anecdote in La Capilla. The desperate screams of the driver woke up the entire Navarro family, except for the three daughters who were deaf-mute. Only the fourth daughter, who did not have that condition, also got up alarmed.

Cacheras, the eldest son of the Navarros, used to recount this story, perhaps with some exaggeration, but it always provoked laughter. He said that his father, Don José, and the rest of the family hurried out upon hearing the screams. They went to knock on the room's door and looked for Don Juan Casillas to open it.

Once inside, they illuminated the terrified guest with flashlights. The poor man, realizing he was not in a coffin, calmed down. The next day, Cacheras narrated the events, causing laughter among the neighbors. He particularly remembered when the man shouted, "Get me out of here, I'm alive!", thinking he had been buried alive in a coffin due to the narrow space of the room.

Undoubtedly, the driver's reaction and Cacheras's subsequent jest, with his unforgettable laughter and tendency to embellish stories, became part of the endearing and humorous memories of the town.

Chepo's Radio and Memories of the Time

In those days, when there were still no televisions for entertainment, people often exaggerated stories to make them more interesting, as my uncle Eulogio, my father's brother, did. Radios, which looked like large boxes with bulbs, were beginning to be common.

There was a man named Chepo, who lived in the same house where Gregorio Trujillo had his bakery. This house was huge and belonged to two elderly ladies, aunts of Concha Martín, Gregorio's wife. Chepo, their nephew and the house owner, was a man in his forties who never married.

In that same house also lived two of Chepo's sisters. One of them was Mariquilla, mother of a boy our age nicknamed Tite. The other sister was Pachita, whose husband, Federico, was a renowned jeweler who made gold jewelry. They were all refined, kind people.

We lived in a large house that spanned the entire block and also housed a bakery. But what I want to tell you about is Chepo's radio, which was one of the few in the neighborhood at that time. Chepo often invited us to listen to important events, especially football matches. I vividly remember the broadcasts of Guadalajara matches against visiting teams. At that time, the three major league teams were Oro, Atlas, and Guadalajara, our favorite, affectionately nicknamed "las Chivas."

The excitement peaked when Chepo announced that on Sunday, Guadalajara would play against América, the classic match of those times. We would gather around the radio, biting our nails with excitement, while Chepo, as passionate as we were, delighted in our company. Together, we cheered for Guadalajara.

I also remember a famous boxing match broadcast on the radio around 1944 and 1946. They were two fearsome heavyweights, real "destructive tanks," and people were eager to know who would be the best. That day, Chepo's radio became the focal point of the whole neighborhood, everyone wanting to hear the outcome of that great fight.

Chepo's radio was the neighborhood's central gathering spot for significant events, and one such memorable moment was the broadcast of a boxing match that captivated not just Mexico, but the entire world. Chepo, with his usual generosity, invited us in advance to listen to the fight between Joe Louis and another prominent boxer, whose names echoed as champions in our ears.

That Saturday afternoon, we gathered early at his house, eager to see who would be the best. The fight was intense, with each of us following every punch and round attentively. Chepo's house was packed; even Gregorio Trujillo and his sons, Goyo chico and Chava, joined us. We were all football fans and played together on the "El Nacional" youth team. Goyo and Chava, though not as mischievous as I was, were excellent teammates.

The excitement during the fight was palpable. I believe Joe Louis, a great black champion, emerged victorious. Louis maintained his title for twelve years, from 1937 to 1949, thanks to his technique and intelligence in the ring. His powerful punches were akin to mule kicks.

That night, as we listened to the fight, we enjoyed the famous "picones" that Don Gregorio had brought, making the evening an unforgettable experience.

Memories at My Grandfather Tacho's Carpentry Shop

My days were filled not only with mischief but also with moments of calm and tranquility, especially between the ages of 8 and 14. During that time, I spent much time with my grandmother María, my father's mother. In her golden years, she and my grandfather Tacho were alone, as all their children had married.

I was my grandmother María's favorite grandson, and my parents allowed me live with them to help her with daily chores and keep her company at night. I was not afraid in that huge house, with its vast patios and two large corrals illuminated only by moonlight, except for a light bulb that provided some light to the patio.

Though we later moved to San Luis Potosí, I vividly remember the times when, staying with my grandmother, we lit the house with oil lamps. These were round containers with a thick wick that absorbed the kerosene. If the lamp stayed on too long, we would wake up with black nostrils due to the soot released by the device.

My days were not just about mischief; they were also filled with learning and household chores. From ages eight to fourteen, I spent a lot of time with my grandmother María, helping her in every way I could, from cleaning the pigsties, a task that required daily attention, to feeding the animals twice a day.

My grandmother prepared the pigs' food with yellow corn which she soaked from the day before, mixed with whey cheese. We got this whey from Doña Cuca, a close cousin of my grandmother on both parents' sides, also related to Don Pancho González, the tailor, and the family from Rancho el 53.

Every day, I was tasked with fetching the whey from Doña Cuca. I carried two large buckets, about ten liters each, as they milked many cows and produced plenty of whey. I liked going to that house; upon entering, I always greeted with a loud "Good morning! Do you have whey?". Doña Cuca's daughters, very kind and just a bit older than me, welcomed me with a warm smile and kindly responded, inviting me inside.

Memories of My Aunt Cuca and Her Homemade Delights

I often found my Aunt Cuca's daughters grinding cottage cheese on a grinding stone. They were always busy, yet they never failed to roll a fresh ball of cottage cheese for me, a gesture I adored and a reason I enjoyed visiting.

I would fill two buckets with whey and embark on the return journey to my grandmother's house, which was about four blocks away. It was a walk I usually did on foot, and due to the weight, I had to rest at every corner, particularly since I was still a child.

My Aunt Cuca, a widow after her husband passed away leaving her with six children, was a strong and resilient woman. Her eldest son, Antonio, whom we called Uncle Toño, married my grandparents' youngest daughter, María de Jesús, affectionately known as Aunt Chuy. Her brother Lilis never married, as was common among many single men in La Capilla. Juanito, the youngest, along with his three sisters, completed the family. One of them married a Mr. Jiménez, a family known for being good merchants and for a time owners of the finest racehorses in Mexico.

Memories of My Grandparents and Their Lessons

I fondly remember two young ladies who used to gift me fresh cheese. They, like many others in La Capilla, chose to remain single, even being very beautiful. They believed that if they did not find the right man, it was better to live their entire lives unmarried.

Now, returning to my grandparents, both had immense affection for me. My grandfather owned his carpentry shop, a magical place for me. There, I spent hours crafting wooden trucks, wheelbarrows, and small petaquillas, to which I attached yokes with oxen I molded myself from the black clay of Tajoy. I was also his helper, in charge of buying red powder glue for painting the petaquillas, nails, tacks, and any other materials he needed.

My grandmother María also entrusted me with tasks. Whenever she wanted to buy something, she would say: "Go see if the chickens have laid eggs. Sell them and keep something for yourself." My grandfather, for his part, spent much time napping in the carpentry shop or, when awake, devoted to playing and practicing...

Memories of My Grandfather Tacho and His Baritone

My life was not limited to mischief; it was also filled with meaningful moments with my grandfather Tacho. I vividly remember his fondness for playing the baritone, a wind instrument similar to the bass but slightly smaller and more melodic. Among his daily activities, besides making petaquillas, was the constant practice of his instrument.

He was particularly fond of piloncillo, those small cones of cane sugar, despite having lost most of his teeth and being about seventy five years old. He had a particular taste for onions, not knowing that this food is excellent for strengthening the heart. Perhaps that contributed to his longevity; he passed away at ninety six years old, having been born in 1867, during Benito Juárez's presidency, and dying in 1963.

Now, resuming my childhood activities outside the house with my grandmother, I remember that, after leaving school, my brother Miguel and I would go home where my mother urged us to learn the catechism. We loved listening to the biblical stories, which were part of our religious and cultural education.

The Birthright: A Plate of Lentils

The birthright, a special chapter featuring a plate of lentils. This story is set in the Old Testament, spanning from Adam to Moses, including Abraham, David, and other sacred history heroes. One day, we learned about Esau selling his birthright to Jacob for a simple plate of lentils.

Esau, the elder brother, arrived hungry one day after a long day in the field. Jacob was enjoying a modest dish of lentils. Hungry, Esau asked Jacob for some of those delicious lentils in exchange for his birthright. Jacob agreed, and thus, the price of the birthright became a mere plate of lentils.

In this way, Jacob became the firstborn, and this story was etched in our minds when we were taught it in catechism, even as children.

Curiously, something similar happened with my brother Miguel and me. But what I'm about to tell you is the absolute truth. After attending the temple and participating in catechism, we returned home where our mother was cooking lentils. Before letting us eat, she tasked us with sweeping the pens and said, "When you finish, you can come to eat."

Miguel and I started sweeping, though he was less enthusiastic about it.

My father was away from La Capilla, busy with his work, making me reluctant to sweep. I was eager to finish quickly to enjoy the lentils I loved so much, which I still adore today. Miguel was stubborn and didn't want to help; he insisted that I should be the one to sweep both large pens.

At that moment, something crossed my mind. I remembered the story of the birthright and the plate of lentils. I told Miguel: "Fine, I'll sweep both pens, but you'll give me your birthright." He hesitated at first, but since he also loved the lentils, he eventually agreed. We agreed that he would give me his birthright in exchange for my plate of lentils.

So, by sweeping both pens, I became, at least for that moment, the firstborn of the family. In everyday life, I acted as if I were the trusted heir. Truthfully, I don't know if it was a coincidence or a twist of fate, but as we grew older, we reminisced about this biblical (and proven) event and laughed at the coincidence that bonded us. I hope you find this more eloquent version to your liking.

CHAPTER 18

Seeking Treasures in My Childhood - Memories with Tachín, Carlos, and the Carpentry Shop

My cousin Tacho often visited me at my grandmother's house. Since he was her grandson too, it was no problem, and together we would embark on adventures in my Grandfather Tacho's carpentry workshop. Sometimes, another cousin, Carlos, would join us. Carlos was Tacho's brother and the son of my Aunt Chuy, the youngest daughter of my grandmother who married my Uncle Toño Groscoy, and for a while, they lived with my grandmother María to accompany her. That's how Carlos joined us, being the only boy among Uncle Toño's four daughters.

From a young age, Carlos proved to be a kind person, just like Tacho. I never saw them angry; Tacho was always full of laughter. In those days, I remember they bought Tacho his famous hat. He had a skin tone very similar to Carlos's, akin to Grandfather Tacho's color, which was due to their indigenous ancestry, although I was a bit lighter-skinned due to my mother.

Continuing with our adventures in Grandfather Tacho's carpentry workshop, we would always ask him many questions, though I tended to be the most curious. He loved our inquiries. From him, I learned most of the family stories, including those about his parents. His mother was Martina Cortés, and his father was Don Abundio Gutiérrez.

In Search of Treasures - The Fox of La Capilla

Throughout my life, I learned practically everything from my grandfather Tacho. I won't repeat those details to stay on track with the story. Let's continue with our treasure-hunting adventures, Tachín and I.

Our quest for treasures stemmed from the stories my grandfather Tacho told us about our great-great-grandfather, Felipe Navarro. He died without revealing the location of his buried and hidden gold. My grandfather, who spent most of his life in that large house, dedicated his days to the relentless search for this buried gold, turning it into his daily pastime. Despite never finding anything, he never lost hope. His stories thrilled us, and Tachín and I decided to join in this hobby.

We began digging everywhere except the bedrooms, as our grandmother would scold us for that. One day, we took some shovels to a spacious corral, a room next to a barn. Almost daily, we dug where we thought it sounded hollow, and that particular day, inside that room, we hit the ground, and it sounded hollow. We began to excavate and dug a hole similar to those of rabbits. Gradually, we ventured into the tunnel, removing the soil. The deeper we dug, the deeper the pit seemed.

The thrill of treasure hunting led us to unimaginable places. On that day of our adventures, I was immersed in tunnel excavation. My body was almost entirely inside the hole, leaving only my feet outside. The only visible things were my shoes as I continued digging with the rod and tossing the soil into a bucket beside me. When the bucket filled, I pulled it out slowly, and Tachín assisted me in this task. I was so absorbed in the digging that I lost track of time.

However, at one point, something unexpected happened that left me almost breathless. The tunnel I was digging suddenly collapsed, burying me under the earth. I could barely breathe and felt the soil pressing down on me. What saved me was that my feet remained outside the hole. Tachín, shocked by the situation, was unsure what to do, but he finally gathered the courage and began pulling my feet. It was a strenuous task, but he managed to pull me out. I emerged struggling and panting, and when I finally came out completely, my face was so covered in dirt that I hardly recognized myself.

After the scare, we couldn't help but laugh at the situation and our own illusions. We had agreed to keep our expeditions secret, but even we didn't understand why we continued dreaming of finding the gold that Felipe, our great-great-grandfather, had buried. At other times, Tachín and I embarked on new adventures, following the exciting stories of treasures and gold burials that my grandfather Tacho had just begun to tell us.

One day, Tachín and I were exploring an old stable that stretched to the ceiling, revealing its age with every creak. Suddenly, we found a spot on the floor that resonated peculiarly. Our excitement overflowed, and without wasting time, we began digging with the rod, this time without creating a tunnel. Over time, we dug a half-meter-deep hole, and the soil became looser.

Excited, I kept digging relentlessly. Then, suddenly, the rod made contact with something solid. My heart raced as I noticed the rod encountering a plate, similar to that of a boat. I pierced it with the rod, moving it up and down, and the metallic sound resonated in the air. Tachín also noticed and shared my excitement. We thought we had found a treasure chest.

Without delay, we ran to the carpentry where my grandfather was and told him the exciting news. He came quickly to verify if it was true. Seeing the rod pierced through the boat, his excitement surpassed ours. He pulled out a rosary he always carried in his pocket and placed it next to the rod. He warned us not to turn our backs on the rosary or the rod because if there was gold there, it could turn into coal if neglected.

This experience filled us with excitement and anticipation as we explored the mysteries the old stable had to offer.

My grandfather Tacho had certain superstitions, perhaps due to an experience from his childhood that marked his life. Once, when my father was just a child, he was outside the house, near a rose bush, digging for treasures. At one point, he encountered a strange clay pot buried in the ground. To his disappointment, instead of gold, the pot was filled with coal. Popular belief said it should have contained gold, but my grandfather thought his lack of faith in the search had turned it into coal.

What happened next is that my grandfather Tacho quickly brought a pickaxe and a shovel to expand the hole we were digging. We all felt excited and were sure we had found a golden treasure. We continued digging enthusiastically, praying and feeling like we owned a treasure at that moment.

However, when we finally reached the object we had assumed, our excitement turned into surprise. Upon seeing it, our faces shifted from excitement to confusion. It wasn't a golden chest, but an old and worn-out toilet. We realized that, at some point in the past, a toilet had been buried there and covered. Amidst so much excitement, we had unearthed an ancient latrine. Life at my grandmother's house, in the carpentry with my grandfather Tacho and my cousin Tachín, sometimes had unexpected surprises.

After this peculiar discovery, my grandmother scolded us and told us we had dug enough and that the house was completely turned upside down.

Soledad Gutiérrez de Navarro: The Woman of Courage - The Cristero War

My aunt Chole, as we affectionately called her, though her real name was Soledad Gutiérrez de Navarro, was my grandparents' eldest daughter. She married a notable man named José Navarro. In those days, when they married, José was barely making ends meet as a carpenter. It was during the peak of the Cristero War that their first son was born, whom they named Reynaldo.

In that historical period, Mexico was engulfed in intense strife. There were protests against President Plutarco Elías Calles' policies, whom some called "Satan." Calles had ordered the closure of churches, the persecution of priests and nuns, and sought to align Mexico with the atheistic communist government of Russia. He aimed to eradicate Christianity and follow the purge model that occurred in Russia in the 1930s. However, God was with our people, and though there were many martyrs, the Mexican people resisted valiantly.

The Cristeros, like ants across all the central regions of Mexico, rose in defense of their faith. They faced adversity with courage, recalling the deeds of Christians against the Moors in Spain. The struggle was intense, and although the government tried to impose its agenda, it could never subdue the determination of our people.

Aunt Chole and José, like many others, joined this cause bravely, defending their beliefs and fighting for religious freedom in Mexico. Their story is an example of courage and faith in difficult times.

Aunt Chole in La Capilla

In this account, the influence of our Spanish ancestry, particularly the Castilians from the highlands of Jalisco, becomes more apparent. These Castilians never yielded to adversity and fought with strategy and courage in challenging times.

The setting is La Capilla and its surroundings, where protests erupted courageously. My Uncle José was commissioned as a promoter of these causes, but the government became aware of his involvement and started to persecute him. This marked the beginning of his exile to the United States, specifically in San Francisco, California, where he lived for the rest of his life.

Before emigrating, Uncle José was accompanied by Aunt Chole and their son Reynaldo Chico. Many people in those times emigrated and sought refuge in such unusual places as entire convents. In fact, I got to visit some of these people in the convent they reached in San Francisco, California.

During their time in San Francisco, Aunt Chole and Uncle José became guardian angels for the family, tirelessly fighting amidst the difficult economic situation we were going through. The first to make the decision to join the exile was my Uncle Liborio, followed by my Uncle Elodio, who faced a particularly significant challenge when dealing with a bull at that time. Their stories are a testament to the strength and courage that characterize our family in times of adversity.

Aunt Chole in La Capilla and Uncle Liborio in the North

During this stage of the story, both my Uncle Liborio and my grandfather Tacho decided to join us. When they arrived, my Aunt Chole and Uncle José, two kind-hearted souls, were filled with joy. We welcomed them enthusiastically, providing them with food and a home until they could find employment. They never complained, and there was always room for those who arrived at our door.

Aunt Chole was an exceptional cook, and Reynaldo and his three children were equally wonderful. All were kind and helpful, ready to assist us at any time, even with English when needed, as we did not speak it. My uncles were willing to collaborate and were an essential part of our extended family.

Before deciding to emigrate, my uncles had gone through many trials and tribulations. I learned a lot from them, especially from Aunt Chole, who had an excellent memory and enjoyed sharing stories of what they lived through during the Cristero days. Much of my knowledge about this crucial period comes from the conversations that took place around La Capilla, which I have mostly recounted in these pages.

Continuing with the stories about the Cristeros and our life in La Capilla, I want to recount an episode that occurred after a long time without visiting the place. About twenty years had passed since our last visit, around 1947. At that time, I was about eight or nine years old and spent most of my time with my grandmother María.

One day, my grandmother announced that Aunt Chole was coming to La Capilla. She was excited and began purchasing many new things to make the house look splendid. She bought large beds for everyone to rest comfortably and a wardrobe to organize the clothes. She did her best to ensure they enjoyed their stay to the fullest.

Finally, the awaited day arrived. Accompanying Aunt Chole were Uncle José and Hester, the eldest daughter of the women. When they arrived, I was at my grandmother's house. They entered along with my Uncle Eulogio, who had gone to pick them up in Guadalajara and had traveled together on the truck. The reunion was a true feast of emotions and affection. There were hugs and tears of joy.

As just a child, I watched these relatives who dressed elegantly and seemed very sophisticated. In my young mind, I was impressed by their presence and style.

My daily life was full of adventures and dirt, especially during the visit of my relatives. Hester, whom we affectionately called Hestercita, seemed especially charming to me. After greeting us, she and my aunt paid attention to us, the young ones of the house.

I fondly remember the moment when Hestercita looked at me and said, "Look, you are Liborio!" with an expression full of affection. It tickled my heart, and I experienced an emotion that made me feel as if the tickles would never go away. For eight days, I avoided washing my face so that those feelings wouldn't leave. I truly felt handsome, even like a king.

Hestercita even participated in celebrations in San Francisco and stood out for her beauty. It was a curious detail that, when she spoke with my Uncle Eulogio, she did so in English, as he spoke the language fluently after spending much time in the north. There, his first three children were born: Rafael, Concha, and my dear friend Tachín.

In La Capilla, the news of my uncles' arrival attracted many people, and every day they came to visit, mostly relatives. Don José Navarro and Doña María Navarro, close relatives, were especially cherished in the family. Doña María was a first cousin of my grandmother María. During the days they were in La Capilla, the house was overflowing with love and constant visits.

In those times in La Capilla, there were also other notable characters who left a mark on my memories. One of them was Don Ramoncito Barba, a kind-hearted gentleman and one of the well-off individuals in the area. He had three sons, all excellent boys. The eldest was named Ramón, nicknamed "Moral," the next was Arnoldo, and the name of the youngest escapes me at the moment. What I do remember clearly is that he always dressed elegantly in black, probably as a sign of mourning for his mother's passing.

All of Don Ramoncito's sons studied to become priests, though none of them ultimately embraced the priesthood. Among the anecdotes I fondly remember, one stands out where Don Ramoncito asked me for help with something and, in return, offered me some "patolas." Patolas were like beans, but much larger, about six times larger than a common bean. They were like the pinto cows, of various shapes.

We played a game called "Garambullo" with the patolas. To play, we placed a bunch of patolas in the palm of the hand, then closed the fist and raised it quickly. The player in turn named a quantity, and if they guessed the exact number of patolas remaining in their hand after making the movement, those patolas were theirs.

It was a simple but entertaining game that we enjoyed during those fun moments in La Capilla. These memories remain valuable in my memory.

I especially remember one day when Don Ramoncito invited me to his house. He wanted me to shuck some corn cobs he had stored in one of the rooms of his house. Although I only shucked a small amount that he needed for something specific, Don Ramoncito generously thanked me with a pile of patolas. I left his house happy and satisfied with the reward.

Besides playing with patolas, I was also fond of making paper balloons that we would fly with a sponge soaked in ignited kerosene. This was something I shared with my cousins Casillas and Cleofas, who were sons of Don Juan Cacillas.

Another moment I clearly remember is one Sunday when the "sardos," a group of army soldiers, came to recruit young men aged eighteen for military service. Since Sundays were mass days and the plaza was full of people and youngsters, the situation became chaotic. It was then that I saw Mon, a slim and agile young man who looked like a deer running swiftly. At that moment, Mon dashed away like an arrow escaping from the soldiers. Did they ever catch him? Never! Mon always managed to evade them admirably. The soldiers had no idea where the "little ball" went and failed to catch anyone.

I remember the day when Don Ramoncito invited us all to his ranch, located about two kilometers east of La Capilla. His ranch was beautiful, with an extensive orchard and a large pond where the cattle drank water daily. The water in the pond had a reddish hue, similar to the soil surrounding it, and we used to call it "Don Ramoncito's pond." Occasionally, we dared to bathe in it, though we didn't like it much due to the murky water and the many leeches that stuck to our skin. However, what we did enjoy were the peaches, which we tried to access by jumping and stealing them.

In that beautiful setting, filled with friends and fun, was Mon, who was quite smitten with Hestercita. How could he not be? Hestercita was truly charming. I remember her father, Don Ramoncito, entrusted Mon to bring something to La Capilla one day. She was a bit shy and did not open up when Mon arrived at her door.

Mon, slim, tall, and agile like a deer, didn't hesitate to jump the gate that led to the orchard. He undoubtedly had all the qualities of a champion and was determined to impress Hestercita.

The outings organized by Don Ramoncito Barba were memorable. I recall a day when they prepared a delicious grilled meat feast. They also cooked corn on the cob, accompanied by tasty fresh cheese. Since Don Ramoncito had a good number of cows, there was never a shortage of fresh cheese at his home. My father was also present, having obtained permission to join the gathering with my uncles. My Uncle Eulogio and Don Toño Navarro, brother of my Uncle José and father of Angelina, Eusebio Paredes' wife, were there as well. Besides them, my mother, Mariquilla, and many others joined the gathering.

I remember they brought a basket full of prickly pears and a jug of pulque from the harvest of some agave plants they had in the area for those who wished to enjoy it. Oh my God! The memory of those delicious grilled meat tacos with spicy sauce makes me hungry again.

And for dessert, the royal prickly pears from the nopals found in the basket. These prickly pears were also known as "tunas mausas" due to their considerable size and exquisite taste.

That day when Don Ramoncito Barba invited us to his ranch must have been in early September, as the corn was at its peak. The corn cobs were ripe but still tender, perfect for cooking. Along the road to La Capilla, amid the maize fields' margins, the vegetation was in full bloom. Flowers of blue, yellow, and white hues, resembling little bells, adorned the landscape in abundance. The countryside's beauty in my region at that time was genuinely remarkable. I even keep a photograph from that day when my mother brought the camera and captured Don José Navarro, my father, a cousin of my father named Cristóbal Martín del Campo, and my Uncle José enjoying the outing.

After that pleasant outing, my father invited my uncles to tour several cities using the "Red Buses of Los Altos" routes. Family ties were very strong, as my father had lived three years in my uncles' home in Wister. They all cared deeply for each other, and when it was time to say goodbye, I remember Hestercita shedding some tears. She gave us children hugs and, in some cases, even a kiss. She gave me a kiss.

However, before washing my face, I must mention how beautiful and kind Aunt Chole was. She had a delightful laugh and a very likable personality that we all enjoyed. It saddened me and the other children greatly when they left. Even Father Morales came to see them off, showing how much they cared for each other. He was the one who recommended Uncle José move to the United States during the Cristero War times.

Twenty years after my uncles returned, Father Morales invited them to a meal at his house. On this occasion, many familiar faces attended, and although I was not directly involved in the conversation, I could see that almost all who had gone on the outing with Don Ramoncito Barba were also present.

After their departure, we all felt a sense of sadness. Good people leave pleasant memories. After that episode, my grandfather and a young musician formed a musical band. My grandfather Tacho introduced me and my brother Miguel, along with several youths and two or three more children, to the band. Next, I will describe our experience in the musical band and how long we lasted in it.

Musical Band

Ezequiel Gutiérrez, as he was called, arrived at La Capilla and talked with Father Morales. He was impressed by the offer he received: besides a salary, they provided him with a house adjacent to ours. Soon, his entire family moved in: his father, Don Juanito Gutiérrez, his mother Doña Juanita, and his brothers, Adalberto and Abundio, who also became members of the Band.

In what is now the residence of the new priest, there was a spacious hall where conferences were held. That place served to start learning from scratch, though some, like my grandfather — who was called "el Chore" and played the trumpet — and the teacher Ezequiel, already had musical knowledge.

Soon, we began studying solfege from the first book. Ezequiel was an excellent teacher, just like my granddad. We spent several months practicing solfege until, once ready, they brought all the instruments to begin our practices. This learning period extended for quite some time until the teacher considered us prepared. I was assigned a wind instrument known as the Harmony.

Being the youngest and shortest in stature, I was assigned the Harmony, a wind instrument. It was a challenging task, as I had to constantly coordinate with the Bass. This instrument, with its deep and resonant tone, was part of the melodic section along with another, played by a young man two years older than me, known as "el Palillo" whose real name was Manuel Miguel. My brother played the flute, and my granddad Tacho, the baritone, an instrument similar to the bass but smaller in size.

Our band had a wide variety of instruments: piccolos, cymbals, bass drums, snare drums, trumpets, trombones, even a triangle, among others I now can't recall. We were about fifteen members in total. This great band became a refuge for many of us, steering us away from youthful mischief.

I remember one day, having already made significant progress, Ezequiel, our teacher, urged us to learn faster and with more dedication. The festivities were approaching, and he planned for us to debut playing at the kiosk in the square. The excitement overwhelmed us, and we began to practice with renewed zeal. I even stopped hanging out with my usual friends in the square, completely absorbed and excited by our band.

I already felt like a great musician and excitedly told my mother that we were about to start playing at the parties. It was then that she had my first shoes made for me. I remember a man coming occasionally, a cobbler who took measurements and returned after a month with a large order. When I wore these shoes, I found it hard to walk; I was used to wearing huaraches every day. The new shoes were so stiff and sturdy that I felt like a cat with thorns on its paws. To tame them, it was necessary to walk a lot, and sometimes I even got blisters. I preferred my huaraches, but to play in the band, I had to wear shoes.

The day arrived when we began to play in the square, in front of the temple's portico, right before the festivities. It was a Sunday because Ezequiel wanted us to get used to playing outdoors. We had learned and practiced about ten musical pieces, and among them was the famous Marcha de Zacatecas. I don't remember which piece we started with, but I remember when we played the Marcha de Zacatecas.

We, with our music, had elevated the Marcha de Zacatecas to the status of a second national anthem. We started playing and, to our surprise, a crowd began to surround us. They even applauded us. My friends were amazed, exclaiming, "Look at Zorrito! He can play!" The Harmony, almost my size, impressed everyone, both young and old. I heard their murmurs of astonishment.

When we finished the Marcha de Zacatecas, Don Ramoncito Barba came up excitedly, congratulating Ezequiel and asking him how much it would cost to repeat the piece. I don't know how much he charged, but we ended up playing it three times in honor of Don Ramoncito, and the people were delighted. Finally, there was in La Capilla a band worthy of its name.

Foundation of the Music Band: Agustín "El Cucho"

Then, another gentleman, whose name I don't remember, requested "El Quelite," which was also well received. It was at this time I received my first salary, something I didn't expect. Ezequiel distributed the money, and I could hardly believe the amount. Although it wasn't much, it represented a fortune to me. I would have been satisfied with ten or twenty, but holding the bills in my hands, I got so scared that I ran home and handed the money to my mother. "What is this?" she asked in surprise. I explained that I had been paid for playing in the band, which filled her with pride. I decided not to spend it and felt satisfied to contribute something to our family.

As the festivities approached, my mother used that money to have a suit made for me. It was black, an item that my uncle José, my father Chole's brother, had left before heading north. From that suit, mine was adapted. I don't remember well who made it, but I think it was Luis Muñoz, whom we called "El Chimo." He was an excellent tailor and owned the famous greyhound, "El Tiro."

With the band, we continued practicing during the week and playing in the kiosk on Sundays before the festivities. During that period, we experienced many memorable events, some quite curious. One of them involved a character known as Agustín "El Cucho."

It was a Sunday, and we had not yet started to play. We had left our instruments in the kiosk and were sitting on the square's benches. Suddenly, some greyhounds began to fight, causing a great uproar. The church was open, and the rosary was about to start. The early parishioners were beginning to enter, and the dogs, amidst their fight, ran into the church. One of them, chased by the other, went up to the altar, where they continued their struggle.

At that moment, there was Agustín, known as "El Cucho." He was born with a cleft palate, and although an operation had partially corrected it, he still had difficulties speaking clearly. That day, he ran out of the temple, shouting at the top of his lungs. Someone asked him what was happening, and he, panting, tried to explain: "A fierce dog fight at the parish altar!" But, due to his difficulty in pronouncing certain words, his message was not clearly understood.

Another curious person, not understanding him, asked: "What do you say, Cucho?" Agustín, already annoyed for not being understood, got even more irritated when called "Cucho," and complained: "Why do you call me Cucho?"

The situation became even more chaotic when Agustín, unable to pronounce "Cucho" correctly, became enraged by the mockery of others. The crowd, surrounding them and cheering for a fight, shouted: "Go for it, Cucho! Come on, Chale! Hit him hard, Cucho!" In a tense moment, Agustín, rising from the ground while having the other man down, yelled out: "Well, that's the fight, because he called me Jucho!" Realizing he couldn't take on everyone, he decided to withdraw. This incident became an anecdote that would be remembered for years.

The long-awaited festivities finally arrived. At that time, they were celebrated in February, although December 12 was always dedicated to honoring the Virgin of Guadalupe with Las Mañanitas. That day, only the 12th was celebrated, and I got to participate with the music band. Throughout the day, dancers arrived, and masses were celebrated, a true festivity throughout Mexico, even declared a National Holiday.

The first day of the festivities, which I had already explained how they were celebrated, I awaited eagerly. I felt important. The people of La Capilla were extremely happy with us, as for the first time, they had a formal and quality band. Believe me when I say we played at the same level as the municipal band of Tepatitlán. The color and excitement that began to be felt on the serenade nights were indescribable. We started playing just before the rosary and, during it, we rested a bit. When the church began to sing the last song, we climbed up to the kiosk and started to play just as people were leaving the temple.

The young men and women began to walk around, while the adults, seated, enjoyed our music. They even surrounded the kiosk, attentive to how we played. That's how we spent the entire festival, with everyone enjoying our presence. The youths and ladies walked around, throwing confetti and streamers, giving carnations and gardenias in abundance, enhancing the beauty of the present girls, who were truly lovely.

Even I had admirers. In the brightness and bustle surrounding the kiosk, there was a presence that captured my attention: "the blondie from Doroteo," a very pretty young girl with blonde hair. I noticed that, while I was playing, she stood in front of me, lost in the music, but her eyes insistently fixed on me. One day, I noticed her gaze and, to be honest, I found her very pretty and she attracted me. During a break, I gathered courage, approached her, and we started to chat, simple conversations typical of children.

At that time, I got a carnation and gave it to her. I had not yet set my sights on Victoria's redhead. At that moment, with the redhead, we were just kids, unaware of the complexities of love, living in that beautiful age of innocence. We simply liked each other and got along, nothing more.

I also remember that she was the daughter of a wealthy man, Doroteo Navarro, who had moved to Guadalajara but did not forget his homeland and returned for the festivities. Doroteo, the older brother of José María Navarro, who was the delegate at that time I mentioned during the national festivities, had this beautiful girl and other older, equally attractive children.

The Music Band: La Güera de Doroteo

Doroteo's sister's brother went to the seminary and might have even become a priest. Hopefully, he is one of the good ones. His sister, with somewhat reddish hair, I believe was named Esther. But let's continue with the festival story. It was around the fifth day when I returned home, and my mom said, "They've brought your suit, try it on to see how it fits." It fit me very well. I decided to wear it out to show it off. It was around three in the afternoon, I remember well because I had already eaten, and even my dad was at home.

I headed to the square, showing off my almost new shoes. My goodness! I felt like a peacock, all proud, thinking about playing with the band that night. Esther would see me in my new suit. I had already gone to the square to show off to my friends and was returning home, walking on the sidewalk, puffed up with pride in my suit, swaying from side to side, aimlessly but very satisfied. At that moment, a lady was coming from the opposite direction, carrying a brazier and a ten-liter glass carboy full of alcohol.

She was coming to sell cinnamon with alcohol, a typical drink brought by merchants during the festivities. Absorbed in my own image and she in her task, neither of us foresaw the imminent collision. My suit snagged on the corner of her arm, and in an instant, the carboy fell to the ground, spilling alcohol everywhere.

The situation turned into chaos. The lady, desperate, screamed: "Darn boy! Son of a...! Stop! Stop, damn you!" Known as "El Zorrito," I could not allow that name to be discredited, so I began to run. While thinking about what would happen when she caught me, I passed by some children playing outside Pedro Manos's house, brother of Luis "el Chino." Among them were a boy named Alfonso and a girl named Teresa.

I ran like lightning past them, and I remember one shouted, "Don't give up, Zorrito!" while the lady continued behind, furious and swift, thinking that at any moment I would tire. My goal was to reach my grandmother María's house, about four blocks away, more than a kilometer. Halfway there, I turned to look at her, and there she was, closer, looking like a marathon runner with her skirts billowing in the wind. You could even see her undergarments from so much running, and she kept yelling at me: "Stop, boy!" The closer I got to my grandmother's house, the more tired I became, and the lady was almost catching up. I was even more frightened thinking she wouldn't get tired.

Knowing every corner of my grandmother's house, I crossed the block from side to side and entered like a flash through the open door, closely followed by the tireless lady. Without respecting anything, she ran after me to where my grandmother was feeding the pigs in the pens at the back of the property. I ran through the whole place, and although I looked for my grandmother, I didn't see her in the pen. I kept going to the pigsties and, upon arriving there, was completely scared but didn't stop running.

While desperately fleeing from the swift lady, my grandmother shouted, "Boy, wait!" I wondered, "Wait? How could I wait?" I just managed to shout back, "A lady is following me and wants to catch me!" I crossed a vast orchard at the house, running like a hare, terrified. Knowing every corner of that property, I reached the end, where my father Felipe had built a bullring. Now demolished, only walls remained of what was going to be a house, but it was never finished. I got there, desperate, and knowing my way out, used my hiding spots in the wall, jumped like a ghost to the other street, and kept running the same way I had come.

I arrived home but just passed by, because I was afraid my dad would scold me. So, I headed to the house where teacher Ezequiel lived. There were Don Juanito, his wife Doña Juanita, and also Adalberto and

Abundio. I told them what had happened, although at first, they pretended to know nothing. Later, they confessed they were already aware, but being so kind, they reassured me, saying, "Don't worry, stay here, things will sort themselves out," they told me while I took refuge in teacher Ezequiel's house. They understood it had been an accident and managed to calm me down.

I was exhausted. Later, my mom and dad found out where I was and were already informed about everything. They sent for me; it was Don Juanito who told them I was at his house. It relieved me to know that my dad had gone to talk to the lady and had paid for the spilled alcohol.

Later, I learned what happened when the lady entered my grandmother María's house, chasing me furiously. She crossed the patio, the corral, and reached the pigsties where my grandmother was. The lady, still angry and searching everywhere, didn't know I had already hidden among the many trees in the orchard.

My grandmother, though already about sixty years old, upon seeing the lady and knowing she was after me, instead of getting scared, brought out the courage of the Gonzales and other surnames she carried. She confronted the lady, argued with her, and even threatened her. That made the lady lose her nerve, and my granddad Tacho, informed in the square of what was happening, hurried home. Upon arrival, he saw the swift lady running in, and he also hastened his pace to the pigsties, just when my grandmother was confronting the lady. "Calm down, María! I'll handle this," he told my grandmother, taking the lady outside.

The desperate lady sought help from the delegate, Don José María Navarro, whom she found in his large store, located south of the square. The poor woman was distressed: the alcohol she was carrying was her hope of earning some money. Fortunately, everything was resolved when they even paid for the damaged purse.

Thus, the festivities continued, and that night I returned to play in the music band, hoping to see Doroteo's blondie again. I didn't wear the new suit because it had wrinkled and dirtied in the incident. With that suit, something similar happened to me as with my aunt Cleta's dog: it never barked, but the day it did, its snout got broken. And I, who had never worn a suit before, the day I did, that happened; although the incident with the swift lady left me astonished, and I was just a sigh away from being genuinely scared. That suit, which I avoided wearing for a while, caused me a kind of fear. In those days, in La Capilla, few children dared to wear suits, and if I did, there were always mockeries around.

Indeed, we used to make fun of everything; we were mischievous in our daily escapades, even when it came to mocking those dressed elegantly. I remember one occasion when a very distinguished lady, whom we affectionately called "Catrina," arrived at La Capilla. Her elegant dress and a hat adorned with feathers left us astonished. It was as if the bishop himself had arrived.

From the moment she alighted from the bus, we began to gather around her. As she walked, two blocks later, we were nearly fifty boys following her. I never knew what went through the lady's mind.

She wore a somewhat tattered dress with purple hues and shoes of the same color, with heels so high she could barely walk on the cobblestones of the square. She draped her shoulders with a coyote fur that seemed to have traveled far, and her hat boasted a feather that stood out as a symbol of grandeur.

Her attire suggested she was about to attend an important event, as if she were there to announce something momentous. Yet, she walked away toward the north of the square, crossing a street that formed a closed block. She had the appearance of someone from the United States, where dressing in that manner was common in northern cities.

It seemed she had decided to adopt the same style she wore from where she came, perhaps to impress.

As she moved on, a group of boys followed her in silence, with admiration in their eyes. It was something they had never witnessed before and it left them speechless. However, at one point, the lady stopped and turned around, startled to see so many boys following her. She shouted: "You are following me! Go away!"

Lady Catrina

The anecdote of "Catrina" in our Chapel was a memory we cherished. Though she was beautiful, her attire was overly flashy and peculiar. We decided to leave her alone, as her colorful and extravagant look made us laugh.

This story of the lady happened just before I began studying music in the Musical Band. We continued playing joyfully, and one day we were told we were going to have our photograph taken. We dressed up carefully, and Don Gregorio Trujillo allowed us to take the photo near the Bakery. Each of us received a copy of that photo.

We continued playing enthusiastically, and the community of La Capilla was happy and lively. They counted on us to liven up their Sunday celebrations. The Band was thriving, and we had been playing together for about a year.

However, there was an unpleasant incident at some point. A conflict arose between Ezequiel, the conductor, and a young man with similar features. They started to fight, and Ezequiel pulled out a small knife during the altercation.

Music Band's Decline

In a regrettable turn of events, the Music Band experienced its decline. A dispute between Ezequiel, the conductor, and another young man almost ended in tragedy. Ezequiel, amid the scuffle, caused some injuries to the other boy in self-defense, fortunately not very serious.

Herminio Alcalá, our commander, intervened and decided to put Ezequiel in jail, not as punishment, but to protect him. The father of the other young man was completely outraged and even carried a gun, intending to harm Ezequiel. Herminio managed to calm the situation, but to avoid retaliation, Ezequiel agreed to a mediation agreement to keep the peace.

Both Ezequiel and the other involved family were known to be good people. Ezequiel had contributed positively and joyfully to the life of La Capilla. The other family was also respected in the community. However, sometimes disputes can dismantle the good, and we all deeply regretted the departure of Ezequiel and his family.

My grandpa Tacho, who was enjoying his role as the second conductor and was happy to teach us by his side, was affected by this unfortunate situation. He and I were learning together in the Music Band. That's how the Band disbanded, and the music that once united us faded away.

The disbandment of the Music Band marked a period of uncertainty and change in La Capilla. After Ezequiel's departure and without another conductor to match his passion and talent, music seemed destined to lose its splendor. I continued with my mischief, not understanding why Father Morales did not undertake the task of forming a new band.

The musical instruments, which were property of the temple, were stored once more in the Curato. No one knew what fate awaited them.

After the death of Father Morales, the other priests did not take the initiative to revive the music.

Perhaps the reason lay in the lack of instruments or uncertainty about their ownership. However, I think there was potential to bring joy back to La Capilla. The Delegation had the capacity to lead this initiative, and if money was lacking, the community of La Capilla could contribute to organizing it.

The merchants and bakers in the area also had musical talent, and although they did not sing badly, they often were not willing to share their skills. The Ranchera, a popular genre, resonated in their voices. With effort and organization, the Music Band could rise again and sustain itself.

The music, which had once united the community's youth in the Music Band, had dissipated, leaving room for other distractions.

CHAPTER 19

Rafael and the Slaughter of Don Martín

Rafael was the eldest among the children of my Uncle Eulogio and his wife, Emilia Torres, who in turn was the daughter of Don Martín Torres. Don Martín led a comfortable life thanks to his butcher shop, located southwest of the square, just a few houses from my home on Guerrero Street. When it was time to slaughter cattle or pigs, he would raise his red flag early, a sign of his work.

At that time, I maintained a close friendship with my cousin Tachín. At about eleven years old, we were at a crossroads after the dissolution of the Music Band. We needed to find new forms of entertainment when we were not in school. Tachín, who was already actively helping in the butcher shop and in Don Martín's slaughter, invited me to join him and Rafael in these activities.

Don Martín, a skilled slaughterer, used to slaughter both cattle and pigs, introducing us to the art of skinning, removing their hide, and butchering them. It was an enriching experience, as I learned to strip the animals of their leather and participated in this task enthusiastically. I also enjoyed tasting the delicious beef and pork cracklings, whose preparation was a real tradition in the family.

The kitchen of Don Martín was a cozy corner, where these delicacies were prepared with great skill. He used a wooden lathe and a press to compress the meat, carefully eliminating the excess fat. The resulting cracklings were firm and free of excess lard, a true delight for the palate.

These cracklings turned into a delicacy when cooked in a broth with tomato sauce, creating an unmatched flavor. Accompanied by freshly made tortillas, skillfully prepared by hand, these culinary delights completely satisfied us. It was a true culinary pleasure that helped us overcome hunger.

Don Martín used to send Rafael and Tachín to nearby farms to get fresh livestock. On some occasions, I joined Tachín on these expeditions, and we set off on donkey back through our town's alleys. Donkeys were an invaluable resource for transporting the livestock back home, and these adventures became memorable.

Don Martín, owner of donkeys and a mare he cherished, had several animals that accompanied us on our journeys. Along Jones's alleys, we enjoyed our feats, using our slingshots to knock down lizards resting on the fence stones. While traveling the road, abundant nopales surrounded us, and we delighted in the prickly pears we found, satisfying our cravings.

Upon reaching the farms where we went to acquire the pigs, we began the herding process with patience. Sometimes, Don Martín took care of slaughtering the pigs at the ranches, splitting them in half in the abdominal area before loading them on the donkeys. This task—albeit time-consuming and demanding—was entertaining because the pigs were well-fed and did not move quickly.

Thus life went on in the butcher shop alongside Tachín, Rafael, and me. Rafael, at about thirteen, had already reached an age where he experienced certain freedoms, like smoking. He used to buy "Carmencitas" brand cigarettes. Don Martín trusted him and did not skimp on resources to buy them. I remember one particular day when we were at the lagoon, not far from the slaughter. Tachín and I, accompanied by Rafael, dedicated ourselves to hunting pichicuates.

Tachín, Rafael, and the Butchery

Near the Tajo, next to a water puddle, there were some large rocks emerging from the water level. In that environment, lived a harmless type of snake. We had fun throwing projectiles at it with our slingshots. It was during one of these encounters that we noticed Rafael smoking. I said to Tachín, "Look, the mischievous Cepillo is smoking." We called Rafael "Cepillo" because his hair was often disheveled, resembling the bristles of a brush.

As for Tachín, we nicknamed him "Beiby" because he was born in the United States and had acquired that name. Most of us had peculiar nicknames. When we met Rafael, he suggested we try smoking. Tachín and I initially rejected the idea, but my curiosity led me to give the cigarette a chance. Over time, I developed the habit of smoking and even stole money to buy the famous "Carmencitas" cigarettes occasionally.

The vice persisted for about twenty-five years until I began to experience its harmful effects. That's when I realized I had to quit this habit and change my lifestyle.

When I decided to quit smoking, I succeeded with determination and perhaps a bit of luck. I had fallen into such a deep habit that I smoked up to three packs of cigarettes a day. There was no break, even during sleep, as I mechanically lit one after another. However, I gathered the necessary willpower and imposed the challenge of leaving it behind.

I remember it has been twenty five years since then, and I am grateful for not having followed the tragic fate of a friend who could not free himself from the cigarette vice. Whenever I saw him, I warned him about the health risks, but he responded with disdain. Sadly, he died of lung cancer, joining the sad statistics of thousands who succumb to this disease every year.

This concludes the story of Tachín and Rafael, and Rafael's nickname "el Cepillo," who unwittingly introduced me to the world of tobacco. Despite everything, Rafael had the necessary willpower to quit smoking.

If he hadn't, he would have gone to meet Saint Peter earlier. Such is life here in heaven, where we all must adapt to the same rules. Now, I continue with another episode I had forgotten to mention: the times my mother took me very close to Tepatitlán.

Tepatitlán

During that time in Tepatitlán, my uncle Silviano, my father's elder brother, had moved there since he became a partner in "Camiones de los Altos." He played a crucial role in the company, serving as a coordinator at its main offices. One of the advantages of having relatives involved in the transport business was that we did not have to pay bus fares. All the partners' families could travel for free on all the routes.

When we visited Tepatitlán, we arrived at my uncle Silviano's house. He had a son, also named Silviano, but we affectionately called him "el Chato." He too had become a partner in "Camiones de los Altos" and had three wonderful sisters: Sara, Socorro, and Chavela. These sisters were like our mothers, especially aunt Chavela. We felt that we were not only cousins but rather siblings. When we visited their house, it was always a joyous occasion. They invited us to stay longer, but since the church was nearby, we eventually returned home. My cousins attended church occasionally, but not as frequently as we did.

Shooting at the Presidency

My Uncle Silviano's house was situated just half a block south of the Presidential Palace in Tepatitlán. He was the eldest in the family, about twenty years older than my father. He was the family pioneer, and my father was born later, followed by my Aunt Chuy. We were fourteen in total, and what a beautiful bounty it was. My grandmother, María, used to say that God's will is indeed kind.

My uncle had a generous wife named Chavela, a truly kind-hearted person. I remember one particular meal that my brother Miguel and I shared, enjoying our food while Aunt Chavela engaged in her usual lively conversation. Suddenly, we heard shots fired. Aunt Chavela calmly reassured us, mentioning that gunfire was not unusual in the area due to the frequent gun tests at the Presidential Palace.

I was accustomed to hearing gunfire in Tepatitlán, especially on Sundays when the ranchers came to mass. Whenever the booming sounds echoed, we darted away like arrows. This time, I was sitting in the dining room, feeling the vibrations in my chair. I stood up and heard my mother calling me. In any case, it was just another day in Tepatitlán, where gunfire was part of life, and we continued as usual.

While walking by the Presidential Palace, I noticed a commotion near the corner. A crowd had gathered, and curiosity got the better of me. Unable to bear staying in the dark, I hurried toward the corner.

The crowd was restless, and I heard someone say, "There goes Baby Bottie." The street sloped sharply from that point, leading towards the river, and what I vividly remember is a person riding a sorrel horse at full speed. The rider, a small figure, was struggling to control the galloping horse, probably with all their might.

It became clear that there had been a shooting, and a young man lay wounded in the cart. As a curious onlooker, I couldn't resist listening to the conversations. I saw that the young man had been shot in the chest, and a young woman, dressed as a bride, was holding him, crying. She was not just his bride; she was his wife. They had just exited the Presidential Palace after getting married.

Apparently, the shooter had warned them not to get married, but they had ignored the threat. Tragically, the young bride became a widow before they could even start their honeymoon. Such disputes were not uncommon and sometimes escalated to physical violence. In each altercation, there were always those who suffered the consequences.

On numerous occasions, we made trips to Tepatitlán, and it often felt like escaping to another world. Tepatitlán had turned into a picturesque city, the capital of the municipality. It seemed to have everything one might need, resembling bustling Guadalajara. In fact, it ranked third in population in Jalisco, just after Guadalajara and Ciudad Guzmán.

The central square of Tepatitlán was a sight to behold. Its unique kiosk stood proudly, surrounded by a blend of classical Castilian architecture. To the north of the central square, the grand parish church towered, a magnificent and precious testimony to classical Spanish design.

The city boasted a large market, brimming with a wide variety of products. It was a bustling hub of commerce. The market offered a rich array of items, from fresh fruits and vegetables of all kinds to exotic spices and ingredients.

As we wandered through the market, our senses were overwhelmed by the aromas of delicious Mexican cuisine. The stalls were adorned with large clay pots filled with tasty traditional dishes. There were stalls specializing in goat birria, slow-cooked until tender and served with a hot, savory sauce. Eating this dish was an experience, a laborious but delightful endeavor that left you craving more.

In the midst of the market's maze, you could also find lamb birria, each bite an explosion of flavor. These culinary delights were a testament to Mexico's rich and diverse cuisine, where each dish had a story to tell.

Tepatitlán, a city of culinary wonders! It never ceased to amaze me with its delicious offerings. One could not help but be drawn to the enticing aroma of the region's signature dish, birria. Whether goat or lamb, there was something enchanting about how these birrias were prepared here.

While strolling through the streets, especially near the market, we would encounter friendly vendors, often elderly ladies, selling grilled nopales. These nopales were cut into small pieces, perfectly grilled to capture the essence of the tender cactus leaves. They were arranged in large baskets, next to a pot full of tortillas, carefully covered with towels to keep them warm. It was a spectacle to behold, and the nopales, paired with sautéed onion, tomato, and fresh cilantro, left our palates wanting more.

And then there were the butcheries, almost all of them, selling the famous Tepatitlán carnitas. These pork carnitas were a divine creation, skillfully prepared to perfection, becoming crispy and golden. The renown of Tepatitlán's carnitas was well-deserved, and they were a local treasure.

But the culinary delights did not stop there. You would also encounter pressed pork rinds, prepared with such skill that they practically melted in your mouth. A tempting sauce, cooked with just the right spices, adorned these crispy wonders, making them irresistible.

In the bustling Tepatitlán market, when busy housewives found themselves without the time or desire to cook, this was their sanctuary. The market was a place where Tepatitlán's culinary riches were at one's fingertips, a testament to the gastronomic talent of this charming city.

Tepatitlán: Celebration and Music

Tepatitlán, a city that knows how to celebrate! Among its many treasures, it boasts a great municipal band that dazzles the crowd every Sunday during ceremonies and on special occasions. Whether at bullfights or during the annual festivities like the "Lord of Mercy" celebration, which peaks on April 30 and starts nine days earlier, this city knows how to revel in style.

The festivities commence with a lively pilgrimage lasting two days, April 28 and 29. The streets swell with people, making it nearly impossible to walk. Pilgrims first visit the charming church of San Antonio, located north of Tepatitlán. They then return to the parish and continue their journey to the Sanctuary of Guadalupe, west of the church, eventually making their way back to their own Sanctuary, south of the parish. These celebrations in Tepatitlán are a marvel to behold, drawing even larger crowds than those I described in La Capilla.

Amidst the celebrations, one can witness the city's vibrant activities, including parades of beautifully decorated floats. Charros and various groups participate as well, parading proudly in their distinctive attire. The "Colegio Morelos," with its magnificent military band, plays a significant role in the city and is affiliated with the International Organization of Marist Religious.

Tepatitlán truly knows how to come alive, where music and celebration are intertwined with its very essence, making it an extraordinary place.

Tepatitlán: Lord of Mercy

When I was returning from La Capilla to Tepa and was about to arrive, I could see Tepa ahead. A tall hill rose majestically, and I couldn't help but sigh at its beauty. It's like a dream come true, especially at night. In those moments, Tepa looked like a vast Christmas tree, aglow with many lights.

When the temple lights came on, the bodies of the churches, their towers, and domes, which were imposing, looked gorgeous. But the Sanctuary of the Lord of Mercy stood out even more. This Christ has a history dating back to 1847, give or take a year or two, but to this day, the Sanctuary houses hundreds of granted miracles depicted on plaques from the second half of the 19th century, showing gratitude for the requested and granted miracles.

The story of this wonderful Christ begins on a ranch close to Cerro Gordo, to the west, near the Rancho del Aguacate. I lived around there at the time.

In the 1840s, a man named Pedro Medina lived in this place. He resided next to the imposing Cerro Gordo, immersed in nature. One day, while cutting oak and redwood for his family, something caught his attention among the trees: a thick branch forming a Cross. Without hesitation, he cut it down carefully, preserving it intact.

Pedro Medina, head of a deeply religious family, full of faith and love for God, decided to bring the Cross home. He loaded the robust piece onto an ox-drawn cart, and although he didn't know how to carve a Christ, he kept it in his home. Time passed, and the Cross remained untouched.

One day, two weary travelers crossed paths with Pedro Medina. Being a good man, he invited them to rest and eat at his house. The travelers, learning about the Cross Pedro had, offered to create a Crucifix with Christ on it, claiming they had the expertise and wished to express their gratitude in some way.

Though it would take a bit more time, don Pedro immediately agreed when the young artisans offered to carve a Christ sculpture for his chapel, as that was his wish. Plus, he promised to pay them well for their work. Thus, with the skill of experts, they began the task, increasing don Pedro's joy with every chisel stroke.

As he later recounted, the artisans worked tirelessly for about ten days, creating a beautiful and inspired masterpiece unlike any ever seen before. When don Pedro had to leave to attend to some matters at his estate, he said upon departure, "I'll return tonight. Stay at home, and if you need anything, my family will attend to you."

Upon his return at dusk, he saw the completed Christ. The sculpture was so beautiful and lifelike that don Pedro was nearly brought to tears in admiration. He removed his hat in respect and then inquired about the young men. He was told, "We don't know. They left a while ago and haven't returned." Don Pedro thought to wait for them to give them a good reward for their excellent work. Everyone at home was amazed and said, "We have never seen something so sublime."

When don Pedro went to tell the young artisans how wonderful the Christ turned out, he was in for a surprise. They had vanished without a goodbye or collecting their payment. He searched everywhere, but there was no trace of them. Who were these mysterious young men? To this day, it remains a mystery. Popular belief holds that they were actually angels who descended to Earth to expertly carve that miraculous image of Christ. Then, asking for nothing in return, they vanished into thin air. What clearer proof of their heavenly origin could there be?

The image stayed at don Pedro's home for quite some time before he decided to take it to Tepatitlán to be baptized, along with two or three other beautifully carved Christs. That was when it was named "The Lord of Mercy," and don Pedro Medina built a grand sanctuary for it, where to this day, believers flock to ask for the urgent miracles they need. With the intercession of this divine image carved by angels, many have seen their prayers answered.

Tepatitlán Dear

Tepatitlán, beloved and beautiful town that even inspired the famous song every mariachi in Mexico knows, "Let's go to Tepa." Now I return to my Chapel, my childhood town with its beautiful memories and sometimes sadness and scares. Like when I was almost drowning in La

Grifa's pond or when the blond girls drowned. Or that time when a malignant fever nearly took me.

I was about eight or nine years old. I was playing marbles near the house, on the bare ground. It must have been in April or May when I caught such a high fever that I didn't die only because God didn't want it. When the doctor came, he told my mom he didn't know what strange illness had struck me, but to prepare because I was going to die. My mom accepted it with Christian resignation.

Three days passed, feeling like three centuries, burning with fever, delirious with terrifying visions. Everything was spinning, and my body felt as heavy as lead. My mom prayed the rosary day and night. On the fourth day, the fever subsided a bit. By the fifth, I could sit up. It was a great miracle! When the doctor returned, he couldn't believe it. He said something very powerful had saved me.

Malignant Fever

I consoled myself thinking, "don't worry, son, if you die, you'll go straight to heaven." I didn't feel like I was going to die; I just felt sick, nothing more.

However, the word quickly spread, first, that I was very ill; then, that I was dying; and finally, that "Cica's boy had died of a malignant fever." My goodness! With the commotion that ensued, it seemed like the world was ending.

In the end, the doctor was wrong: either he was a novice, or God performed the miracle of healing me, for I had to write this book. "Surely, boy, get up, you have nothing, stop playing dead, you have a lot of work and responsibilities in your future," he told me.

And here I still am, thanks to God. Better ask for permission to write so many other things. With illnesses, there is no prognosis blinder than

God's will. This time I got up after two days as if nothing had happened. My mom sent me to Doña Aurelia's house, from Don Tomás Torres, the one who told me about the baby Jesus at Christmas.

I knocked on the door, and when she saw me, her eyes nearly popped out. She couldn't even speak until I started to tell her, "My mom sent me to you." And she says, "Liborio, you didn't die! Didn't you die?" I thought I was really dying.

Doña Aurelia was a very kind and charitable lady, the opposite of her husband Don Tomás Torres. Anyway, what she told me is that, if I hadn't died, not to even consider it. So, I continued with my misadventures and exploring La Capilla.

Among my older friends were Cocorilla, Cepillo, Sanduriga, Alfonso Martín del Campo. He was my second cousin, but a bit simple. He said such funny things that he made all his friends laugh. All those I mention were about thirteen or fourteen years old.

Alfonso helped Chepillo Castellanos with the task of making candles. Cocorilla had a machine to make noodles in a room at the entrance of her house. One day Cisto and I entered that room, and Alfonso and Cocorilla had met I don't know where.

That so-called Pedorrón was a relative and friend of ours, from the same gang with Sanduriga, Cocorilla, Alfonso Trinegallinas, and Rafael el Cepillo. They were like two or three years older than Cisto and me.

It turns out that one Sunday night, after having fun at the fair and having gone to the rosary, this boy went home. As he was very hungry, he went straight to the kitchen without telling anyone. There he found a chicken that had been out all day (because there were no refrigerators at that time). And since chicken meat spoils quickly when left out too long, well, he grabbed it and ate it.

Just like that! He enters the kitchen and sees a chicken that had been cooked since the morning. As he was very hungry, he didn't think of notifying his mom so as not to risk her saying no. And he started eating it in a hurry because he was starving.

After he finished it all, satiated and burping from being so full, it turns out they then went to look for the chicken and there was no chicken. He had hidden it in his belly! To not name names and then get kicked if he sees me. The problem was that he ate it too quickly, without chewing it properly. And then, from sheer exhaustion, he fell deeply asleep, the thing is that at night he began to digest, releasing farts every so often. His mom asks him, "What's wrong with you?" and there she discovers where the chicken was.

He had eaten it without chewing. Then they gave him a homemade medicine for colic and to sleep, thinking he would be better the next day. But no, he spent the whole night straining and farting nonstop. Early in the morning, they send for the doctor, Don Isidro Ruiz, a very good person and excellent doctor. He examines him, asks questions, and sees he's poisoned. Then he prescribes a medicine.

CHAPTER 20

Story of Pedorrón

At that moment when they were administering the medicine, Cocorilla and Cacheras entered the house, having planned to meet in the morning to go somewhere. However, Babilonio was still in bed, suffering from the havoc the chicken was causing in his stomach. Imagine the rottenness brewing inside him.

Luckily, the medicine prescribed by Don Isidro, who was still present, arrived. He gave instructions on how to take it, and it began to work, purging his insides. Amid the noise of the medicine's effects, he experienced a cramp and released a fart that was not just any fart, but an enormous one.

Everyone was in the room, which resembled a windowless storage space where Babilonio slept, leaving no escape. When the stinking blast escaped, chaos ensued. The stench was as if a stink bomb had been detonated.

Don Isidro, dizzied, stumbled out, while Cacheras, next to Babilonio, screamed: "The Pedorrón!" and all fled in terror shouting "Every man for himself!"

Even a small Chihuahua bolted out barking, and a cat, previously resting peacefully, jumped up, its fur bristling, howling in distress. Cacheras said that even the mice fled the room due to the overwhelming stench, leaving with the cat and dog, paying no heed to the filth.

Crickets, scorpions, and cockroaches evacuated in single file. Not a single creature remained. Even Babilonio, left alone amidst the stink, began to cry out, "Don't do this to me! Don't be ungrateful!" unable to endure it himself. He rushed to the bathroom as the purgative Don Isidro had given him started to take effect. That was his salvation. And from then on, he was nicknamed Pedorrón.

La Tinaja

Now I will tell you about a delightful ranch I loved in my childhood, La Tinaja de los Navarro, founded when the Castillo colonizers arrived in 1712 or 1713. I visited many times as a boy.

La Tinaja, a magnificent ranch established in the 18th century when Spanish settlers named Castellanos arrived with their families, was where the Navarro family set up this enchanting place they named La Tinaja.

When lands were distributed under a viceregal order, they were given a set time to fence their allotted land to confirm ownership. The area's abundance of stones meant fencing wasn't an issue. However, if someone failed to fence in time, another community member could do so and legally claim the land.

I am well acquainted with the region and its vast pastures, perfectly demarcated by stone walls, flat and green like soccer fields. During the rainy season, these meadows become lush gardens full of blooming flowers, scenting the air.

La Tinaja and its surroundings are just as described. On my first visit at about nine or ten years old, I was struck by the beautiful green and yellow landscapes. Houses with red tile roofs and flower-filled courtyards, and birds chirping everywhere truly make it a paradise.

My mother took me along because she was invited by a relative of hers, one of her best friends, named María de Nina. María's father was Aureliano Navarro, related to Chepillo, Cisto's father. They called her La

Canaleta. María had relatives in La Tinaja we were visiting. She was still unmarried. Other friendly families joined us too.

We walked there happily. La Tinaja is about a league east of La Capilla, roughly five kilometers away. My mother enjoyed these excursions with relatives, especially during the season of tender, freshly crested corn, with all flowers blooming, scenting the fields.

What I remember most upon arrival was the beauty of everything. I don't recall exactly who we were with, but we passed through peach orchards brimming with fruit. We ate our fill, reaching out our hands. Then, we encountered an ox-drawn cart with children and their father - a dreamlike scene.

Walking, we were suddenly greeted by the children on the cart shouting: "Aunt María!" They rushed down to greet us. Their father, María's close relative, stopped the oxen and greeted us warmly. He invited us onto the cart, suggesting we must be tired - a welcome respite since the women were laden with bags. About ten of us climbed aboard, including María's children and friends like Cuca, another single lady.

We reached the aforementioned house, large with several barns, carts, stables with horses, and cattle-filled corrals. I, being nosy, counted the cows by a pond in front of the house, shaded by some ash trees. On the other side stood a massive white sapote tree, providing magnificent shade.

The women gathered there the next day to chat. The tree had beautiful foliage and thick trunks ideal for leaning against while knitting or engaging in other activities. Being unfamiliar, everything seemed extraordinary to me. At that time, many ash trees dotted the area, enhancing the beautiful scenery. I remember cattle grazing nearby, hearing calves bellowing and birds singing. Carts passed along a path, and the joyful commotion of people in nearby ranches and riders herding cattle filled the air.

"How beautiful," one would sigh, admiring those green pastures full of flowers, with grazing cattle and bustling people around. The women were making cheese in the adobe buildings - an essential task.

Later, more townspeople gathered, including very pretty young ladies who started singing, forming choirs with lovely songs. Our hearts swelled with emotion. The atmosphere was quite different from that in La Capilla. I had never felt so happy. Though we only stayed two days, I will never forget that particular day, especially because two extraordinary things happened...

I fell from a zapote tree

I was thoroughly enjoying the landscape and, to get a better view, I climbed the large white zapote tree I mentioned before—this majestic tree, a wonder only God can create, had captured my attention. I couldn't resist the urge to climb it; somehow, I felt compelled. I had been on a thick branch for a while when I decided to climb higher. Zapote trees have very smooth bark. As a result, I slipped and fell.

The problem was that below there was a jutting-out stone, buried yet protruding. I landed right on it, seated, hitting the base of my spine, right where the lumbar vertebrae end. The pain was horrific! I saw stars and couldn't even speak.

My mother, having seen me fall, rushed over in fright. I was pale from the pain, and she kept asking me, "Speak, son! What's wrong?" Gradually, the intense agony subsided. But I swore never to climb a zapote tree again!

The scare wore off, and we continued to enjoy the beautiful setting until the evening when we returned in the cart. Oh, what times those were in lovely La Tinaja!

On our way back to La Capilla, we passed through orchards full of blooming peach trees, their fragrance wafting through the air. The women, especially María de Nina with her beautiful voice, sang melodiously. As we caught sight of the church towers in the distance, the vast, orange sun began to set behind the peach trees.

We sighed, having only been away from our beloved Capilla for a short while, yet already missing it. Upon arrival, we were provided with cots to sleep on, lit by oil lamps. When called to dinner, we were greeted with a pot of boiled corn, fresh cheese in slices, and newly made beans that melted in the mouth, all topped with melted cheese.

There were a couple of molcajetes with borracha salsa, another green with crushed tomato, and hot tortillas that a lady was making right then on a large clay comal over the wood stove. And there, they were roasting wide chili peppers to complete the feast.

What a delicious dinner we had! Then, to sleep peacefully while listening to the crickets' chirping. The next day awaited me with another surprise. We dined so heartily that we could eat no more. The local families, also relatives, urged us, "Eat up, you've eaten nothing!" forcing us to have seconds. That night we could barely sleep, so full were we.

After dinner, the conversations lingered, which was beneficial for alleviating the heaviness in our stomachs. It was then when we remembered a beautiful tradition: praying the rosary. This custom was practiced on all the ranches in the region of Los Altos de Jalisco. As they began to pray, my brother Miguel and I, with the gentle murmur of prayers in the background, drifted off to sleep. My mother tenderly stroked our hair to wake us up.

When they finished, it was late, so we went to our bedrooms. In mine, there were skylights through which the moonlight entered, reflecting off the walls. Between the tiredness and full stomach, sleep quickly overcame us.

In La Tinaja, the heart of the kitchen was a special place. There, a huge table hosted the preparation of delicacies. I remember a young man in a corner grinding nixtamal in a manual machine, skillfully turning the handle to produce the dough needed for tortillas. The same lady who had welcomed us the night before was in charge of shaping and cooking the tortillas on the griddle, using the same stove she fed with wood and splinters, which were the residue of tree felling, becoming fuel.

The breakfast we enjoyed was magnificent, as was the dinner the night before. We savored fried eggs and chilaquiles that roared with pleasure, so delicious they were. But what truly amazed me was a grilled meat, finely chopped and served with freshly made tortillas, accompanied by a tomatillo and roasted tree chili sauce. Each bite was a true delight for the palate.

The night in La Tinaja was prolonged with songs and lively conversations. People shared stories of La Capilla and the various events happening in the region. The evening was enjoyable, and we all seemed to have forgotten about dinner. It was then when a little girl, barely visible in the dim light, arrived with unexpected news: they invited us to her house.

Following the girl, we reached her home to an extraordinary surprise: they had slaughtered a calf. Without a word, they prepared an exceptional barbecue, the kind that falls apart easily. The meat was cooked so skillfully it could be separated with just two fingers. While we waited, they offered us tortillas wrapped in corn leaves to keep them warm. The patience was worth it, as the meat was seasoned with local herbs and spices, and the flavor was exquisite.

The satisfaction was such that it seemed we had never been hungry. Yet, we couldn't rest our stomachs, and we continued the evening in the courtyard, rejoicing over the meal and the stories shared on this unforgettable night in La Tinaja.

The next day brought me another surprise. Very early, some uncles of mine from Teocaltiche came to visit the family. They were the husbands of two of my father's sisters, whom we hardly saw. My mother was very happy, but for me, it meant that we had to return soon to La Capilla. And I did not want to leave.

La Tinaja: A Memorable Farewell

The evening at La Tinaja reached its climax when we were offered an unusual dessert: peaches. We were almost bursting from how full we were, but, as always, the hospitality of our hosts encouraged us to continue savoring these delights. We went to bed late that night, knowing that an early departure awaited us the next day.

We woke at dawn, with the new day's light flooding our surroundings. We rose carefully, trying not to disturb the sleep of those who were still resting. As we prepared to leave, I remembered María's uncle, though his name escaped me at that moment. What I would never forget is the image of that family, as beautiful as they were kind.

Among the farm workers, there was a young man named Juan de la Torre, whom I remembered clearly. During our stay at Zapote Blanco, an incident occurred that made him an unforgettable figure. A majestic golden eagle tried to take a newborn calf, but Juan ran to the big house and managed to shoot it down with a shotgun. The winged creature lay dead, its wingspan larger than my own height.

La Tinaja: The Farewell and the Special Peaches

The departure from La Tinaja was approaching, but before leaving that place full of memories, I had the opportunity to learn more about the eagle I mentioned earlier. Its claws were so huge that they exceeded the size of an adult's hands. I learned they had been cut off and preserved as a trophy. At that time, I was about eight or nine years old, full of curiosity, and asked Juan de la Torre, the young man who had shot the eagle, about the claws. He told me he had kept them and had even made a keychain with them, which still exists somewhere.

But, as time goes by, we realized it was time to say goodbye. Around ten in the morning, we left in an ox-drawn cart painted red that María's uncle had prepared for us. The bags of peaches we had collected in the basket were placed next to us.

The farewells were emotional, and almost all the inhabitants of the ranch came to say goodbye. Some even encouraged us to stay a few more days. As we left, the special taste of La Tinaja's peaches, whose fruits, nourished by that red and brown earth, had a unique and strong flavor, quite different from those I had tasted elsewhere.

During the journey, we enjoyed the peaches we carried with us, courtesy of María de Nina's uncle. His generosity provided us a comforting path, almost to the doors of La Capilla, where Saltillo lies, near Charco Hondo.

We carried the sacks full of peaches and prickly pears that had also been generously gifted to us. This trip was a chapter full of happy moments that I will never forget, one of the most pleasant experiences of my life.

Felipe, the Agrarian

Felipe the agrarian was a profoundly popular figure in La Capilla, uncle to Luis Muñoz, the owner of the greyhound "El Tiro," which, sadly, was poisoned at one point.

Felipe was also deeply passionate about hare hunting and always had at his disposal a mule renowned for its excellent trot. This mule only found its match in Don Juan Torres' horse, famed for its peerless trot. Felipe, a straightforward man, neither wealthy nor impoverished, left an indelible impression in La Tinaja with his enthusiasm for hunting and his expertise in trotting.

Felipe, the agrarian, was a man capable of sustaining himself, possessing a modest ranch. His dwelling, almost at the heart of La Capilla, was a routine view for me as I traveled from his ranch. On those streets, I would observe him on his mule, advancing with a resolute step and a pure trot that outpaced any man running. One day, we decided to hunt hares on a ranch to the west of La Capilla.

Typically, Felipe arrived atop his mule while the rest of us crammed into a pickup truck. The ranch, located six kilometers west, was reached by dirt roads, yet Felipe was already there waiting for us upon arrival. I can distinctly recall his adeptness with spurs on his mule, which proved to be exceptionally suited for traversing the terrain.

We spent the entire day absorbed in the hunting excitement, reveling in thrilling pursuits and capturing numerous hares. When we eventually grew tired and prepared to leave, Felipe and the truck owner concocted a bet to see who would get back first, capping off a day brimming with adventure at the ranch.

Felipe the Agrarian and Don Juan Gazapa

In the square, Felipe appeared with his mule, and I remember that the truck belonged to a man named Andrés, the father of a young man our age named "Jilo." When we were ready to leave, Felipe mounted his mule and started trotting at a speed that seemed like that of a motorcycle. He delved into a rugged path he knew very well. The truck couldn't keep up with his pace, and all of us, standing in the back, clung on tightly as the dirt road was full of stones, potholes, and sharp turns.

Despite the obstacles, Felipe progressed with determination, navigating the difficult terrain. Upon reaching the cattle grids, he had to stop to give his weary mule a break. Cooling off was crucial to prevent overheating, as an exhausted animal can collapse if not properly cooled down after exertion.

Finally, when we arrived at La Capilla square, there was Don Felipe, sitting on a bench, waiting for us. His mule, spent, did not need to be walked around, having exerted itself enough to get there. Felipe, a nephew of a brave and respected man, once again demonstrated his skill and prowess on that memorable day.

In the peaceful La Capilla, lived a man named Juan Gazapa, likely with Muñoz as his last name, but everyone knew him as Gazapa. My aunt Chole shared an anecdote about him that revealed his amiable personality but also his intolerance for disdain.

Don Juan Gazapa had a greyhound, like many in La Capilla, and his dog often roamed the square. One day, the dog approached a table where a man was dining and tried to snatch some cheese. In response, the man shot the poor dog in the head, thinking it was a stray. Little did he know, the dog belonged to Don Juan Gazapa.

When someone rushed to inform Don Juan Gazapa of the incident, he quickly arrived at the scene with a blanket over his shoulder and a pistol at his waist, bumping into it as he ran. There, he found the man who had shot the dog sitting arrogantly. The dog lay dead on the ground. This event took place in the early 1720s in La Capilla, showcasing that Don Juan Gazapa would not tolerate disrespect toward his belongings.

He asked the man who had killed his dog if he was the perpetrator, to which the man replied defiantly. Amidst their conversation, the man tried to draw his gun, but Don Juan Gazapa was quick and skilled. In the blink of an eye, he shot the man in the head, resulting in his instant death.

The unknown man, whose origin remained a mystery, fell to the ground beside the dog, both bearing fatal head wounds. This tragedy unfolded from a fatal misunderstanding, where the man who had killed the dog threatened Don Juan Gazapa, a stranger to him. In his homeland, this man might have been feared, but in La Capilla, he had made a dire mistake.

This true story exemplifies how threats can lead to tragic consequences when one does not fully understand the circumstances.

CHAPTER 21

The Cacalote of the Alcalás: A Ranch with History

Let me tell you about the Cacalote, an ancient ranch established in the 18th century by the same Castilian colonizers who arrived in the Altense region. It was here that the Alcalás settled, brave and resolute men known for their friendliness but also for their fierce enmity when offended. Throughout my life, I've had the chance to witness their deeds and relationships in this place.

Among the Alcalás, I had a friend named Jesús Alcalá, known as "Chuy." He was involved in numerous perilous events while serving as commander in my town. On several occasions, he miraculously escaped dangerous situations. Jesús Alcalá was the nephew of Don Herminio Alcalá, whom I've previously mentioned in my story. Don Herminio was the commander of La Capilla during my childhood and held the position for a long time. However, before taking on the role of commander, Jesús Alcalá was involved in a tragic incident.

The first confrontation Jesús Alcalá took part in was revenge for the death of Don Herminio's uncle, who lived in the Cacalote. This uncle had a serious conflict with another person, who ultimately killed him. In response, Herminio Alcalá, as the nephew, sought out his uncle's murderer and killed him as well. This story reflects the firmness of character and determination that characterized the Alcalás, who did not hesitate to take drastic measures to seek justice for their loved ones. The Cacalote stands witness to these stories passed down through generations, leaving an indelible mark on the region's history.

After avenging his uncle's death, Jesús Alcalá was appointed commander of La Capilla. Like Don Herminio, he also served in this role for an extended term, and La Capilla enjoyed a period of relative peace.

However, as commander, Jesús Alcalá occasionally had to take drastic actions against those who committed severe offenses against the community. Despite his leadership, some defiant individuals faced consequences on the "other side," as it was commonly referred to in the region. Jesús Alcalá was known for his firmness and determination in maintaining the town's safety.

During his tenure as commander, La Capilla experienced peace that lasted for many years. However, Jesús Alcalá also earned the enmity of those he exiled for their harmful deeds. Some of them tried to return to the town clandestinely, but Don Herminio, a cunning man loved by all, was always vigilant. When he learned of someone with ill intentions, he acted swiftly to neutralize any threat.

Despite his advanced age, Don Herminio never stopped protecting his community. Although some wanted him to continue as commander, he eventually chose to retire voluntarily. His legacy of wisdom and leadership endures in the memory of La Capilla.

Following his departure, another commander took his place, but his term was short-lived. Later, another commander from San Miguel el Alto arrived, whose name I don't recall, and he had a subordinate whose name also escapes me at the moment. The story of La Capilla and the Alcalás continues, full of intrigues and leadership changes, but always marked by the determination to protect and preserve the community.

A new commander succeeded Jesús Alcalá, drastically changing the town's dynamics. This new leader proved ruthless with the populace, occasionally treating the villagers unfairly. He seemed determined to prove he could be tougher than his predecessor, Don Herminio Alcalá.

However, his harsh and unjust approach proved ineffective and, in my view, revealed his lack of wisdom.

I recall witnessing some of his injustices, even though I was far from Don Herminio's influence. Later, he was appointed commander of La Capilla, worsening the situation. He seemed intent on ruling with an iron fist, leading to an increase in abuses against the people. Eventually, some residents decided to end his injustices.

One day, in the square, a group of people approached him with hostile intentions, clearly armed. Faced with an imminent threat, the commander sought refuge in Don Luis Gutiérrez's store. However, due to the store's three doors, he couldn't escape the surrounding crowd. Tragically, he was shot dead in an act of justice by those who had suffered under his command.

This sad episode left La Capilla without a commander for a while. The community was hesitant to appoint another flawed leader, and thus, the story of La Capilla continued, marked by changes in leadership and struggles to maintain peace and justice in the region.

After the tragic death of the previous commander, my friend Jesús Alcalá was named commander, and his term lasted several years. Later, another commander took over for a while, and eventually, Jesús Alcalá was reinstated.

During his last term as commander, Jesús and I became closer friends. I also met his brother Salvador, nicknamed Chava, with whom I established great trust. Jesús shared many anecdotes from his life and the history of Cacalote, including some incidents involving his uncles and neighbors.

One of the stories he told involved a serious conflict between the Alcalás and their neighbors at a nearby ranch. There was a dispute that escalated, resulting in the tragic death of one of the Alcalá elders. This occurred around the second decade of the 1720s, and it seems there was also a casualty among the neighbors in that conflict.

Rivalries and tensions in the region were common at that time, and these stories illustrate the complexity of relationships between families and communities in La Capilla.

Tensions and rivalries between the Alcalás and their neighbors are revealed. Following the tragic events in which members of both families died, the Alcalá neighbors were not satisfied. Often, when the Alcalás returned to their ranch at night, they saw neighbors hiding around the stone fences, apparently trying to intimidate the Alcalás to drive them out of the region.

The Alcalás, in turn, pretended not to notice and loudly commented that they saw "bunches" near the stone fences, leaving the neighbors puzzled. My friend Chuy shared this situation, mentioning that the neighbors were always lurking, looking for an opportunity to settle their differences violently. Although the neighbors were brave, Chuy noted there is no reason to act impulsively when the consequences are known.

In a related incident, Chuy and some of his cousins were practicing horseback riding on a flat field as part of their training in case they faced government army soldiers during the Cristera War. This war was still ongoing, and the young men were preparing for possible scenarios. Their willingness to face danger and their determination are evident in these stories.

The tensions and dangers faced by the Alcalás during that time illustrate the complexity of life in the region and the importance of staying calm in conflict situations.

An unexpected encounter in a prickly pear cactus field is narrated. The Alcalás, who were practicing horseback riding on a flat field as part of their preparation for the Cristera War, decided to stop in a prickly pear cactus field full of prickly pears to enjoy this desert fruit.

Interestingly, two of the mysterious "bunches" that had been stalking the Alcalás were in the field, cutting prickly pears. Suringly, they had hidden their pistols due to the noise of the approaching horses, thinking it was the government army. When the Alcalás entered the field, they were stunned to see these individuals. One of Chuy's cousins reacted swiftly, believing they might be attacked, but nobody knew that the stalkers had concealed their weapons.

In this tense moment, Chuy's cousin drew his pistol and started shooting at the individuals who had surprised them. One fell wounded, while the other, injured yet furious, tried to retaliate against the cousin shooting at them. This narrative illustrates the Alcalás' quick response in an unforeseen and perilous situation. Each shot from the cousin was accompanied by a curse, aiming to repel the aggressor and defend themselves.

This thrilling episode in the prickly pear field highlights the tension and risks the Alcalás faced during this turbulent period in history.

A Moment of Danger in La Capilla

Chuy, sitting at the bar in his uncle Herminio's store in the center of La Capilla, was aware of the potential conflicts and vendettas that could arise at any moment. On this particular day, while looking in the mirror behind him, he noticed the tip of a gun peeking through the door. His instinct led him to react swiftly, knowing he needed to move adeptly.

Chuy rose from the round seat he was in and dove to the floor. By the time he hit the ground, he had already drawn his own gun. The attacker, surprised by Chuy's quick reaction, fired in the direction where he had been seated but ceased firing upon not finding him there.

Chuy, on his way to the floor, fired two shots without aiming specifically, forcing the attacker to hide in the doorway. This incident highlights the dangerous reality faced by those in positions of authority at the time, where violence could erupt at any moment, and quick reaction was crucial for survival.

The Cacalote of the Alcalás: A Duel in La Capilla

An exciting confrontation that took place in La Capilla is narrated, showcasing Chuy's courage and survival instinct during a moment of great danger.

Waiting patiently in his position, Chuy carefully assessed the situation. He knew he needed to act swiftly and accurately. When the aggressor peeked out, Chuy did not hesitate to fire his gun. However, the attacker dodged the shots due to a step at the door.

The confrontation continued with an exchange of gunfire, but eventually, both ran out of bullets. The attacker tried to flee, running across the square, while Chuy pursued him, determined to catch him. Eventually, Chuy got close enough and aimed his gun, only to realize he had no bullets left. Nevertheless, the attacker, unaware of Chuy's empty gun, chose to surrender.

This thrilling narrative demonstrates Chuy's skill and bravery during a tense moment and also provides details about life in the Cacalote, like the presence of a large house and an orchard with fruit trees, adding context to the story.

Chuy's Farewell

This narrative depicts a touching episode that highlights the close relationship between Chuy and his sister during his final moments.

While I have not had the chance to visit Cacalote personally, I hope to do so one day to learn more about this place that holds special significance in the Alcalá family's history. During my visits to La Capilla, however, I spoke with Chuy's brother, Chava, a friend of mine and a cockfighting enthusiast.

Chava shared the poignant story of Chuy's illness, which affected his heart. One day, feeling unwell, Chuy came to Chava's house, and his concerned sister immediately sent for a doctor. Chuy, aware of his condition, joked about being buried to reassure his sister.

The story concludes with the doctor's arrival, but sadly, Chuy passed away, maintaining his sense of humor until the end. This anecdote underscores Chuy's courage and spirit, as well as the support and emotional connection within the Alcalá family.

Herminio's Tavern: Cockfight Duel

The narrative recounts a memorable episode at Herminio Alcalá's tavern, where card games and disputes often lasted for days and nights. On this occasion, however, the situation escalated dangerously as Herminio Alcalá confronted Máximo González in a cockfight duel.

Both men, renowned for their sharp-spurred roosters, drew their guns amidst the altercation. Thankfully, the presence of numerous friends participating in the game prevented a tragedy. The friends intervened just in time, managing to snatch the guns away before any triggers were pulled, thus defusing the potentially fatal scenario.

This episode illustrates how passion and rivalry at Herminio Alcalá's tavern could lead to perilous situations but also highlights the crucial role of friends' intervention that averted a tragedy at that moment.

The story unveils the passions and rivalries that typically arose in this iconic place. It begins with the narrator fetching whey buckets for his grandmother's pigs, only to be distracted by a commotion at Herminio Alcalá's tavern.

Despite the tensions, the narrative emphasizes that, the following day, Herminio and Máximo resumed playing cards together, showcasing how the tavern's rivalries were often fleeting. It also introduces a peculiar character nicknamed "Vinaco," who, despite his boldness, aimed to ingratiate himself with Herminio, aspiring to marry one of his daughters.

This tale reveals how Herminio Alcalá's tavern was a hotspot for clashing passions yet also a place where human relationships and camaraderie held significant value amidst rivalries and card games.

Among the tavern's characters stands out Don Tereso, a committed gambler and bachelor, known for his friendliness. Don Tereso was a cherished community member, and his generosity shined brightest when he shared his winnings with the youths gathered in the square.

Active in the tavern's card games, Don Tereso often left with bags full of coins or notes. Yet, what he enjoyed most was spreading joy among the village children. Exiting the tavern, he would approach the kids and scatter coins on the ground, creating moments of delight.

This generosity and his willingness to engage with the children made him a beloved figure. The children awaited him eagerly, their faces brightening with each of his appearances. Don Tereso took pleasure in their happiness, becoming a beacon of joy in the village.

However, the narrative takes a sorrowful turn when Don Tereso vanishes for a while. Upon his return, he is seen wandering barefoot, seemingly disoriented. It's revealed that a grave financial loss from gambling led to his mental decline.

Despite their sympathy, there was little the children could do. Don Tereso's tale serves as a caution about the perils of unchecked passions and the enduring impact of one's generosity, even through challenging times.

The Night Encounter at the Corner: "El Tinaco"

Herminio's story tells of an incident involving a character known as "El Tinaco," then serving as a local policeman.

The scene unfolds as "El Tinaco" exits Don Herminio's tavern, heading home. Walking along the sidewalk near Don Juanillo Franco's house, westward, he notices a menacing figure at the opposite corner.

The figure, adopting a threatening stance, draws a gun. Luckily, a van parked nearby on the sidewalk provides "El Tinaco" with cover, shielding him from the initial shots fired in his direction.

Chaos ensues, with bullets hitting the van's tires and rims, but "El Tinaco" remains unharmed behind his makeshift barrier. Bystanders' shouts urge him to move to the square's portal for safety, as shots could come at any moment.

Eventually, the assailant flees, running down the street and vanishing into the night. Despite the danger and tension, "El Tinaco" emerges unscathed from this nocturnal corner encounter, narrowly avoiding a potentially tragic outcome.

The Gonzales de la Cruz: A Duel on South Street

The story of the Gonzales de la Cruz recounts a confrontation that marked their legacy at La Cruz ranch. The Gonzales de la Cruz were two renowned brothers in the region, and their ranch bore the same name, La Cruz.

The plot unfolds on the street where two key characters in the narrative resided, my friend Cisto and my uncle Felipe González, near the parish, heading south. These distinguished brothers were known for their elegance and gentlemanly demeanor, always impeccably dressed, showcasing their riding boots, quality saddles, and elegant silver spurs.

Their wide-brimmed, leather-trimmed hats identified them as genuine cowboys.

However, one day near the parish, an unexpected situation arose. After dismounting their horses, an individual named Dávila started firing stray bullets at them down the southbound street. The Gonzales, aware of their reputation and armed with reliable pistols and holsters, did not hesitate to return fire.

The encounter escalated into a duel of bullets and bravery on the sunny southern street. The Gonzales de la Cruz, with their experience and weaponry, stood their ground firmly. This scene became an indelible memory of courage and skill, highlighted by the leather trimmings of their hats glistening with each gunshot flare.

Despite the tension and violence, the Gonzales de la Cruz proved their mettle, earning respect from those who witnessed the duel on South Street. Although one of the Gonzales was injured, their indomitable spirit remained unbroken as they continued to confront the threat resolutely. Their legacy endures as a testament to valor in La Cruz's history.

The scene symbolizes the tenacity and courage of the Gonzales de la Ruiz, who never surrendered to adversity. Their legacy continues as a testament to the unyielding will of a family that bravely defended its honor and land on that historic southern street.

The Sorceress of Tonalá: A Desperate Healing Attempt

This captivating story unveils a moving episode featuring a brave police officer. It transports us to a time where hope and despair intertwined in the quest for healing a loved one.

The officer, known for his courage and dedication, was in anguish. His beloved wife was gravely ill, and the doctor's efforts had not eased her suffering. Overcome with desperation, he sought an unusual solution: seeking aid in Tonalá.

Tonalá, a town near Guadalajara renowned for its indigenous "Sorcerers" or "Verberos" since time immemorial, was famed for its mystical and ancestral practices. The officer embarked on a journey to Tonalá, seeking a sorceress's aid in a desperate bid to heal his wife.

Upon her arrival, the sorceress was met by a crowd in the streets and town portals, stirring excitement and gathering people to witness this extraordinary event. Even the author remembers feeling the excitement at school.

The sorceress, skilled in herbs and spells, assured the officer of healing his ailing wife. She immediately started ancestral rituals, igniting a fire, chanting meaningful indigenous words, and concocted an ointment for the afflicted area, along with oral remedies.

Yet, despite the hope stirred, fate had different plans. The wife's condition worsened rapidly, and she passed away. The intervention seemed to hasten her demise.

Subsequently, the crowd turned aggressive towards the sorceress. Tension mounted, and Herminio, the police commander, felt overwhelmed. Fearing the situation might escalate and harm the sorceress, he decided to protect her.

News of this tragedy reached Herminio, prompting him to visit the officer's home with the community's support. They collectively mourned the loss.

Eventually, the mob led the sorceress to a nearby lagoon, immersing her. The shocking scene ended with her rescue, soaked and frightened. Herminio, driven by justice and humanity, chose to safeguard and care for her.

This story echoes the desperate fight for life and hope amidst adversity. Turning to witchcraft reflects the depth of love and despair when seeking to alleviate loved ones' suffering. Although it ended tragically, the officer's bravery and the community's unity leave an indelible mark on this tale.

CHAPTER 22

Another Adventure with Tacho: Chasing Rabbits on a Bicycle

There was a time when "Manita Roja" bicycles were a coveted treasure, and adventures in nature were the pastime of choice.

The story begins with the excitement of receiving a "Manita Roja" bicycle, a brand that represented excellence at that time. The gift of this bicycle brought me great joy, as well as to my brother Miguel, who shared the fun of riding it.

On that particular day, Tacho and I decided to embark on a bicycle adventure to follow the rabbit hunters to the Llano pasture. The path was a trail that had once been part of the old Royal Road, used by both vehicles and carts. The thrill of the hunt and exploration drove us, even though we had never been to that place before.

The day's conditions added an extra element of challenge, as it had rained copiously the night before. However, this did not deter us from continuing our adventure on "Manita Roja" bicycles, and we pedaled with determination through puddles and muddy roads.

Suddenly, we encountered a puddle that, at first glance, seemed just like the others, but turned out to be much deeper. My bicycle got stuck in the water, and I fell, first landing on the seat and then hitting the ground in a subsequent fall.

I was in a state of pain and dizziness. Meanwhile, Tacho, who was some distance away, stopped upon realizing the situation.

What followed was a comical scene, as Tacho, seeing me tumbling on the ground, began to laugh heartily. His laughter was uncontrollable and infectious, making me feel even more uncomfortable and embarrassed. Tacho couldn't contain his amusement and was clueless about what had caused the fall.

I was suffering from pain in my "colita" due to the fall, feeling unable to move. Eventually, when the pain subsided, I managed to stand up and continue our bike ride to the Llano pasture, a mountainous terrain where more adventures awaited us.

However, we did not manage to find the rabbit hunters or locate the town of Mirandilla. Despite this, we kept pedaling with determination and enjoyed beautiful landscapes, such as a small lake where we spotted birds like mallards and geese.

This tale takes us back to a time when outdoor adventures were the epitome of fun and excitement. The "Manita Roja" bicycle was a faithful companion on these journeys, and each adventure, including the unexpected falls, became a cherished part of our memories and lived experiences.

On these rides, we enjoyed the natural beauty of the rainy season and the diversity of fauna that inhabits the region.

We also passed through a ranch called El Terrero, known to be the land of the Casillas, and another called San Francisco, where we made friends who became our compadres in the future. This bike ride was not only a physical adventure but also an opportunity to explore nature and connect with the people of the region.

Elpidio Navarro and His Tragic Fate

I will now share a bit about the life of Elpidio Navarro and his tragic end. Elpidio Navarro was a prominent figure in the community, a man around 35 years old, known for his physical appearance: tall, white, blue-eyed, and presentable. He was also a relative of the author and other community members, a typical Navarro.

Don Elpidio had three sons and several daughters. The eldest son, also named Elpidio, often called "Pillo," was my friend; I remember he was just a year or two younger than me.

One day, Pillo and other children were playing soccer in the field. Suddenly, a conflict arose between Pillo and another boy, apparently over a disagreement during the game.

What followed was an episode that ended in tragedy. Elpidio Navarro, learning of the conflict between his son Pillo and the other boy, decided to take drastic measures. Instead of seeking a peaceful solution, Elpidio reacted violently upon encountering the other boy on the street. The boy was carrying a bucket of water with two cans hanging from a hoop, and upon seeing him, Elpidio confronts, snatches the bucket, and hits him with it.

The aggrieved boy's mother, witnessing her son coming home injured, inquires about what happened. The boy, tears in his eyes, confesses Elpidio assaulted him. The mother, distressed by the situation, decides to relay the incident to her husband, who was absent at the time, away in La Capilla.

This series of events damaged the relationships between the families, putting everyone on the defensive; indeed, Don Elpidio since then would not leave his house unarmed. One day, he visited Don Luis Gutiérrez's store, where both men were seen talking at the back of the establishment, leaning on the counter.

Unexpectedly and without warning, Elpidio draws his gun and shoots Don Luis Gutiérrez at point-blank range, who falls dead instantly. The action was quick and ruthless, leaving all onlookers astounded by the act's violence. Elpidio, after committing the murder, flees the scene as a fugitive.

At that moment, there was no nearby police presence to chase the murderer. However, Cacheras, Elpidio's nephew and Don José Navarro's brother, was in the vicinity, soon to learn about the crime and the perpetrator's identity. Cacheras, young and brave, decides to pursue his uncle.

With courage and resolve, Cacheras disarms Elpidio and hands him over to the authorities. The murderer is arrested and later transferred to the infamous Guadalajara Penitentiary, the largest and most notorious prison in the region. Although it is not mentioned how long Elpidio would spend behind bars, it is clear that his fate is sealed.

These unfortunate events lead us to reflect on the tragic course of events and challenge us to question if there was any alternative that could have prevented these misfortunes.

Pillo, despite his youth, was deeply affected by his father's death and experienced profound guilt. This led him to seek solace in alcohol, turning him into a chronic alcoholic. At his core, Pillo was a kind and friendly young man, and I fondly remember the times we shared.

Trips to Guadalajara

The trips to Guadalajara were a source of excitement for me; I enjoyed every journey on the bus, marveling at the places we passed. These trips usually ended at my Aunt Carmen's house, and my Uncle Lorenzo's, who were a kind and loving family. The hosts were the parents of my cousins Alfonzo and Lencho, with whom I formed very deep family bonds.

My Uncle Lorenzo owned a grocery store known as "La Concha," located opposite the Purísima Concepción church.

Aunt Carmen and Uncle Lorenzo always made us feel at home, their generosity and affection were evident, always ensuring that the children ate well during our visit.

Aunt Carmen was like a second mother to me, a woman with a big heart who never appeared angry with anyone. Her relationship with Uncle Lorenzo was a prime example of marital love. My grandmother Chita also lived in their house and had her separate room.

During my visit to Guadalajara, I enjoyed the company of my beloved grandmother Chita. This wise and loving woman played a fundamental role in my life; she would tell me stories and share knowledge about my father, my grandparents, and other ancestors. Much of the information I have included in this book came from Mama Chita. Additionally, she was a devout woman who often prayed the rosary, which I occasionally joined. Her spirituality and devotion to the Virgin of Guadalupe profoundly impacted me, as she fervently prayed to the "Morenita Guadalupana."

Mama Chita also had a passion for bullfighting and enthusiastically followed the broadcasts on the radio, demonstrating a deep understanding of bullfighting rules and movements.

In Guadalajara, my Uncle Antonio also lived, my grandfather's brother. These visits were special moments in my life, helping me to strengthen ties with this part of my family and enriching me with their wonderful traditions.

I remember a walking trip with Aunt Carmen to my Uncle Rafael's house. This picturesque journey allowed us to explore the route's details and the unforgettable encounters along the way.

One memorable stop on this journey was a stand where they sold various flavored snow cones. In fact, a funny anecdote happened there; my aunt bought me a snow cone, and as it was so tasty, I hurried to eat it, which caused a freeze in my throat. Seeing this, the stall owner offered me a glass of water, making the pain disappear as if by magic. This story reflects the simplicity and kindness of the people we met along those paths.

I was also impressed by the "Cuartel Colorado," a large Federal Army barracks with red walls, from which it got its name. There were many horses of the same color: light coat with white legs. And I remember the presence of hundreds of well-uniformed soldiers and a military band that set the pace during parades, an unforgettable image.

My Dear Capilla - Meeting with Tachín

Returning to my beloved Capilla was an exhilarating moment, brimming with mixed emotions only someone yearning for their homeland can experience. As I neared, my heart quickened, and a sense of belonging and familiarity enveloped me. The profound bond one shares with their birthplace is unparalleled, and upon arriving in Capilla, I felt the warmth of home.

My dear friend Tachín greeted me with open arms, his happiness evident in his smile. He always wore his signature hat, which, over time, had borne the brunt of the rain, now nearly covering his eyes. Nonetheless, it didn't matter; he remained the Tachín I remembered.

I reminisced about shared moments with Tachín, like the time in the square when I would snatch his hat, and he'd playfully chase after me. There were also instances when I challenged Tachín to a fight, despite my lack of boxing expertise. Initially hesitant, he eventually accepted, resulting in a memorable encounter that brought us laughter and strengthened our bond.

Returning to La Capilla filled me with nostalgia but also provided the chance to reconnect with old friends and relive cherished memories.

Every corner of my beloved Capilla held stories and experiences I would treasure forever.

My Dearest Capilla - A Dream Made Reality

During that time of my life, I was no longer the fearless child I once was. As I grew, so did my understanding of the world, expanding through varied experiences. At around thirteen, nearly fourteen years old, my fondness for my beloved Chapel only intensified. Reflecting on those days fills me with longing, for it was then that my appreciation for my town and its enchanting ranches deepened.

With adolescence came novel sentiments and emotions. I began to take more notice of the charming young ladies and women in La Capilla. Among them, girls with black and blonde hair stood out distinctly. It was then that I fell for a girl my age, who reciprocated my feelings. She was stunning, with fair skin, green eyes, and blonde hair—a true gem.

Our romance flourished in an idyllic setting, transforming every day in La Capilla into an adventure, each corner of the town rich with cherished memories. Adolescence unveiled a realm of feelings and discoveries, with my dear Chapel bearing witness to each phase of my growth. In this chapter, I celebrate this realized dream, a youthful love in a place so dear to my heart.

My Beloved Capilla and Victoria's Fair Maiden

Victoria's Fair Maiden, as we affectionately called her, was a name that resonated deeply within me. I recall a joyful Sunday in the plaza, surrounded by youths and maidens, all reveling in a serenade. That was when I encountered Victoria's Fair Maiden, blossoming into womanhood, and a connection that had been forming over time.

She was beautiful, with fair skin and blonde hair, her rosy cheeks leaving me breathless. I believed we were courting, and one day, mustering courage amidst excitement and nerves, I confessed my feelings. Asking her to be my girlfriend was daunting, yet her affirmative smile filled my heart with elation.

Our meetings were simple but meaningful. Once, I gathered a large bouquet from my grandmother María's garden and presented it to Victoria's Fair Maiden during another plaza serenade. It was an innocent gesture of affection that symbolized the love and tenderness I felt during those youthful days. The thrill of giving her the flowers was overwhelming.

She seemed like an angel descended from heaven, with her rosy cheeks and bright green eyes shining like precious gems. Her beauty was so captivating it left me breathless.

One day, at Don Luis Gutiérrez's store, I saw her again. She was with a friend, Josefina Navarro, Don Luis's niece. Our conversation was pleasant. Victoria's Fair Maiden gifted me a portrait, a memento I still cherish. Life, however, has its twists, and I learned she suffered from a heart condition. She passed away young, and I remained unaware of her departure.

Back then, La güera de Victoria had another boyfriend. To that young man who captured her heart at that time and whom I never got to meet, I congratulate him, for he must have been someone truly special to win her affection. A girl as beautiful as she must have had many suitors.

In 1949, we moved to San Luis Potosí, and since then, I have continued to remember La güera de Victoria with pure and sincere fondness, without any malice. At that age, sometimes God decides to take someone early to heaven. I hope that one day, when my time comes, I'll find her there, in that place of peace and eternal love. Her affection was fleeting, but it left an indelible mark on my heart.

CHAPTER 23

La Presa de Gómez

To fend off sadness, I prefer to talk about the ranch at La Presa de Gómez, which was part of our lives during those same years when la güera de Victoria and I shared dreams. What can I say about La Presa de Gómez? It is a beautiful place, but even more beautiful are its people. The inhabitants of this place have generous hearts, ready to extend a friendly hand to anyone of good heart.

They are deeply religious without being fanatical, and they show their love for God and the Virgin of Guadalupe with their daily prayers of the rosary and other traditional prayers. They follow the same customs that our Castilian ancestors brought from Castile, Spain, and keep alive that connection with their spiritual heritage.

In La Presa de Gómez, people are exceptionally kind and generous. They are hospitable and always willing to help their neighbor with justice and joy. When someone comes to visit, they are received with enthusiasm. I want to share this because when I was about thirteen years old, I had the opportunity to spend a few days in this wonderful place.

The presence of Gómez is felt everywhere in La Presa de Gómez, with surnames like Aceves and Martín being predominant. In this place, joy is contagious, and almost everyone knows how to play the guitar, including women, who sing beautifully. The Aceves, in particular, seem to have been born to sing and brighten the world.

I remember that during one of my visits, they lent me a horse to explore the area with an older friend they called Uncle Domiro, who was also known as Atilano Gómez. Atilano owned vast lands and a large number of cattle. It was here that I learned to handle the plow with a yoke of oxen. They taught me how to draw furrows for sowing and also to take care of the oxen, placing the yokes on their horns and directing them with the plow. During the milking season, I learned to perform this task effectively.

At La Presa de Gómez, I learned many new things. They taught me how to milk cows, extracting fresh milk from their udders. I also got involved in working with the calves, but sometimes I found myself in comical situations, being thrown into the air like a leaf carried by the wind. I laughed along with the others as I fell to the ground after being shaken by the calves' kicks.

Despite the challenges, I greatly enjoyed this rural environment. Even though the sowing season had not yet begun and the fields were not green, the early mornings were beautiful. I especially remember the dawns, which were truly lovely.

Before leaving, we stopped at an Aceves house, where we were invited to a special event. It seemed to be a celebration, possibly a birthday, with music from some guitars and two accordions, and many people had gathered.

When we arrived, the house was full of people, and some were already dancing. Someone called me "Chaparrito" because I was not yet tall enough and only reached the shoulders of the others. It was a joyful and festive moment at La Presa de Gómez.

At La Presa de Gómez, I experienced unforgettable moments. I recall a particular occasion when we were invited to an Aceves family home. There, I enjoyed the music and the party's joy. There was a beautiful tall girl from the family who stood out. It was a day full of fun and laughter.

The music played a zapateado, and despite my lack of skill in dancing with the tall girl, everyone laughed at my unrestrained enthusiasm. I jumped and kicked in all directions without coordination, but I was happy. They said that this is how one learns, and the tall girl also laughed at my uncoordinated movements. They even stopped dancing to watch us.

I had boundless energy and thoroughly enjoyed the music and fun, jumping around like a happy kid. Although I was not an expert dancer, people applauded my enthusiasm and the good time we were having.

This memorable day at La Presa de Gómez felt like an unintended farewell, as my father would soon take me to San Luis Potosí to assist him in the truck loading office in Los Altos. At thirteen or fourteen, I was already useful in that task.

Before leaving, I remember two particular things. The first was a dispute I had with a friend nicknamed "el Carioca" about how to place the steel rings on the carts.

El Carioca

The Carioca was a youth like me, around thirteen or fourteen years old. On an ordinary afternoon, we found ourselves in the square, surrounded by other boys, seeking ideas for some mischief. As we had no ideas at the time, it seemed a good idea to some boys to provoke a fight between Carioca and me. They loved organizing fights between peers for amusement.

Two boys approached me, saying, "Carioca claims he's better than you in fights and could break your mouth anytime." Without thinking, I responded overconfidently, "We'll see about that; he can come whenever he wants." I soon realized I had been naive to fall for their provocation without Carioca saying anything.

Then, they told Carioca the same. I think, at his age, he was smarter than me. He instantly replied that he wasn't afraid of me but only said so to not please the others. Eventually, they realized they couldn't have their fun at our expense, so they gradually left us alone.

At that moment, I recognized my recklessness and how I'd fallen into the other boys' trap.

Carioca approached me, appearing more mature, and said, "You know, Zorro (they no longer called me Zorrito then), I'm not afraid of you, but I won't gratify them by fighting you." By then, I no longer wished to fight, yet I stood firm in my reply, "Alright, anytime you want." He suggested, "No, let's go to the town's edge; that way, no one will notice, and we'll avoid trouble."

I agreed to his proposal, and as we walked toward the town's edge, we encountered Pillo González on one of his father's fine horses. Pillo had been in the square with us and, seeing us walk in silence, asked where we were going. I answered evasively, and without further words, Pillo followed us on his horse to the town's edge.

We reached the town's edge, near a stone fence. The last house was Agustín's, the cook I mentioned by the paddock. We jumped the fence and proceeded to the next house, likely belonging to Don Feliciano Navarro. Pillo watched from his horse as we started exchanging blows, enjoying the scene.

However, a severe storm broke out then. Carioca said we should take shelter to avoid getting wet, so we ran to a shed in a corral across from Agustín's house. Waiting for the storm to pass under the shed, I noticed many wood splinters likely meant for kindling and placing iron rings on wagon wheels.

While there with Carioca, waiting for the storm to pass before resuming our fight, I contemplated stopping the fight. But he showed no signs of halting despite the blows exchanged. Then, I remembered the festival at La Capilla, where his father managed the fireworks, referred to as "coheteros."

Carioca worked with the "coheteros," hired for powder castles and fireworks at festivities. At one of La Capilla's events, I encountered him near the square. Seeing me, he seemed displeased and made it known. He told me he would kiss me, which I rudely rebuffed. Then, he approached me, challenging me to a fight. Unsure how to react, I stepped up to face him.

The fight began, and at one point, Carioca delivered a blow that dimmed my vision and made me see stars. Feeling intense pain, I conceded his victory. It was then, while waiting under the shed to avoid the rain, I thought to do unto him what he did to me at La Capilla's festival. We decided to fight again, this time alone, exchanging blows like true boxers.

Pillo had left due to the storm, leaving us alone in our bout. At one moment, I managed a solid hit on Carioca, stunning him and securing my victory.

After our fight, we both were seeing stars from the pain. Eventually, Carioca sat down, acknowledging my win. I waited for his pain to subside, and then we solidified our friendship, having not mingled much before.

We decided to leave by jumping the fence, but bad luck struck when a dog, owned by Agustín – the same one that bit me when younger, leaving a scar on my leg – confronted us. We often teased it and climbed the window railings. However, this time, when delivering an errand, the dog recognized and bit me.

Despite this, we managed to escape and took refuge in a nearby shed. There, a large corral seemed to store fuel. José, the blacksmith, was busy fitting rings on wooden cartwheels, but since they awaited a furniture piece blocking the way, it appeared we'd have to wait longer.

The last confrontation of my childhood was with Carioca, a fight I'll never forget. After leaving the shed, we passed the first corner beside Agustín "el Cucho"'s house. There was José's blacksmith shop, and we paused to watch him forge bits, heating and masterfully striking them.

José had assistants fitting horseshoes, while he forged a cartwheel ring. Watching him bend the metal gradually with heat and shape it precisely was fascinating. He explained his work process and invited us to watch him place the rings that evening.

José, the Blacksmith

Don José, the blacksmith, was a marvelous craftsman who had two assistants whose names I cannot recall precisely. I explained to them where the blacksmith shop, often referred to as "the Anvil," was located. José and his helpers performed commendable work there, and I was eager to learn more about their trade.

José's blacksmith shop was always bustling with horses since, at that time, people frequently traveled from one place to another, relying heavily on these animals for transportation in the area. There were many carts back then because few people owned pickup trucks, and the roads were not as developed for vehicles.

The blacksmith workshop was a spacious area with two large furnaces. José was a very kind person who sometimes let me operate the bellows, used to intensify the coal and keep the flame alive in the furnaces. He was an expert in his craft, often receiving nets from ranchers needing repairs. He also created ornamental bars for the tips of fences and windows, as well as large locks for house doors, all handmade with great skill.

Don José also made rings that could even be used for personal defense; they were not luxury jewels but weighed about half a kilogram each. As mentioned earlier, he also crafted steel rings for cartwheels. I remember once, Carioca and I took shelter in the smithy's shed while it rained. There were some wooden wheels, steel rings, and many mesquite branches, as they were waiting for the rain to stop to light a bonfire and heat the rings.

Almost every day, Carioca and I would go to don José's blacksmith shop to enjoy watching him forge iron and shoe the horses. Sometimes, we even helped hold the horses' legs while they were fitted with horseshoes and nailed the nails. One day, we heard don José say that they would place the rings on the cartwheels that night, as there would be a full moon, and everything was prepared for when it got dark. This was because the incandescent color of the rings is more visible in the dark, allowing them to be placed by gently hammering them while simultaneously burning the wood to fit them perfectly.

Thus, they created two wheels with grooves and wood of the same measure as the rings. They carefully placed the rings on them and lit a bonfire. Despite the beautiful full moon, the bonfire's light perfectly illuminated the scene. They had also prepared some wooden wheels nearby for when the rings were ready.

After chatting for a while to wait for the embers to become more incandescent, they were ready. Don José the blacksmith, his assistants, and the wheel owner with special handles (to avoid getting burned) removed the first ring and placed it precisely on the wheel I had prepared with wood. While they held the ring, four people with hammers waited, and upon placing the ring on the hot wheel, they struck the four sides simultaneously. The ring fit perfectly in the center of the wheel without moving at all. Once they finished with the first, they proceeded with the second ring.

After everything was in order with the wheels, don José the blacksmith knew it was time to enjoy a delicious meal. He had brought a sack full of yellow corn cobs to prepare an "esquitada." He asked us boys to help him shuck the corn, and soon we had enough wood embers ready since the corn was shucked.

We began to throw the corn onto the embers, crushing it to ensure it did not burn. Soon, the popcorn began to pop, and we were happy eating esquites. Our faces were covered in ash due to the heat, but we were content enjoying the meal. That concluded the operation alongside don José the blacksmith and the cart owner, who was satisfied knowing he would soon debut his cart in the town. This was the type of dynamism that characterized don José.

As time passed, competition in daily life began to change the scene at don José's blacksmith shop. Fewer horses arrived to be shoed as they were replaced by pickup trucks and even more modern vehicles. The only thing that lasted longer were the oxen teams, until they too were replaced by tractors.

Faced with this situation, don José decided to switch directions and took up pig farming, a business that proved to be more profitable for him in modern times.

Severo's Inn

Severo's Inn, affectionately known as "the Hee-Haws," deserves special mention. This inn was always filled with donkeys, mules, horses, and muleteers arriving from other places with their loads or just looking for a place to rest and feed their animals before spending the night. Besides serving as a shelter for the muleteers, the inn also had rooms available for them.

This place was a crucial meeting point for travelers, and it was always brimming with activity and life.

I remember the first time I entered the inn back in 1942. Upon entering, a broad cobblestone corridor leading to Severo's office welcomed me. In that office, there were saddles and harnesses for the donkeys and mules, all piled up in the corridor.

The corrals were full of animals enjoying their meal, and this inn was the only hotel in the area at that time. An anecdote that still lingers in my memory is the arrival of don Pedro Chico's mules on that date. They came in wildly, herded along that road which they had to pass in front of the Hee-Haws. In a moment of chaos, some of the mules managed to enter the inn, although not all could do so due to the large number in the herd. It was a scene worth remembering.

Severo's Inn, known as "the Hee-Haws," was a place where all the muleteers gathered, and on a particular occasion, they faced a complicated situation. Severo, despite being a straightforward person, showed his mettle when the mules got frightened and became trapped while trying to remove them from a cart.

At that moment, all the muleteers came together to solve the problem. They removed the cart and began freeing the mules. I also remember that Severo lived near the inn, at the same corner. His wife shared his kindness, and they had a beautiful religious painting known as the "Divine Face" in their home, naturally and beautifully adorning it.

One day, at Rancho El Palenque, they built a small chapel and dedicated a lovely altar to it. I remember the inauguration, attended by people from La Capilla and myself. We went together with Tachín, who wore his famous hat. We participated in the slaughter with the permission of his grandfather Mártir, as my uncle Eulogio was busy in the north. It was an unforgettable day where I shared special moments with my sister.

Severo's Inn: The Pilgrimage

One day, I borrowed a donkey, and we set off on a pilgrimage that seemed like a scene from Don Quixote and Sancho Panza. The pilgrimage was full of people singing and carrying flowers, indicating it was early September when the celebrations began. After the procession, some people, including Tachín and me, continued forward.

We walked leisurely through a pasture known as "El Potrero de la Nopalera." However, the lack of action bored us a bit. That's when Tachín, with his playful spirit, began to prod the donkey he was riding, urging it to run. I was on the donkey and couldn't control it, as I only had one rein and a lasso in my hand.

Eventually, the donkey started to sprint, and I couldn't stop it. In a moment of desperation, I leaped backward from the donkey, clinging firmly to its rump to avoid falling. However, I believe I squeezed a sensitive spot, causing the donkey to react unexpectedly.

That journey on the donkey became even more thrilling when the wind caused me to turn around and fall backward onto the animal. It was like a brief flight, but this time it was worse because I landed on the donkey's rump, hitting my back hard and emitting another cry. Finally, I fell to the ground seated, gasping and feeling courage flowing through me.

My cousin Tachín and I, eager to fight, were angry about the situation, but there wasn't much we could do. Moreover, our embarrassment increased when we realized that a group from La Capilla, also going to the inauguration, witnessed us in the midst of this comical scene.

They watched, laughing heartily at seeing me fly through the air and fall to the ground. Some of them shouted playful nicknames like "Cacheras" at me, while others offered to help me stand. Among them was Simón Navarro, a very kind and funny person. Simón had a brother named Liob, both part of the "Cacheras" gang. They also had another brother known as "la Lepora," and their father was named Simón, if I recall correctly.

The laughter of the Navarros was contagious and distinctive, a joyful trait I always associated with the Navarro family from La Capilla. Imagine the scene when they finally managed to restrain the donkey and lift me from the ground. The laughter didn't stop, but at least I earned some laughs along with my bruised pride.

After that unexpected flying episode from the donkey, I got up and picked up some stones, in case Tachín tried to hit me again. We both continued on the donkey, each with a stone in our pocket just in case.

Finally, we arrived at the beautiful little chapel of "Palenque," and the inauguration was a true marvel. They had decorated arches with flowers, most of them dedicated to Santa María. The mass that followed was beautifully sung, and afterward, we all enjoyed a delicious roast meat. They had cooked a large number of corn cobs and prepared a significant amount of cheese adoberas, filling us with joy and satisfaction.

After enjoying the meal, Tachín mounted his horse "Panzón," lent by his grandfather "Pito." We decided to take a ride to Cerro Gordo, but soon realized we were not alone. We walked about a kilometer uphill and began encountering many rattlesnakes. The further we advanced, the more snakes appeared. To defend ourselves, we cut some jarra sticks, the best weapons against venomous snakes. We managed to kill three or four of them, roasting them to eat and make ornaments with their rattles.

Thus, we continued our day, filled with unexpected and thrilling adventures, in that special place where life was full of surprises and memorable moments.

That day, at the inauguration of the beautiful chapel in Palenque, with the Divine Face that don Severo generously donated, we lived special moments. We ate corn, hunted some snakes, and enjoyed the Chapel of my town. So the years passed, and then don José the blacksmith arrived, marking a new chapter in our lives.

It was in June 1948 when don José proposed an exciting trip to San Luis Potosí. We embarked on this adventure, leaving behind the fair-haired girl from Victoria, and thus began a new chapter in my life.

That same year, at the beginning of 1948, my father received a job offer in San Luis Potosí, an opportunity that would improve our lives. With his rising success, he participated in the formation of a cargo transport service, and soon he was sent to San Luis Potosí to oversee the freight service. After several months of work, he called my mother to join him in this new stage of our life.

Chapter 24

San Luis Potosí: My First Impressions

When my father took me to San Luis Potosí, Miguel and Rubén stayed under the care of my grandmother Chita in La Capilla. I was almost fourteen years old, but I still looked like I was ten. My growth was gradual, and I was always concerned about remaining short, but I was slowly growing.

San Luis Potosí, what a beautiful city. I loved exploring and learning more about it. It had a unique charm that captivated me and that I still remember fondly. One of the most notable features was its streets; instead of being paved, they were made of quarry blocks, giving the city a unique and beautiful character.

I also had the chance to visit the Alameda, a large park in front of the train station. All the park benches were made of concrete and had special work that made them look like real stone. It was a lovely place to walk and enjoy the city's beauty.

San Luis Potosí: A Charming City

San Luis Potosí, a city that left a deep impression on me. Upon arrival, I was amazed by the beauty of its streets, all constructed with quarry blocks instead of pavement, giving the city a unique and charming character. But what stood out the most were the Alameda's benches, made of concrete, yet meticulously designed to mimic tree trunks. The detail was astounding, even the color of the tree barks was perfectly recreated.

The genius behind this design deserves an award for their skill in imitation. The city should honor them for their talent. Moreover, the proximity to the train station made San Luis Potosí even more special for me. The train whistles became a beloved part of my daily life. There is nothing like the sound of a train anywhere else that makes you think of this wonderful city.

However, the San Luis Potosí train station also holds intriguing stories. It is said that in 1914, General Thomas Urbina, a compadre of Pancho Villa, invaded the city to loot and steal the riches of the citizens, including gold, silver, and dollars. This treasure became a point of conflict between Urbina and Pancho Villa, who claimed it later. This city has a fascinating history that continues to amaze me to this day.

San Luis Potosí: Land of Legends

San Luis Potosí, a land filled with legends and intriguing historical episodes. One of the most notable moments in history occurred during the Mexican Revolution when General Álvaro Obregón lost an arm due to cannon fire. However, the story also involves another influential character, Pancho Villa, who, instead of following the advice of his gunner, Miguel Ángel, lost a crucial battle and fled to Sonora.

In his defeat, Villa encircled Chihuahua, hoping to reach a hacienda where his compadre, Thomas Urbina, kept a vast treasure he had plundered in San Luis Potosí. Villa sought Urbina's help, arguing he needed the treasure to continue his fight. However, driven by greed, Urbina refused to assist his compadre, leaving Pancho Villa disheartened by his friend's betrayal.

The situation became even more tense when General Fierro, Villa's right hand, tried to retaliate against Urbina, but Villa stopped him, respecting their relationship. Despite everything, they continued their journey in search of new horizons. However, during their travels, General Fierro's anger grew to an unsustainable point, and he eventually returned to confront Thomas Urbina and seize the accumulated treasure of San Luis Potosí.

This story, filled with intrigue and betrayal, is just one of many that surround San Luis Potosí, a land rich in history and mystery.

San Luis Potosí: The Transforming City

San Luis Potosí, a city in constant evolution, welcomed me with open arms when I first visited. As I mentioned earlier, I told you about the majesty of the Alameda and the train station, but there was much more to discover.

Crossing the street to the west from the Alameda, I encountered the passenger station of the Camiones de los Altos. At that time, they were finishing the construction of an impressive five-story building. On the ground floor, a hotel was being created, while the terminal and ticket office were located on the upper floors. The freight office, on the other hand, was situated a few kilometers to the west, in front of a beautiful park.

This park left a lasting impression on me, as the tree trunks were impressively thick, and at its center stood an old church with classic and beautiful architecture. Additionally, at that time, I will always remember the site cars parked in the park, although my memory betrays me a bit about the exact colors, I believe they were blue with yellow details.

One day, while walking through the park toward the church, I passed by one of the site cars and, upon touching it with my left hand, I received an electric shock that made me jump like a startled goat. It seemed that the driver had placed some electric trap on the vehicle, which led me to wonder if this was something they commonly did to children.

My first impulse was to get angry and want to hit the driver, who was sitting at the back of the vehicle. However, given my young age at that time, I limited myself to feeling annoyed by the experience.

San Luis Potosí, a city transforming before my eyes, provided me with both astonishing and curious memories. Every corner of this city had something special to offer.

San Luis Potosí: A Place of Notable People

At the passenger ticket office of the station, I met a close friend of my father, who was also from La Capilla. His name was San Cevenatas de La Capilla, and like my father, he had been sent to San Luis Potosí. This friend had come to the city with his family, including his wife, Doña Lupe, who was from the Ranch of Juanacasco, the same ranch that belonged to my great-grandfather, Don Miguel Franco el Grande.

Doña Lupe was an exceptionally kind lady, and her marriage to Don Santiago had resulted in several sons and daughters. Don Santiago, for his part, was a close friend of my father and one of the best friends he ever had. He was always ready to make everyone around him laugh and was known for his joyfulness.

Don Santiago worked in the passenger office in rotating shifts, being one of the three employees tasked with this duty. His presence in San Luis Potosí added a special touch to my experience in this ever-changing city.

In San Luis Potosí, I encountered a number of notable people who left a lasting impression on my memory. At the Camiones de Los Altos passenger station, where I was working at the time, I met several individuals who stood out for their kindness and character.

One of the station workers, Mr. González from Tepatitlán, worked twenty four-hour shifts. He was an exceptionally kind and hardworking person. Another gentleman joining this team was equally a good person. Both were partners and affectionately known as "el Quemado" and "Roberto." The nickname of the second employee, Roberto, emerged after an accident in which he was burned with acid in a truck collision in Tepatitlán. This accident left him with scars on his face and body, similar to another man from Tepatitlán known as "el Quemado," who suffered a similar fate in the same accident.

Despite their facial disfigurements, both men were considered beautiful people, and the community in San Luis Potosí appreciated them for their kindness. Besides these two individuals, my father and other team members had been sent to work in San Luis Potosí as part of their job responsibilities.

During our stay in the city, my mother and I had some remarkable experiences. On one occasion, my mother visited a relative residing in San Luis Potosí. I remember we took a city bus to get there, and upon getting off, we encountered a crowd of men causing a commotion in the square.

San Luis Potosí: An Unforgettable Encounter

In San Luis Potosí, I experienced an unforgettable encounter in front of a business establishment. As I was passing by, one of the men present decided to throw flowers at my mother, although I was still quite young. Despite being almost fourteen years old, I looked only ten or eleven. The situation surprised and caught me off guard.

What happened next left me baffled. One of the men, boldly, tried to grab my hair. He nearly succeeded in pulling out a tuft, but at that moment, my survival instinct kicked in, and I was about to fight back. However, I thought better of it and realized confronting those men would only lead to trouble.

Despite the awkward situation, the surrounding people couldn't help but laugh. I decided to walk away and continue with my day. Eventually, we reached my mother's relative's place, a kind lady who lent me a ball to play outside in the street. The street belonged to her children, and I set out to kick the ball against the wall.

While playing alone, two young fellows about my age approached. They were friendly and asked if I wanted to join them in playing ball together. It was a kind gesture that made me feel more at ease in an unfamiliar environment, but I soon discovered they had ulterior motives: they planned to steal the ball.

When I agreed to join them, they quickly grabbed the ball and ran, leaving me perplexed. However, instead of getting carried away by the situation, I remembered the survival lessons I had learned in La Capilla. A mix of courage and determination filled me, and I decided not to succumb to their theft attempt.

Instead of chasing them desperately, I stood still, watching them as they moved away. They ran almost two blocks, laughing at their prank, but I remained unflappable. It seemed they had underestimated me, but I wasn't going to give up so easily.

When they turned the corner, I seized my chance. I ran three additional blocks, one beyond where they had turned. Then, I stopped at the second corner where they had turned. From there, I watched them playing with the ball, making sure they didn't see me cross the street. Taking advantage of my strategic position, I planned to catch them at the next corner.

Finally, I reached the corner where I awaited them, hidden. I saw them approaching, unaware of my presence. I felt like a cat stalking its prey, ready to retrieve my ball.

When they were close enough, I sprang, grabbed the ball, and ran off. I left them standing there with their mouths open, running like a champion.

However, they didn't give up easily and chased me determinedly. They were older and nearly caught up with me. In desperation, I reached a crowded place near a market with many people walking around. I approached an older man and asked for help. I explained that those boys were trying to rob me of my ball. While the two boys approached and denied my accusations, the older man decided to intervene and support me.

He told the boys to leave, mentioning he had called a nearby policeman. Terrified of facing the authorities, the youths decided to turn around and disappear. I thanked the man who became my guardian angel at that moment.

As I continued walking, I reflected on how to face new situations life presented to me in this unfamiliar place.

San Luis Potosí: An Odyssey

My arrival in San Luis Potosí was full of surprises and challenges. As I explored the new neighborhood, I lost sight of the ball and felt disoriented. The house my mother had headed to seemed like a labyrinth at that moment.

I remembered seeing a firefighter's water pump at the corner of the house, so I quickly headed towards it looking for direction. However, the house was not in sight, which confused me even more. I wandered through different blocks, desperately searching for the house, but found water pumps of the same color at almost every corner. Fear began to take over me, and my mother also started to worry about my whereabouts.

After going around in circles, I finally found the house. Upon arrival, my mother and the kind lady hosting us were very worried. The lady's husband was at work, and the children were at school, so they were clueless about what to do during my temporary disappearance.

I explained what had happened, and the lady, with her characteristic kindness, comforted me, saying that a ball was nothing and I should have come back earlier. Though the ball might have been lost, my safe return and the concern of my mother and the hostess showed that true wealth lies in the love and unity of the family.

An Unbreakable Bond with My People and My Roots

Every time I think back on San Luis Potosí, I can't help but feel a deep connection with my people and my roots. Whether good or bad experiences, they all are part of my family, of my very blood. I also feel the presence of my ancestors' spirits, whom I deeply love and know they await me with open arms when the time comes for me to embark on the journey towards a better life.

However, sometimes I digress from the narrative about San Luis Potosí to share other experiences from that period when my mother and I were together. One such experience was when someone brought concerning news. Silviano, my father's older brother and a partner in the Cooperative, informed my father that my brother Miguel had gotten into a confrontation with a boy his age in La Capilla, my hometown. This news shocked my mother, and tears began to stream from her eyes. My father, in his role as a comforter, sought to gather more information about the incident.

My uncle Eulogio arrived with additional details, as he also worked as a collector for Camiones de Los Altos. According to him, Miguel, staying with Mans and Chita along with Rubén, got involved in a skirmish. Worried about the situation, my father took out his pistol, which belonged to my uncle Liborio and was aged over time, but still laden with meaning and memories.

An Incident That Changed the Course of Things

On that occasion, I was in the midst of preparation (as if awaiting a brief respite) when an incident occurred that would change the course of things. It seems that Miguel was at home playing with a friend, and the pistol he was handling accidentally discharged. The bullet went through his ribs, a twist of fate that allowed him to survive. Miguel acted swiftly, disposing of the weapon as if nothing had happened.

At that moment, Don Herminio, the commander whom I have mentioned before, passed by. Miguel took some silver coins that my father had in his pocket and quickly headed to the portal, in front of Don Herminio Alcalá's Cantina, the commander. There, he found a cargo truck, quickly boarded it, and departed for Guadalajara.

From Guadalajara, he reached my grandfather Antonio's house, who was my mother's father. Later, he moved to Mexico City, where some acquaintances from La Capilla worked in construction. Miguel was just sixteen years old at that time, and although I don't know exactly what he did during that period, I know he lived for a while in a building in the city.

CHAPTER 25

A Return to La Capilla After a Sad Incident

The address was Mezones Street #33, in a building that I later learned was called "Edificio Alfonso." However, after the tragedy that occurred with my brother Miguel, my mother had to return to La Capilla. She had left my younger brother, Rubén, in the care of my grandmother Chita. At that time, I stayed in San Luis with my father, who worked in the Freight Transport office.

I soon learned to help him efficiently in his work, and one day he decided to take a short vacation to settle some matters in La Capilla and move the whole family to San Luis Potosí. Thus, after working together for just over two months, we headed to my hometown, and I was excited.

The return trip to La Capilla coincided with the rainy season, probably in September, as I could see that the corn crops were mature and ready for harvest. When we arrived in Tepatitlán, my heart was filled with joy, as I felt close to my beloved Capilla again. However, as fate had prepared for me, things had changed since my last visit.

The Return to La Capilla: A Journey Filled with Emotion

The bus that usually went to Arandas and passed through La Capilla had already left, and there wouldn't be another until the afternoon. It was then that my father decided to opt for a hired car and went to look for his friend, nicknamed "El Indio." I remember his name well, Antonio Gómez, a person of great quality. Without hesitation, Antonio gladly offered to help us, as they held great mutual esteem.

The road was not yet fully paved, and about sixty four kilometers before reaching La Capilla, the road turned into pure dirt. Moreover, there were areas where vehicles got stuck due to deep puddles. Drivers had to navigate these obstacles by going off the road. At one point, the car got stuck. To overcome this hurdle, a pair of oxen, brought from somewhere nearby known as "La Paleta Grande," was needed. Despite these setbacks, I felt an indescribable excitement when I glimpsed La Capilla's horizon from atop the road.

It was around eleven in the morning, and my longing to reach La Capilla grew increasingly intense. I felt a magnet calling me back to my beloved Capilla, where my friends, whom I greatly missed, awaited.

At that time, La Capilla's church had only one tower, and it felt like years had passed since my last visit, although it had only been three months. I felt an unstoppable urge to run and arrive as soon as possible.

Upon reaching La Capilla's entrance, my father's friend, El Indio Gómez, was engrossed in lively conversation with him, as they were close friends. However, he didn't notice other jams that had formed due to the rains and the continuous passage of heavy vehicles. El Indio suggested we get out of the car to inspect the situation. While we were outside, we had an unexpected encounter.

A friend known as "Chuy," riding his sorrel horse, approached. Chuy was coming from his ranch in Coleto, near Don Victoriano Navarro's ranch, a close relative of my father. Chuy used to make this journey daily, and his presence at that moment was a pleasant reunion.

He greeted me with joy and spoke of his skills as a horseman, mentioning that he was a prominent member of La Capilla's Association of Charros. I remembered how, during festivities, he would dress elegantly as a charro, standing out with his distinctive mustache and his impeccable sorrel horse. His passion for horseback riding and charro tradition was reflected in his attire and his horse, also a sorrel.

This encounter with Chuy marked the beginning of our return to La Capilla, a journey full of emotions and reunions with the people and places we hold dear.

The Return to La Capilla: An Encounter with the Morenita Guadalupana

Our journey back to La Capilla continued smoothly, and upon reaching the plaza, "El Indio" decided to return to Tepatitlán. However, my father had an important purpose in mind before going home: to visit the Morenita Guadalupana at the local church.

As was his custom, my father affectionately referred to the Virgin of Guadalupe as "Mi Morenita." He had deep respect and devotion for the Virgin and did not want to arrive home without paying homage to her. It was a beautiful Sunday, and the plaza was bustling with activity, with fruit and typical food stalls appearing weekly.

Upon arriving at the church, my heart raced with excitement. It was a special Sunday, and the church was filled with worshippers. As we entered, my father urged me to move forward and greet the Morenita Guadalupana. Just ahead, I saw Victoria, a young girl with blond hair who had a smile like an angel. My heart nearly burst, and emotions welled up inside me.

We greeted each other from afar, as she was with her family and I was with my father. However, her joy at seeing me was evident. Then, we went to see my grandmother Chita and my mother, who were also thrilled about our return, despite the haste caused by the accident.

This encounter in the church with the Morenita Guadalupana and loved ones at La Capilla marked a special moment in our return, filled with emotions and pleasant reunions.

Our return was overshadowed by my mother's concerns for my brother Miquel, who was in Mexico City following the shooting incident. Although his friend was recovering well, my mother continually worried about him and wondered how he was faring in the big city.

Meanwhile, my parents began to discuss their future plans and options. My father had received a job offer as a freight transport manager, necessitating our move to San Luis Potosí. This decision meant a temporary separation from my grandmother Chita, who moved to live with my aunt Carmen and uncle Lorenzo in Guadalajara.

Our arrival in San Luis Potosí was somewhat chaotic as we were adapting to a new life without Miguel. Nonetheless, we gradually settled into our new environment. We were assigned a house near the office and cargo warehouse, enabling us to establish ourselves in the city.

This chapter of our lives was marked by changes and adaptations to a new place and routine in San Luis Potosí. Our stay was very comfortable; we found accommodation that provided us with comfort and well-being. My father was pleased with his job, and I thoroughly enjoyed helping in the office. I quickly learned and felt important serving the customers and making new friends among my father's acquaintances. There was always time for engaging conversations.

Recognizing the importance of education, my father decided we should both enroll in school. I attended Instituto Potosino, a Marist Catholic school, which offered an excellent education and dedicated teaching. Besides academic subjects, we received half an hour of religious education, which I found deeply interesting.

In sports, I had the chance to play soccer and joined a team, balancing my office responsibilities with school and sports commitments. This period in San Luis Potosí was filled with many significant events and experiences.

In the office, an elderly man who knew my father from their days in La Capilla would visit, reminding us of our connections and ties to our origin despite starting a new life in the city.

CHAPTER 26

Permanence in San Luis: The Encounter with Don Luis

During our stay in San Luis Potosí, we had the privilege of meeting Don Luis, a man who had decided to settle in the city with his family. Although we don't remember his last name, Don Luis often shared that he had arrived in San Luis as a child. Upon his arrival, his father had started a business in the city.

Don Luis also owned a beautiful ranch in the Huasteca Potosina region, near a town called Río Verde. One day, he invited us to visit his ranch, which was truly spectacular. On the ranch, there was a wide variety of animals, including a significant number of cattle and zebu, typical of the region. Moreover, the area was surrounded by lush vegetation, resembling a jungle, home to diverse wildlife, including deer and occasionally leopards.

The region was impressive, like all the jungles of Mexico, divided into three: Tamaulipeca, Potosina, and Veracruzana. During our visit to the ranch, we enjoyed delicious grilled meat, said to be from a recently hunted deer. The experience also allowed us to meet Don Luis's wife, enriching our time in San Luis Potosí.

Don Luis was a man of distinguished appearance, accompanied by his two sons, who seemed to be around eleven and twelve years old. He was a friendly and sociable gentleman, immediately engaging in lively conversation with my mother.

Later, after enjoying a meal together, my father asked Don Luis about a topic that had piqued our curiosity. We wanted to hear firsthand the dramatic story of how he had experienced death and subsequent resurrection. My father had already shared some details with us, but we were eager to know the complete story.

Don Luis began his account by explaining that when he was around nineteen or twenty years old, he still lived at home with his father and two sisters. His mother had passed away, and at that time, an epidemic ravaged the region, caused by reasons that remain mysterious to this day.

The story of how Don Luis "died and came back to life" left us astonished, and we were eager to hear all the details he had to share. It was a tale that promised to be both amazing and mysterious.

The Epidemic Challenge: The Incredible and Astonishing Story of Don Luis

Amid the crisis sparked by the epidemic, the story of Don Luis, who lived during a time when yellow fever mercilessly struck, emerges as an incredible tale of resilience and wonder. In those dark days, when cemeteries were overwhelmed with the deceased, his life took an unexpected turn.

Don Luis, a young man of about nineteen or twenty years old at that time, still resided in his father's house alongside his two sisters. The epidemic spread fiercely, claiming numerous lives and leading to the overcrowding of cemeteries in Mexico and beyond, including the United States. In this bleak context, Don Luis too fell victim to the disease.

According to his account, yellow fever affected him so severely that he ultimately succumbed to the illness. With his father and his two sisters grieving inconsolably, Don Luis became the sole male of the family. The older sister, overwhelmed by responsibility, also fell gravely ill due to distress.

The dark night loomed over the cemetery, and at dawn, when they brought Don Luis's body for burial, they encountered an overwhelmingly crowded scene. The cemetery was packed with deceased individuals, leaving no room for new burials. The caretaker told them they had to place his tomb atop an existing one due to the lack of space, a scene symbolizing the magnitude of the tragedy.

Don Luis's story becomes even more astonishing when he recounts his experience after being placed in the coffin atop the tomb. Amid the night's darkness, nearly at dawn, with intense cold, he experienced the unthinkable: he came back to life. Opening his eyes in the gloom, he realized he was still alive. His story is a testament to life's fragility and human beings' capacity to overcome seemingly insurmountable circumstances.

The incredible story of Don Luis reminds us of the importance of hope, faith, and resilience in times of adversity, as well as the human spirit's ability to overcome even the most daunting challenges.

Don Luis's tale becomes even more extraordinary when he recounts his experience after being placed in the coffin atop the pre-existing grave. Amid the darkness, with dawn still far off and the morning chill setting in, the unthinkable happened: Don Luis came back to life. Opening his eyes amidst the gloom, he realized he was still alive. His resurrection was a poignant testament to human existence's fragility and the ability to overcome unimaginable circumstances.

The amazing story of Don Luis underscores the significance of hope, faith, and resilience during hard times. His return from the dead serves as a reminder that sometimes life can offer unexpected miracles that defy all logic.

When his sister opened the coffin lid to bid him farewell, she was astounded to see Don Luis's pale, deathlike face. His countenance bore the toll of illness, and he had lost a significant amount of weight. The scene was both moving and eerie. Don Luis, who appeared dead, opened his eyes and tried to communicate with his sister. However, his words barely left his lips before he lost consciousness again.

Startled by this unforeseen return to life, the sister called for her other sibling's assistance. The second sister arrived in haste, equally shocked to see Don Luis in the coffin. As they tried to make sense of the situation, Don Luis regained consciousness briefly, just long enough to inform them he was still alive. Yet, his appearance, with a gaunt face and devoid of strength, made it hard to believe him.

The family, overwhelmed with mixed emotions, tried to rouse the eldest sister, who was sound asleep and unresponsive to their attempts. After several unsuccessful efforts, they decided to seek medical help to understand what was occurring.

Don Luis, still frail but alive, dressed hurriedly and set out to find a doctor. The dawn's light heralded a new day and a second chance for him. The story of Don Luis, a man who defied death and returned from the departed, is a testament to life's fragility and the power of hope to triumph over the grimmest situations.

The dam that triggered a tragedy: San Luis Potosí in danger

In the quiet city of San Luis, a pivotal event shook the lives of its residents and left an indelible mark on their collective memory. The year was 1949, when the community became aware of a tragic incident from years past, a disaster involving the breach of a dam at dawn.

The dam, situated west of San Luis, had kept its secrets for a long time. However, on that fateful early morning, it gave way under the water's pressure, unleashing a deluge that seemed to come from another world. The fierce, merciless waters rushed toward a neighborhood of modest homes, where most people were still asleep, oblivious to the looming danger.

The avalanche, nearly ten meters high, advanced silently as people slept peacefully in their homes. The deafening roar of water colliding with houses finally awoke the populace, plunging them into confusion and fear. Chaos ensued in the streets, and those responsible for children or the elderly were particularly impacted. Many lost their lives, swept away mercilessly by the torrent.

Those who could swim made valiant efforts to survive, while others sought refuge on their rooftops, fighting to stay safe. When the deluge finally receded, the city was engulfed in eerie silence. The tragedy left a trail of destruction and loss that the community would not soon forget.

The death toll was uncertain, as many bodies were trapped or carried away by the waters. Moved by the catastrophe's magnitude, the city mobilized to aid survivors, rescue the trapped, and retrieve the deceased.

Dawn brought no expected relief. The city was in shock as the community strived to rescue survivors and recover the deceased. The final victim count remained uncertain, but the tragedy's scale was etched in everyone's memory.

Criticism arose, questioning the city and its apparent lack of foresight as culprits of the disaster. There were inquiries about why expert engineers had not been consulted before the dam's construction, or if it had been an act of negligence by inexperienced apprentices.

This tragic event, known by few, has faded into the annals of San Luis Potosí's history. Yet, it serves as a reminder of life's fragility and the importance of making responsible decisions concerning infrastructure that affects an entire community.

My Cousin Silviano's Accident: A Dangerous Turn

On the winding road, where danger lurked in every sharp bend, my cousin Silviano embarked on a journey that would forever alter his fate. The passenger truck he drove met a daunting challenge: a treacherous curve soon to become an accident scene.

Fate had other designs for Silviano that ominous day. As he navigated the perilous bend, the truck's brakes failed, plunging the scene into chaos. Despite his efforts to control the vehicle, the curve's force and the brake malfunction proved overpowering.

The truck slid off the road, tumbling toward a small ravine. San Luis, known for its prickly pear cacti, witnessed the dramatic event. Amidst confusion and fear, passengers screamed, a testament to the shared ordeal.

Fortune, however, smiled at Silviano in that critical moment. The truck halted amidst a cactus cluster, preventing a worse tragedy. Despite the initial shock and injuries, the outcome could have been graver had the vehicle plunged deeper.

Realizing he couldn't remain trapped, Silviano, driven by determination, kicked out a window, forging an escape path through the spiny cacti. But imagine the numerous thorns piercing him during this desperate exit! The pain from those penetrating spines was a small price for his survival.

Once free, he encountered another bus from the same company at the accident site. Wasting no time, he hurried aboard, eager to inform transit authorities swiftly.

Back in San Luis, where we awaited anxiously, Silviano's altered appearance was stark. Covered in scratches and cactus spines, he resembled a thorny creature, his gait shaky from the ordeal.

Post-accident, Silviano transitioned within the trucking firm, moving from driver to inspector, a role less fraught with peril.

While Silviano escaped unscathed, he couldn't shake off sadness for those mourning lost loved ones. Life, he realized, exposes its fragile and vulnerable aspects, reminding us to cherish each day as a precious gift.

My Uncle Eulogio's Dinner: Friendship and Anecdotes

One night in San Luis, as the city's hustle yielded to darkness, three great friends gathered at the ticket office. Roberto, nicknamed "El Quemado," who had been a driver before, now worked in the office. Beside him was my Uncle Eulogio, busy collecting fares from those boarding the bus on its journey through the small towns. Completing the trio was Don Santiago Padilla, finishing the afternoon shift.

That evening was special, full of laughter and shared stories. The three friends enjoyed reminiscing about a particular day when they arrived in San Luis on their truck. After their workday, they would head to a spacious neighborhood with plenty of rooms for travelers. The owner was a charming woman named Josefina, affectionately known as "Chepina."

Chepina personally welcomed guests and provided exceptional hospitality. In her kitchen, a talented cook prepared delicious meals that delighted all who were lucky enough to taste them.

That night, "El Quemado" and my Uncle Eulogio arrived at the neighborhood with Don Santiago, who had come early. The atmosphere was joyful and friendly, and the friends shared laughter while enjoying a delicious meal.

Upon reaching the diner, they were pleasantly surprised to find some "pozole" left. Chepina told them there was enough to serve everyone. The servings were generous, as usual there, filled with delicious pozole and accompanied by tostadas, as it was known that pozole was best enjoyed with tostadas instead of tortillas.

Don Santiago and "El Quemado" were pleased with their portions, but my Uncle Eulogio, known for his insatiable appetite, was still hungry. With his characteristic enthusiasm, he inquired if there was more pozole. The cook informed him there was a bit left, but no meat, only two large tongues.

Undeterred by the lack of meat, Eulogio decisively replied, "Put it all in, even without the meat." Thus, he continued to relish his bowl of pozole with the two large tongues while Don Santiago and "El Quemado" shared anecdotes and enjoyable conversations.

When Eulogio finished his second plate of pozole, everyone was amazed at his voracious appetite. They prepared to leave, but Eulogio asked them to wait, claiming he was still a bit hungry. The night carried on with laughter and stories, and Eulogio kept astonishing everyone with his capacity to savor the meal.

They decided to stay and asked for some blankets to lie down on the dining room floor. Quickly, they began to settle in, with "El Quemado" and I laying mats on the ground. The table, which was more comfortable, was reserved for Eulogio, who wanted to enjoy his meal peacefully before resting.

As the night progressed, they finally settled down to sleep. However, sleep eluded them due to worries about whether Eulogio would become congested after eating so much pozole. Around two in the morning, they finally closed their eyes.

But the calm was short-lived. Eulogio, who had eagerly enjoyed the pozole at dinner, began to snore loudly. He would get up, lie down, and rise again in desperation. He made noises like thunder, spewing pozole kernels with such force that they bounced off the walls and ceiling. The bulb light from the kitchen illuminated the scene, and everyone watched in astonishment, waiting for the moment Eulogio would get congested.

We woke him occasionally to make sure he was alright. However, he only murmured in his sleep, and meanwhile, dawn approached.

When we finally decided to wake him, it was already daylight. We called out, "Eulogio, Eulogio," and when he finally opened his eyes, he looked at us in surprise. He had spent the night snoring, unaware of the amusement and concerns he had caused among us.

It was a night of camaraderie and flavors, where Chepina's hospitality and the good food came together to create a special memory in these friends' lives. Chepina's diner became the setting for an unforgettable evening, where friendship and pozole were thoroughly enjoyed.

The Closure of an Unforgettable Dinner

As the dawn's light began to brighten the room, my Uncle Eulogio gave us an intriguing look, boldly inquiring, "Is it time to go for menudo yet?". Don Santiago and El Quemado continued their conversation, laughing, as if nothing had happened.

My father and I were astonished by Eulogio's suggestion. After keeping us awake all night with his snoring, it seemed he had an endless stomach. We wondered if it was indeed time to enjoy a good bowl of menudo.

The dinner at my Uncle Eulogio's became a recurring topic of conversation, and each time we reminisced about that night, we couldn't help but laugh. That dinner turned into an anecdote that entertained us for a long time.

And so concludes this part of my account of our stay in San Luis Potosí. Although it was a relatively short period, about six months or maybe a year, I will never forget the delightful experience we had there.

I wished to stay longer, but circumstances led us to Tepatitlán as my father was promoted to a better position. I will soon share more about my beloved Tepatitlán and our experiences, some filled with joy and others marked by sadness.

WARNING!

Not everything written here is one hundred percent verified, but it is a collection of memories from individuals, books read, and other forms of information gathered throughout the life of

Liborio Gutierrez.

CHAPTER 27

My Last Thoughts and the Nobility of My Life

The sayings I write here, some are mine and others I learned from a book, heard from someone, or from the Bible.

Proverbs, Sayings, and Adages

When a good man makes an effort, evil appears – *Mr. Robert Ward.*

The pen, undoubtedly, is mightier than the sword.

Never ask a blind man which is the right path – *German Proverb.*

Life is a long struggle in the dark – *Lucretius.*

Love is perhaps the only glow we will have in eternity – *Helen Hayes.*

Love makes us extend our time together.

I pray to God that the difference between us never comes – *Gladys Taber.*

Cupid's dart hurts more when it exits than when it enters.

As long as you have a window, life exists.

The high outcomes of education are tolerance.

Man is tougher than iron, stronger than a rock, and more fragile than a rose – *Turkish Proverb.*

A sharp tongue and a dull mind are always found in the same head.

The price of greatness is responsibility – *Winston Churchill.*

What is Politics? Politics is knowing how to explain what was promised and not fulfilled – *Winston Churchill.*

My great aspirations are a challenge to try the impossible – *Albert A. Michelson.*

Many times people have barked at me, but they have never knocked me down, and I continue – *Liborio Gutiérrez.*

The character of a man is taught in his perseverance – *Heraclitus.*

Without love, life has no meaning.

Experience in life is achieved through corrected mistakes.

In my beginning is my end; if you have no beginning, you also have no end.

To truly highlight the most important things in life is the gateway to wisdom – *Bertrand Russell.*

Honesty is the first chapter in the Book of 'Wisdom' – *President Thomas Jefferson.*

I prefer the dreams of the future over the history of the past – *President Thomas Jefferson.*

Beyond imagination is God – *Amerigo Vespucci.*

There is always a sleeping hero in every soul – *Martin Luther King, USA.*

He who has the right to criticize must have the heart to help – *Abraham Lincoln.*

Respect for the rights of others is peace – *Benito Juárez, President of Mexico.*

Ask not what your country can do for you, ask what you can do for your country – *President John F. Kennedy.*

I Prefer to Die Standing Than to Live Always on My Knees – *Emiliano Zapata, San Antonio, Texas.*

Hunger is the best sauce in the world – *Miguel de Cervantes*.

The best gift you can give your grandchildren are the roots of responsibility and the wings of independence – *Denis Waitley*.

Experience in life is achieved through corrected mistakes – *Liborio Gutiérrez*.

Anyone who has the ability to see the world beautifully will never grow old – *Franz Kafka*.

He who likes to kill must be ready to die – *Mr. Robert Ward*.

To be a star, you must shine with your own light, follow your own path, and not worry about the darkness – *Unknown author*.

A man with courage is a majority – *Andrew Jackson*.

Everyone should have a child, plant a tree, and write a book – *Chinese Proverb*.

Work as if you didn't need the money, love as if nobody had ever hurt you, and dance as if nobody was watching.

To be a respectable man and to be respected, you must respect others. Respect is a light that shines on you when you do things right. Or you can also be a bright star with a lot of light in the lives of others – *Willie Johnson*.

Kindness is the golden chain that binds society in good harmony.

When we accept our mistakes, we are able to overcome them.

Gossips lose all their strength through their mouth – *Unknown author*.

Avoid creating problems so as not to receive punishment – *Confucius*.

He who does not punish evil, commands it to be done – *Leonardo da Vinci*.

Minds are like parachutes, they only function when open. Keep your mind open so you can understand what is difficult to grasp and thus avoid causing irreparable harm – *Unknown author, San Antonio, Texas.*

Nothing in the world is more dangerous than ignorance and stupidity – *Martin Luther King.*

"Punishment begins when the sin is committed – *Unknown author.*

Nobody can withstand a cannon shot of ten thousand pesos – *General Álvaro Obregón, 1920.*

Beauty is not discovered with the eyes, but with the heart – *Unknown author.*

Happiness is not something that is given away, it is something that is achieved – *Unknown author.*

The beauty in life is hidden in the small details – *Unknown author.*

It's good to stir up mice so no one knows who is eating the cheese.

Life is a problem to be solved, not a mystery to be lived.

The wise man never says what he thinks, but always thinks what he says.

Ignorance and poor understanding are the springs of bad humor.

Such is the lightness that the wicked think everything goes well for them – *Victor Hugo.*

Patience is a tree with bitter roots.

Idiocy is a standardized disease; the bad thing is that it does not affect them, but it makes everyone around them suffer.

Do not attempt to solve a flood with water, nor try to extinguish a fire with fire – *Confucius.*

The mind is the home of a great treasure.

Memory is a treasure and guardian of all things.

Do the best at every moment because that moment will never return again.

A genius is a man with two ideas – *Jacob Bronowski*.

There is no greatness where there is no simplicity, kindness, and truth – *Leo Tolstoy*.

When doubt provokes courage, be calm and think first so that you do not make a possible mistake – *Liborio Gutiérrez*.

You cannot place great hope in a small soul – *Jan Smith*.

There is no secret to success; it is the result of preparation, hard work, and learning from failure – *Colin Powell*.

Malice uncovers logic, and both strengthen intelligence – *Liborio Gutiérrez*.

Victory is achieving what you have wished for and joyously links what you have achieved – *Liborio Gutiérrez*.

What is Good is always Good, and what is Bad is always Bad – *Liborio Gutiérrez*.

A picture is, without a doubt, worth a thousand words – *Fred Barnard*.

The best thing about animals is that they don't talk much – *Thornton Wilder*.

A life is not significant except for its impact on others – *Jackie Robinson*.

These sayings and quotes reflect the outcomes of preparation, hard work, and what has been learned in defeats. This is no sensational secret.

This is a proverb from a friend in the USA.

> In your life, three things you got to do:
>
> Do the right thing.
>
> Do your best.
>
> Treat people with respect.

Robert Ward

And it also includes these three things:

> The love of God.
>
> Be humble.
>
> Do everything you do with love for others.

Liborio Gutiérrez

My Nourishment

Blessed God, Father of Jesus Christ, King of the Universe,

You, who feed the world with your goodness and provide for all your creatures.

Lord, we thank you for your great name and your power.

Thank you for providing us with nourishment.

www.ingramcontent.com/pod-product-compliance
Lightning Source LLC
Chambersburg PA
CBHW032028290426
44110CB00012B/712